The Incas & Their Ancestors: The
Archaeology of Peru
Michael E. Moseley
Thames & Hudson
June 2001

The Incas

THE INCA EMPIRE
1532
COLOMBIA
BRAZIL
PERU
BOLIVIA
CHILE
ARGENTINA
PACIFIC OCEAN
EQUADOR
QUITO
CAJAMARCA
CUZCO
COCHABAMBA
Legend
Approximate Limits of the Inca Empire:
Tribe Names are Underlined: Chunchos
Modern Political Boundaries:
Modern City Names are Bracketed: [Santiago]
SOUTH AMERICA
N
K. Marlow, 1992.

The Inca Empire, 1532.

The Incas

NIGEL DAVIES

UNIVERSITY PRESS OF COLORADO

Published by the University Press of Colorado
P.O. Box 849
Niwot, Colorado 80544

Printed in the United States of America.

The University Press of Colorado is a cooperative publishing enterprise supported, in part, by Adams State College, Colorado State University, Fort Lewis College, Mesa State College, Metropolitan State College of Denver, University of Colorado, University of Northern Colorado, University of Southern Colorado, and Western State College of Colorado.

The paper used in this publication meets the minimum requirements of the American National Standard for Information Sciences — Permanence of Paper for Printed Library Materials. ANSI Z39.48-1984

Library of Congress Cataloging-in-Publication Data

Davies, Nigel, 1920–
The Incas / Nigel Davies.
p. cm.
Includes bibliographical references (p.) and index.
ISBN 0-87081-360-9 (cloth)
1. Incas — Politics and government. 2. Incas — History — Sources. 3. Incas — Antiquities. 4. Ethnogistory — Andes Region. 5. Andes Region — Antiquities. I. Title.
F3429.3.P65D38 1995
984'.01 — dc20 94-38972
CIP

10 9 8 7 6 5 4 3 2 1

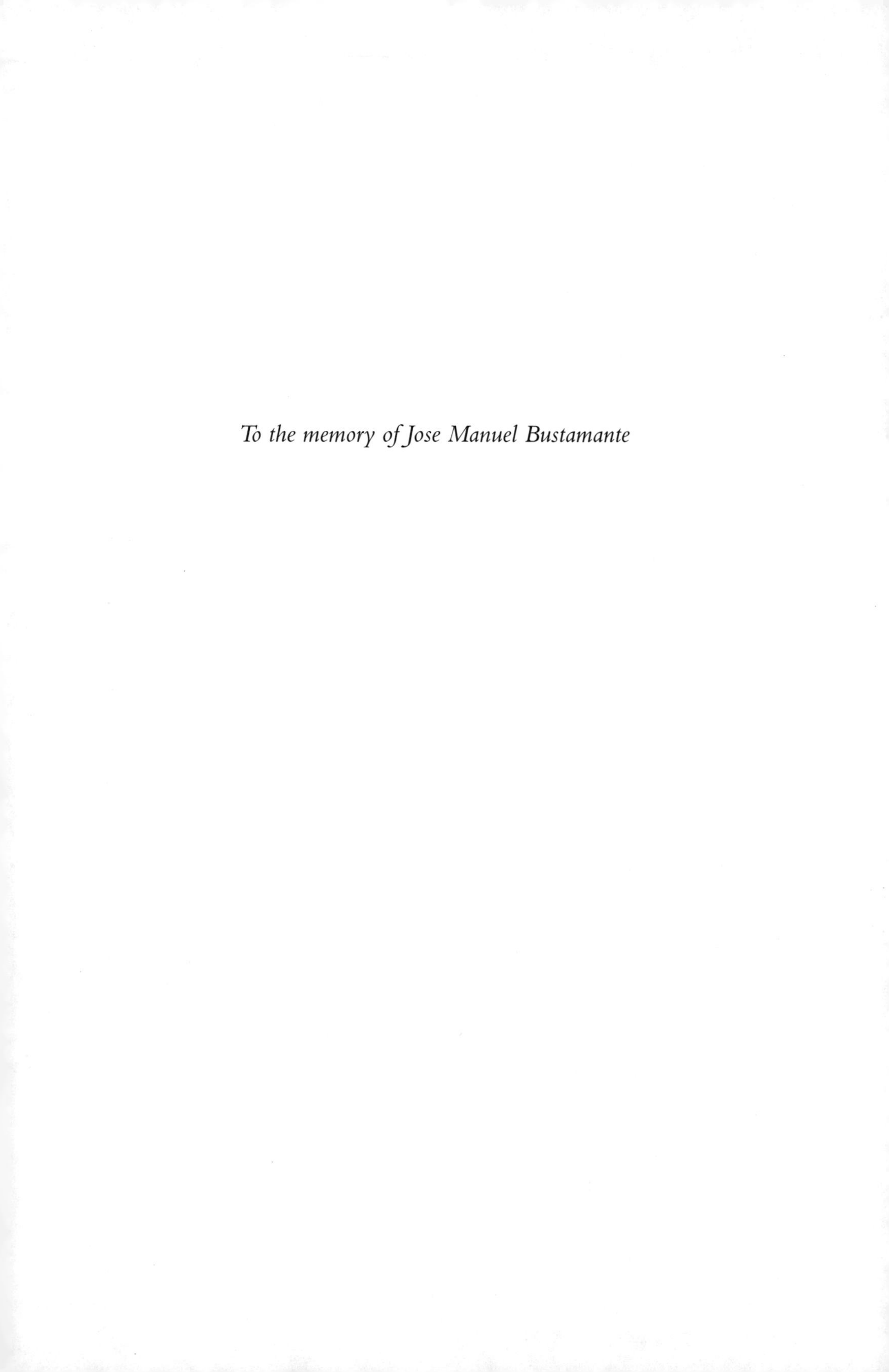

To the memory of Jose Manuel Bustamante

Contents

Maps viii
Prologue ix

1. In Search of the Past 1
2. The First of the Incas 16
3. The Era of Pachacutec 40
4. The Last Conquerors 64
5. The Inca State 103
6. The Empire and Its Infrastructure 127
7. The Imperial System 150
8. The Decline and Fall 181

Appendix A 211
Notes 217
Bibliography 233
Index 249

Maps

The Inca Empire, 1532 ii
The Major Middle Horizon Sites in Peru 10
Cuzco at the Time of Conquest 104
Inca Sites Near Cuzco 108
Plan of Huánuco 138

Prologue

Over the past two decades, in addition to my various works on Aztecs, Toltecs, and other Mesoamericans, I have also written on more general topics, such as human sacrifice throughout the Americas, as well as on the enigmatic problem of possible contacts between the Old World and the New before the voyages of Columbus. During this period, I made fairly prolonged visits to Peru, Ecuador, and Bolivia, journeys that inspired a growing interest in the achievements of the Andean peoples, in particular those of the all-conquering Incas.

In this book I prefer to spare the reader a surfeit of those all-too obvious comparisons between Inca and Aztec. Nonetheless, it may be useful to stress at the outset the almost uncanny resemblances, as well as certain radical differences, between the history of the two peoples. In both instances the traditional sources tell of a humble group of migrants who had fairly recently established themselves in a notably fecund valley, though some authors, including myself, suspect that their arrival was not so recent as such sources tend to imply. By an extraordinary coincidence these two peoples, in a here-or-less contemporaneous process, set out to conquer vast empires, probably far vaster than any that might have preceded them in North and South America. Both then met their doom in the second and third decades of the fifteenth century at the hands of minuscule bands of Spanish invaders.

One major difference confronts scholars who study the two peoples. Unlike the Incas, from the Aztecs and their predecessors we possess pictorial codices relating to many aspects of their past, as well as fairly numerous documents in the native Nahuatl, recorded in early post-Conquest times. For the Incas we tend to rely more exclusively on the Spanish chroniclers, who both in Mexico and Peru, offer a more Europeanized view of events.

For the general reader, this volume aims to offer a lucid overall view, embracing the rare, recent scientific studies of the astonishing achievement of the Incas, who in a short space of time conquered a realm that stretched for well over two thousand miles from north to south. It may be worth noting that for the past three decades no similar work has been attempted, embracing in a single volume the various aspects of the Inca past, not only their political history but also their economy, administration, religion, art, architecture, and daily life.

Equally, I trust that my book will prove useful for Andean scholars. The latter have at their disposal a rich variety of specialized material, focusing on specific aspects of the Inca achievement, for instance their road system, methods of town planning, control of manpower, exploitation of economic resources, as well a class structure and religious beliefs. Such writings mostly tend to take into account the copious, if contradictory, information provided by Spanish chroniclers. Naturally, however, they rely for much of their data on the very extensive archaeological research undertaken in recent decades.

Not only for the general reader, but also for the Andean scholar, an up-to-date overview should prove to be of interest, both for themselves and more particularly for their students. Moreover, from the strictly ethnohistorical point of view, aided by my prolonged studies of the Mesoamerican past, I have sought to achieve a reappraisal of certain aspects of the surviving accounts of Inca history, considering in particular the means whereby the chroniclers accumulated their detailed information, and to reassess the degree to which their accounts may or may not be reliable. Certain fairly positive conclusions have been reached as to the extent to which these works may be related one to another, perhaps to a greater degree than was previously suggested.

Finally, in one respect I shall feel that I have made at least a modest contribution to Andean studies if I can in any way reinforce the acceptance of my conviction, already most evident in the works of so many Andean scholars, as to the need to take into the fullest account the data offered by both archaeological research and by the written sources, in the effort to increase our understanding of the amazing Incas.

The Incas

CHAPTER 1

In Search of the Past

FACT AND FABLE

Sixteenth- and seventeenth-century writing on the Incas was mainly the preserve of Spanish chroniclers. In the absence of abundant data in the native Quechua, much of our knowledge of the Inca past derives from these texts; though their opinions may differ, they all tend to describe native society from a Spanish viewpoint.

As early as the eighteenth century, reports of a boundless realm centered in the High Andes and endowed with fabulous riches began to attract the attention of a wider audience. Voltaire chose Lima as the setting of his *Alzire*, an extremely successful play. His most famous work, *Candide*, published in 1759, offered a rather idealized account of the denizens of an American El Dorado; they supposedly descended from the Incas. Jean François Marmontel's drama *Les Incas o la Destruction de Pérou,* dedicated to King Gustav III of Sweden, was published in 1777. The action, concerned with the fall of Atahualpa (aided by refugees from the kingdom of the Aztec Moctezuma!), takes place in Quito.

Whereas such works were permeated with the notion of the "noble savage" fashionable at the time, William Prescott's *Conquest of Peru*, published in the 1840s, provided a less romantic view. Methodically citing the sources then available, he related in his stately prose the story of Francisco Pizarro's encounter with the Emperor Atahualpa and all that followed.

In the early twentieth century a rather different concept came into vogue. No longer portrayed as greedy and gaudy capitalists obsessed with the urge to increase their immense hoard of gold, Incas were now cast in a new role. Certain authors depicted them as the world's first socialists, at times even describing them as communists! Such notions, as we shall see, are less acceptable to the present generation of ethnohistorians.

Early Accounts

That Europeans were fascinated by Peru is hardly surprising; it was surely among the most exotic of all the lands that their voyagers discovered. The Inca realm was indeed a land of total contrast, stretching two thousand miles from Ecuador to Chile. The coastal land was a stark and lifeless desert intersected by many rivers, whose oases gave sustenance to thriving polities. Wholly different from this bleak shore was the Incas' native habitat. Even the more temperate parts of this forbidding tableland that rises so abruptly from the coast stand at an altitude of nearly 9,000 feet. Though much of this altiplano is fertile, rock is more plentiful than wood, and houses were built more of stone than of timber. Beyond the Andean tableland lies a third ecological zone known as the *montaña*. Embracing the eastern slopes of the great mountain chain and matted with a carpet of lush forest, it is intersected by swiftly running rivers. Into this fetid land, so distinct from their more austere homeland, the Incas feared to tread, and their penetration was limited.

A review of the Inca achievement can hardly be undertaken without a brief résumé of the sources now available and of the problems that they present. The Spanish chroniclers' writings are rich in content but are often ambiguous and at times contradictory. Any quest for truth therefore requires rigorous scrutiny and cautious interpretation. Fortunately, contemporary archaeological research has done much to clarify some of the questions unanswered by earlier writers. Any work on the Incas becomes meaningful only if one takes the fullest account of such research, as well as of renewed studies of certain early colonial sources.

In the absence of native written documents, chroniclers were dependent on oral traditions. Moreover, much of their information derives from the elite of Inca Cuzco and therefore reflects more the state system of the capital than the administration of the Empire as a whole. In such a monolithic society one might presuppose the existence of a single official version of past events. But because of the Incas' bizarre custom of preserving the mortal remains of the previous rulers, each maintained by a vast household of highly placed descendants and retainers, alternative versions tended to survive, perpetuated by the loyal scions of these households *(panacas)*. From these the chroniclers might obtain not so much eyewitness accounts as oral traditions related within a ritual context.[1]

Wedin suggests that the greater part of the available data comes not from official "historians," whose contribution was limited, but from other informants.[2] As a result, the chroniclers tend to offer conflicting evidence, though in certain specific instances they do more or less coincide and appear to follow a single original or official tradition.

Though the Incas did not possess a writing system in the accepted sense, they had an excellent method of compiling data: The *quipu* knotted cords constituted an elaborate means of keeping records. The *quipocamayos* who managed the system were a privileged class of highly skilled specialists. They were able to provide information, for example, on crop yields and storage capacity throughout the Empire, how many men in a given village were available for army service, or how many could work in mines. Shortly after the Conquest, they even recorded the damage done to crops and homes in places where Spanish forces had passed.[3]

Paradoxically, little of their data seems to have become directly available to the Spanish chroniclers. Cieza de León, among the most informative of the earlier sources, writes of the quipocamayos, as well as of other official "historians," yet when he recounts in various instances how he obtained his information he does not mention (except on one occasion) these specialists but rather refers to "Indians" in general, in particular to nobles.[4] Later chroniclers also refer to conversations with quipocamayos, but such statements occur in documents whose material is copied largely from earlier sources. Quipus of which we still have knowledge, taken from cemeteries, unfortunately cannot now be related to the objects with which they were buried.[5]

Only one interview with quipocamayos survives: their declaration to Vaca de Castro. This document, however, offers rather scant information, and the years of reign and of life of the Inca rulers are given in round figures only.[6] Had they so desired, the Incas could surely have recorded more precise dates, but they displayed little interest in chronology, however keenly sought by their European conquerors.

In addition to the quipu knots, a form of verbal history existed in the songs *(cantares)* sung on special occasions to celebrate the events of a ruler's reign. But when a new monarch ascended the throne, he would order that fresh ballads be composed to commemorate his own feats; earlier songs and even quipus were to be set aside, under threat of dire punishment. Dynastic history, far from being preserved, was periodically re-edited and even obliterated.[7]

The Chroniclers

Louis Baudin divided the chroniclers into five chronological categories, starting with the earliest, who took part in the Conquest, and ending with seventeenth-century Spanish historians.[8] However, such categories present obvious difficulties: For instance, Cieza de León, who belongs to Baudin's second category because he arrived after the Conquest, completed his work in the early 1550s, whereas Pedro Pizarro's *Relación*, which as an eyewitness account belongs to the first category, was written in 1571.

Those who took part in the Conquest do offer certain unique descriptions of Inca life and ritual. Francisco de Xerez provides a running commentary on the first meeting between Atahualpa and Francisco Pizarro and describes in some detail the ruler's house in Cajamarca. He also wrote of the great temple of Pachacamac, which he visited when it still functioned as a center of pilgrimage.[9] Pedro Pizarro writes of the vast accumulation of treasure found in Cuzco and gives a fascinating account of the vault below the great fortress of Sacsahuaman containing four thousand bundles of gold objects.[10]

Chroniclers who arrived after the Conquest and who relied on native informants are hard to classify. Of their copious writings, certain are of special interest. Cieza de León reached America in 1535 and served as a soldier in Colombia; his first work, *La Crónica del Peru*, was composed between 1541 and 1550 and printed in 1553 in Seville. It was the only part of his writings to be published in his lifetime and describes his travels throughout Colombia, Ecuador, and Peru. His second book, *El Señorío de los Incas*, written in about 1550, portrays Inca society and government; its great merit is that Cieza names his sources, including interviews with Inca nobles, and at times makes it clear that he is describing what he saw firsthand. His work was shortly followed by that of Juán de Betanzos, who married a sister of Atahualpa.

Among earlier writers, valuable information is also contained in the work of Damián de la Bandera, an official who was named *corregidor* of Potosí and Charcas (1557). In 1563 Hernando de Santillán adapted de la Bandera's account of Huamanga to the Empire as a whole; however, as Wedin has demonstrated, he copied certain of de la Bandera's passages word for word.[11]

Certain other chroniclers merit special attention. Unique among these is Huaman Poma de Ayala, who wrote in the late sixteenth century. His account contains parts written in Quechua and is enriched by sketches offering a vigorous portrayal of every aspect of Inca society. Polo de Ondegardo, a distinguished jurist, is much cited by John Murra in his important studies of social and economic problems. For Inca history and military campaigns, the two principal sources in addition to Cieza de León are Pedro Sarmiento de Gamboa (1572) and Cabello de Balboa (1586); the latter spent several years in Quito and describes at length campaigns in that region.

Belonging to another century are the *Comentarios Reales* of Garcilasco de la Vega, published in Lisbon in 1609; the author was himself of Inca lineage. Though he quotes earlier chroniclers such as Cieza and Polo, his portrayal of his Inca forbears as kindly despots presiding over a vast welfare state acquired with a minimum display of force tends to be treated nowadays with circumspection. Nearly half a century later, in 1663, Padre Bernabé Cobo wrote his *Historia del Nuevo Mundo*. Using all the sources then available, in particular Polo de Ondegardo, Cobo's appraisal is in some ways more that of a historian than of a chronicler; he collected a vast amount of material in Peru as the basis for a lucid, comprehensive study that includes valuable data on natural history and family life.

In the 1960s a new dimension was added to ethnohistoric studies of the Andean past: an intensified focus on regional sources. A rich store of information was made available with the discovery in the Archivo de Indias in Seville of the report of the *visita* of Garci Díez de San Miguel, made in 1567 to the Aymara province of Chucuito, together with the 1562 visita of Iñigo Ortiz de Zúñiga to the province of Huánuco. Scholars were quick to draw attention to the significance of these documents as part of a whole series of visitas now available. These were the product of administrative inspections made by the Spanish authorities after the Conquest. Franklyn Pease, in listing the principal visitas either published or known to scholars, suggests that the study of regional documents has revolutionized Andean historical research.[12]

Special Problems

Because we possess so few transcripts in the Quechua language, we depend upon sources written by Spaniards and, only decades later, by hispanicized natives. Such documents were written from a Spanish viewpoint, in terms intelligible to contemporary European readers. But, as Tom Zuidema points out, any attempt to reconstruct the Inca past must involve the difficult process of first asking how the Incas themselves conceived it.[13]

Unfortunately, however, the basic concepts of native informants bore scant relation to those of the chroniclers. Absolute veracity and precise dates were hardly relevant to informants, and a strictly *historical* view of events in a European sense was of even lesser consequence. Moreover, such a view was scarcely available; as we have already seen, songs, stories, and even quipu records were apt to be re-edited to satisfy the whims of a new ruler. Inca history had already been refashioned by the great ruler Pachacutec, whose reign is traditionally dated from 1438. Salomon points out that the Inca perception of diachrony had little to do with what we call history; the concept of action over time was conceived of not as changing the world but as conveying certain ritual notions based on the use of imagery and on social interaction through ritual.[14]

A further problem was posed by the preconceived notions of the chroniclers themselves, who were ill prepared to face the challenge of alien concepts. Imbued with notions of primogeniture, they paid little attention to the Inca system (or lack thereof) of royal succession. The chroniclers' view of the process of history as the salvation of the world through Christianity, incomprehensible to their informants, impeded efforts to understand Andean religious and social thought.

Another basic question is posed by the sources' attitudes to a recurrent theme: Were the Incas good or bad? Many writers were under pressure to portray Inca religion and government as harshly cruel in order to legitimize the Conquest in face of the indigenous population's prolonged opposition to Spanish control. In 1571 and 1572, following extensive inquiries, the Viceroy Francisco de Toledo sent a series of *informaciones* to King Philip II in which he demonstrated that the Incas were only recent conquerors and therefore had no hereditary claim to rule Peru. His final dispatch, dated January 1572, even cited survivors of tribes who had reportedly occupied the valley of Cuzco before the Incas arrived and still nursed a bitter hatred of the imperial rulers. It was Toledo who commissioned Sarmiento de Gamboa to write his history; though Sarmiento's work was carefully researched, it served to perpetuate Toledo's claim that the Incas were usurpers rather than legitimate rulers.

By contrast, the exponent par excellence of the pro-Inca case is Garcilasco de la Vega, who describes the Incas as benevolent rulers over a realm in which hunger and even poverty were unknown. The works of earlier writers such as Cieza and Polo, as well as the much later account of Cobo, tend to present a more favorable or at least impartial picture of Inca rule.

Modern Studies

As a result of such differences of opinion over the merits of Inca rule, earlier modern studies of Andean history tend to divide the chroniclers into two schools: the Toledan and the Garcilascan. In the early twentieth century the Garcilascan school came into favor, and the concept of the Incas as the world's first socialists enjoyed a certain vogue at a time when Marxist dogma was as yet unsullied by experience and when socialism was often viewed as the ultimate utopia.

Among the first to express such ideas was Louis Baudin, whose work, *A Socialist Empire: The Inca of Peru*, was written in 1928, though not translated into English until 1961. Notwithstanding his title, Baudin offers both praise and criticism, writing, "The Incas plunged their subjects into a sleep that was akin to death and robbed them of all human dignity."[15] In his *Ancient Civilizations of the Andes*, published in 1931, Philip Ainsworth Means tends to accept the Garcilascan view of the Inca state as primarily dedicated to the well-being of its subjects.[16]

Louis Valcárcel, who wrote his two-volume history between 1943 and 1949, has the great merit of being among the first to incorporate the findings of early archaeologists such as Julio Tello into his overall picture. However, he also describes the Incas as socialists and even communists. He affirms that their benign rule, far from pandering to the nobility and other privileged classes, was so structured as to attend to the welfare of the population as a whole.[17]

In addition to differences over the nature of the Inca Empire, further disagreements arose over how it was acquired. Those who lean toward the Garcilascan school regard the process as gradual and generally peaceful. But in the 1940s John Rowe, drawing support from major chroniclers, opposed this view and insisted that the Inca conquest of empire was swift and violent, a notion now heavily supported by archaeological research.

Rowe may be called the pioneer of "modern" Peruvian ethnohistory. His writings sought to evaluate the work of the chroniclers in a more

Andean and less European context. Rowe's description of Inca culture, published in the *Handbook of South American Indians* in 1946, became the standard, or orthodox, version of their past. He did not confine himself to the written sources, having already produced a study of the archaeology of Cuzco.[18]

The 1950s witnessed the outstanding contributions to Andean studies of John Murra and Tom Zuidema. At this time also Richard Schaedel and Maria Rostworowski began to publish; among the latter's principal achievements was her reinterpretation of the significance of the peoples of the south-central coast of Peru based on close study of unpublished documents from Peruvian and Spanish archives. The early 1970s were marked by the first of many contributions by Franklyn Pease and Craig Morris, whose studies have consistently sought to combine archaeological and ethnohistorical data.

In the late 1970s and the 1980s so many scholars from around the world have entered the field and added to our understanding of the Andean past that it would be hard to single out specific names; many will be cited in this work. They generally seek to subject the sources to an objective analysis reinforced by the more recent archaeological findings. Far from being confined to the core region of the Inca Empire, much of their work concerns outlying provinces, ranging from Ecuador in the north to Chile and northwestern Argentina in the south. Increasing attention is also directed to the kingdom of Chimor, seen by some as exercising a major influence on Inca statecraft.

The Findings of Archaeology

The era of modern archaeology began in Peru with the work of the great German archaeologist Max Uhle, who excavated the coastal site of Pachacamac in 1896. His report, published in 1903, was the first truly stratigraphical study in the Americas.[19] Early investigations such as Uhle's tended to concentrate on the civilizations of the coast, including the kingdom of Chimor; a few were also dedicated to the imposing ruins of Tihuanaco. Nonetheless, certain Inca sites, apart from Cuzco itself, attracted attention at a relatively early stage.

Uhle was also the author of a series of studies of the Inca past, the first of which was published in 1909. In addition, he wrote a description of the ruins of Tomebamba in Ecuador, the capital of the emperor Huayna Capac. In 1911 Hiram Bingham first located the spectacular site of Machu Picchu, a discovery that has played a dramatic role in focusing public attention upon the Incas.[20] However, the most prominent field investigators of the 1920s and 1930s — Alfred L. Kroeber, Wendell C. Bennett, and Julio C. Tello — tended to excavate pre-Inca sites, and it was not until 1966 that Cuzco itself was fully treated in Rowe's *An Introduction to the Archaeology of Cuzco.* Rowe, after describing pre-Inca remains in the Cuzco Valley, writes in some detail of the great fortress of Sacsahuaman, drawing attention to major differences in its masonry style as compared with that of Tihuanaco. The latter is built with massive square or rectangular blocks of stone, whereas those of Cuzco are mainly huge irregular polygons.

The modern period, following the end of World War II, has witnessed a notable expansion in field investigation of the Inca past. This research is remarkable both for its extent and depth; almost every facet of the Inca achievement has been studied. Such key factors as the road network and the storage system, so basic to the process of social expansion, have been examined in detail, as have typically Inca sites such as Huánuco Pampa and fortress settlements in more remote parts of the Empire. Numerous studies have also been published of the coastal provinces. In order to better understand the Andean past, archaeologists now also study present-day ways of life. Researchers may compare their own findings not only with tools described in earlier documents but also with those still used in the Andes, some of which have scarcely changed over the centuries.

Apart from the core regions, Ecuador has received close attention as the scene of fierce hostilities between Inca rulers and local tribes. Much fieldwork has also been carried out in the southern reaches of the Empire, stretching as far as Santiago in central Chile. Recently more attention has also been paid to the final boundaries of the Inca domain, on which the sources' information is rather vague.

An additional factor, most relevant to any study of the Inca, is the information provided by archaeological research about the possible role of Huari as a potential conquest state and thus, in a certain sense, a predecessor to the Inca Empire. This vast site twenty-five kilometers northeast of Ayacucho was visited by Tello as long ago as 1932, but he never published his findings, and Huari remained unknown. Rowe, Collier, and Willey made a further reconnaissance in 1946 and produced a report seeking to relate Huari to other Andean sites, including Nazca and Tihuanaco.[21] Ben-

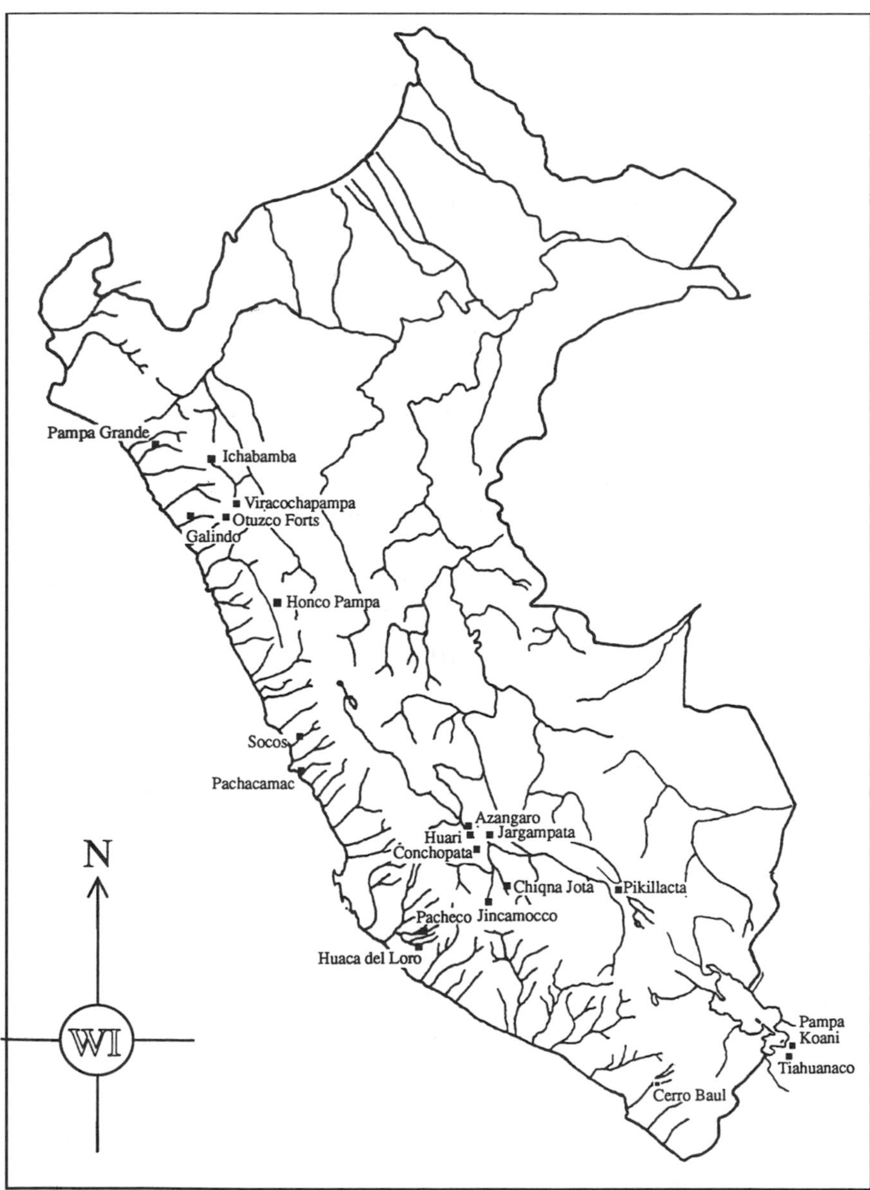

The Major Middle Horizon Sites in Peru. From Huari Administrative Structure *by William H. Isbell and Gordon McEwan, 1991. Dumbarton Oaks. Reprinted by permission of the publisher.*

nett conducted the first excavations, and his published account included a sketch map.[22] Subsequently the Huari Urban Prehistory Project excavated the site under the direction of William Isbell, discovering much evidence of the evolution of state administrative architecture.

Considering that Huari-related ceramics are widely distributed across Peru, archaeologists concluded that Huari constituted a "horizon style" — that is, a style encompassing the whole cultural area. The horizons concept was originally defined by Geoffrey Bushnell, with the major categories identified as Formative, Classic, and Postclassic.[23] The concept was later much modified; the Huari-inspired period is now defined as the Middle Horizon, dated from approximately A.D. 600 to 1000. It is preceded by the Early Intermediate (A.D. 0–600) and followed by the Late Intermediate, or pre-Inca, Period (A.D. 1000–1400). Isbell, who offers an estimate of five hundred occupied hectares for the site of Huari, suggests that a figure of ten thousand to twenty thousand inhabitants is acceptable, though the population might have ranged between twenty thousand and thirty-four thousand.[24] Isbell writes of massive walls that divide Huari into irregular sectors; the complexity and poor preservation of the architectural remains hinder the task of interpreting the settlement's form and organization. These large walled enclosures divided into barracklike residences are the dominant feature of Huari architecture.[25]

In addition to the wide circulation of Huari-inspired ceramics, there also appeared at this time in areas outside the Huari heartland large administrative centers, one of which (Pikillacta) lies in the Valley of Cuzco. The resemblance of their planned enclosures to those of Huari, together with the presence of Huari-style pottery, led Isbell to suggest that they might have belonged to a Huari provincial organization.[26] In another context he wrote that Huari became the capital of a state that had conquered a substantial territory, the control of which would require a bureaucratic hierarchy of administrators.[27] Lumbreras offers a similar interpretation of Huari as a conquest state and even provides a map of the Huari Empire. For Lumbreras, urbanism and militarism began with Huari and gradually affected all central Andean societies.[28]

In many respects, perhaps including road and storage systems, precedents for Inca achievements do exist. However, in contrast to Tula, the pre-Aztec conquest state of Mexico, Huari left behind no written records of any conquests, and the scope of a possible pre-Inca empire is thus harder to define.

Tihuanaco had emerged as an equally powerful highland state. Its earlier phases predate Huari, to which its exact relationship remains rather obscure. According to Isbell, Huari and Tihuanaco display common cultural attributes, and some interaction undoubtedly took place between the two.[29] Moreover, Tihuanaco and Huari shared a common iconography, of which a dominant theme was the classic image of a staffed front-facing deity on a pedestal, flanked by two or more rows of profile attendants. Variants of this image appear on the Gate of the Sun at Tihuanaco and on ceremonial urns and jars from the site of Conchopata, near Huari.[30] A certain rather ill-defined relationship is apparent between the "gateway god" and the Inca creator deity, Viracocha, who according to legend appeared in Tihuanaco at the beginning of the world. Rowe, however, sees the Middle Horizon deity as more related to Illapa, the Inca thunder god, or to his Aymara equivalent, Thunapa.[31]

Hence, one may conclude that some antecedents not only of Inca statecraft but also of Inca religion may be found in the comparatively remote Middle Horizon, which ended in about A.D. 1000. From the Late Intermediate Period, an interval of up to four centuries between the end of the Middle Horizon and the rise of the Inca, no evidence survives that suggests the emergence of a paramount power in the central Andes. Certain aspects of leading principalities that existed during this period, all eventually absorbed into the Inca Empire, will be considered later. Outstanding among these are the kingdom of Chimor, the principalities of the Ica-Chincha coastal culture, and the successor states of Tihuanaco, in particular the independent Colla and Lupaqa kingdoms that arose during the Late Intermediate and were among the early Inca conquests. But because the written sources relate to the period after they had become part of the Empire, their previous history and territorial extent are ill-defined.

A Cautious Approach

Though archaeological research has thus enriched our knowledge both of the Incas themselves and of possible Middle Horizon precedents, in many respects its findings tend to confirm as much as to deny the accounts of the primary sources. These, for instance, generally define the Inca realm as stretching from northern Ecuador to central Chile, thus very approximately corresponding to the traces of Inca occupation as now identified by archaeologists. The latter offer much data, but it would be hard to base an account of the Inca achievement exclusively on either their findings or the reports of the historical sources. The sources are rich in detail but often lack credibility except where more concrete proof is offered. To cite a single example, Cabello's vivid account of the wars waged by Huayna Capac against the tribes of northern Ecuador, in which he describes the tribes' use of a series of mountain fortresses for defensive purposes, might well be dismissed as just another colorful fable.[32] But Plaza Schuller lends support to Cabello's tale in the form of archaeological evidence indicating that defenses of this very kind existed. The evidence includes a map depicting a ring of fourteen simple forts stretching from the northwest to the southeast of Ibarra, situated in the extreme north of Ecuador — in the precise region where Huayna Capac campaigned.[33] Nonetheless, the sources by their very nature pose so many questions as to lead certain scholars to treat them with limited credulity. However, these written sources remain indispensable in the study of certain questions; archaeological research alone simply cannot provide the kind of data needed to examine, say, the role of the Inca ruler or the workings of the Cuzco hierarchy.

Given these fundamental problems, can Inca history be written at all? Or is the would-be historian confronted on the basic issues with little more than an assortment of contrived myths? The dilemma is posed in forthright terms by Tom Zuidema. He argues that the chronicles tend to reflect the differing social classes of their informants and were written by men confused by abstruse and unfamiliar belief systems.[34]

Though many investigators may not share Zuidema's hesitation to accept the historicity of the main sources, few would deny the relevance of the problems he poses, and most would accept the need for caution in assessing the sources' reliability. One may cite Murra, who stresses the need to transform casual reading of the chroniclers into rigorous examination and affirms that a persistent analysis of the primary sources offers the only alternative to outmoded models based on arbitrary selection of quotations and the resulting compilation of reports of questionable value.[35]

As a substitute to any such arbitrary selection of quotations, the temptation may also arise to reach conclusions by a kind of head count, presenting as plausible whichever version of a given episode is supported by the largest number of sources. But because the chroniclers often copied each other's works, a point treated as factual by a whole series of writers may in reality emanate from a single informant.

Even if certain special characteristics of the Andean chronicles compel the modern scholar to offer interpretations that reflect his own subjective judgment, this surely does not wholly negate the possibility of objective analysis of the Inca achievement. The problem, far from being unique, is more or less universal. Few students of antiquity today would deny that attempts to retrieve the past are inevitably influenced by subjective judgment. Claude Lévi-Strauss stresses the point: "No one can even write a history of the French revolution; all the historian can do is to reconstruct a myth based on his own selection of fact. History is never, therefore, history, but 'history for. . . .' "[36]

On man's endeavors to accurately record his past, one may also cite the philosopher Michael Oakeshott: "There is no history that is not a judgment, no event which is not an inference. There is nothing whatever outside the historian's experience." In another passage of the same work, he writes: "If the historical past be knowable, it must belong to the present world of experience; if it be unknowable, history is worse than futile, it is impossible."[37] Such comments may pose in a wider context the question of how far Andean history can indeed be written, as the Incas can hardly be said to belong to the present world of experience.

The lack of precise native-written accounts of what really happened is therefore hardly confined to the Andean region and should not deter the ethnohistorian from at least seeking to outline the actual course of events. Without such an endeavor, social and economic problems become hard to clarify —just as, for instance, it would become almost impossible to define such aspects of late eighteenth- and nineteenth-century European society if doubts prevailed over such basic facts as whether Frederic the Great lived before Napoleon or whether it was he or Napoleon who invaded Russia and took Moscow.

Modern historians rightly place greater emphasis than their predecessors on socioeconomic conditions, as opposed to offering a mere catalogue of political events, a kind of heroic history based on the lives of rulers and the triumphs of their armies. But as part of the process of clarifying those conditions we must first face the complex task of offering at least *some* overall reconstruction of political events. To fulfill this purpose, in Chapter 2 I cover the shadowy reigns of the first seven rulers. In the following two chapters I sift the evidence available on the events of the great period of Inca expansion, beginning with Pachacutec and ending with Huayna Capac. The latter's reign may be somewhat more clearly defined than that of other rulers, as the leading informers of the early chroniclers included various sons and grandsons of Huayna Capac. In subsequent chapters dynastic, social, and economic systems will be studied, first those of the metropolis Cuzco, thereafter those of the Inca Empire. I end the book with an attempt to assess Inca motivations and to account for their remarkable achievements.

It must always be borne in mind that for events to become meaningful they have to be considered in the context of the values attributed to them by participants, values that are at least in part ritual. In the case of the Incas, happenings can only be viewed in the light of their relative significance within the framework of their own society. As Marshall Sahlins, in describing Polynesian society, writes: "Events cannot be understood apart from the values attributed to them: the significance transforms a mere happening into a fateful conjecture. What is for some people a radical event may appear to others as a date for lunch."[38]

CHAPTER 2

The First of the Incas

THE CREATION

Before examining the diverse accounts of the foundation, or occupation, of Cuzco by the Incas, one must first ask: What do we know of their more remote origins? What were their creation myths, and how do these compare with those of other Andean peoples? In more precise terms, did such myths come from the coast, as Demarest suggests, or rather, as Rowe believes, from the Aymara legends of the Lake Titicaca region?

Mircea Eliade aptly describes myth as a form of sacred history in which the actors in the drama are not men but supernatural beings. Myth is thus related to a "creation" that tells how something first came into existence; it reveals that the world and life itself have a supernatural history and that this history is significant, precious, and exemplary.[1] Creation myths, to be found in every part of the globe, are essentially narrative and perform the vital function of anchoring a people's present in their past.

Most of the principal Inca chroniclers write fairly briefly, if at all, of the original creation of man; if mentioned, it tends to be associated with the Lake Titicaca region and often with the site of Tihuanaco. For instance, Betanzos states that at a time when all was still and dark the creator, Tici Viracocha, ruled over certain people, whose name no one recalls. Viracocha, who first emerged from Lake Titicaca, killed these shadowy beings who had offended him and turned them into stone. Then he rose up from the lake once more and, after creating the sun and the moon, fashioned certain new people out of stone, together with many pregnant women and others who had recently given birth. With these he went to Tihuanaco and then dispatched them to different places, including Cuzco.[2]

Cieza de León (the first two chapters of his *Senorío de los Incas* were lost) deals less specifically with the creation of man, focusing on events that occurred when mankind already lived in the Andean region. This omission is scarcely surprising in Peruvian chronicles; it was hard for Spanish Christians, nurtured on the creation story in the Book of Genesis, to admit to a second creation in the New World, complete with its own Adam and Eve living in an Andean version of the Garden of Eden. Reluctant to contemplate such heresies, few chroniclers speculated as to how people descended from a single creation in the Old World had reached Peru. Cieza speaks briefly of a flood in Collao in which only six humans survived. Somewhat confusingly, he also writes of a primordial god who equally arose from the island in Lake Titicaca, a being who was tall and white; he did not create mankind but taught the people he found how they should live, including those who eventually reached Cuzco. This creator was commonly called Tici Viracocha. Though he did not create the world, he first caused the sun to shine upon it; he was able to move mountains and produce huge fountains.[3] Writing some twenty years later, Sarmiento de Gamboa recounts a similar legend of a world inhabited by giants, who were ultimately destroyed by a flood; as in the Betanzos account, the sun and the moon originally produced no light. In the second age of the world, Viracocha created the present Indian race in the region of Lake Titicaca.[4]

Garcilasco de la Vega recounts how he learned of Inca creation legends from sages who visited his mother's house in Cuzco. These sages had survived from pre-Conquest times. He refers to the creator as "Our father, the sun," who took pity on mankind's ignorance and sent two of his sons to earth. They emerged from Lake Titicaca and proceeded to the Cuzco region.[5] But in Andean cosmogony there is really no account of the creation of the world ex nihilo, as there is in so many other cultures. Andean chroniclers tend to write of the appearance of tutelary divinities in a world that already existed.

George Kubler, writing more of the Andean region as a whole than of the Incas in particular, draws attention to stories of multiple creation, or a series of worlds, told by as many as sixteen chroniclers before 1650. Some write of only two creations, or suns; others include as many as four. These sources vividly recall the Mesoamerican accounts of the birth of four or sometimes five suns.[6]

As an example of such chroniclers, Kubler cites López de Gómara, who wrote in 1552 and tells of two primordial gods, Con and Pachacama, for two creations of mankind. Con was a man from the north without bones who called himself Son of the Sun and settled the earth with men and women. Pachacama was also a son of the sun and moon; he exiled Con, turning humans into black cats. A new race of humans was then destroyed by a flood. Thus, two deities were responsible for two creations; these were followed by two more without named sponsors.[7] The legend of Con also occurs in ethnohistorical data gleaned from many coastal sites described by Rostworowski. Con is a water deity whose cult preceded that of Pachacama.[8]

Pedro Gutiérrez de Santa Clara, whose work dates from about 1597, tells of only two creations by Con and Pachacama. They are depicted as a couple who first formed the earth, sun, moon, and sky and engendered all living things before leaving earth for the sky. Many centuries later Pachacama came back and destroyed everything, making men into monkeys (as occurred in some versions of the Mexican accounts of the destruction of four suns). Gutiérrez's account closely resembles that of Gómara in recording a double creation, first by Con and thereafter by Pachacama. Kubler lists other chroniclers who tell of multiple creations, including Murúa. The latter wrote that the Incas were living under the fifth of a series of suns; its emblem was the disk of gold in the Coricancha temple, before which Huayna Capac was crowned. The same scheme is presented in the work of Huaman Poma. Calancha, writing in 1630, also tells the story of five suns. Huaman Poma de Ayala wrote between 1612 and 1615 and, unlike most chroniclers, composed his account mainly in Quechua. He enumerates the successive ages: first the dawn and the cataclysm, and subsequently the five ages of man: primeval, legendary, desolation, growth, warfare, and finally Inca. This scheme was widely diffused in a history written for school use in Peru in 1939.[9]

The Inca myth of human origins appears to comprise a kind of double creation, at times involving two successive worlds and at others one world peopled by two successive races. In the case of other legends, such as the turning of men into monkeys or the creation of four or five worlds instead of two, Kubler finds it hard to avoid the conclusion that they are more of Mesoamerican than of Peruvian origin. Wedin also considers Gutiérrez de Santa Clara's work a reflection of that of Gómara, who was so familiar with Mexican sources.[10] Legends of four or five suns and of the transformation of the inhabitants of past worlds into animals after a series of cataclysms are recorded in detail in classical Nahuatl in the *Legend of the Suns* and other pre-Columbian Mexican texts. Kubler suggests that similar myths from Andean sources might derive from a common ancestry in Asiatic paleolithic times, but such coincidences are surely better explained by the Mexican affiliations of Andean chroniclers who first described them.

Another resemblance to Mesoamerica is also present: the tendency to credit the creator, Viracocha, with attributes remarkably similar to those of the Aztec creator god, Quetzalcoatl. Fernando de Alva Ixtlilxóchitl depicts the latter deity as a Christlike figure, fair-skinned, bearded, and dressed in a long white robe, who traveled through the land preaching repentance and the cult of holiness and performing miracles.[11] He eventually reached the Maya land and departed on a raft. Like Quetzalcoatl, Viracocha is at times portrayed as an itinerant deity, white of skin and dressed in a long robe; at the end of his journey, he also departed by sea.

Myth Becomes Saga

If what survives of Inca mythology offers fewer embellishments than the legends of other peoples, this may be the consequence of the Spaniards' inability or unwillingness to probe deeper. The Andean civilizations as a whole possessed a rich and varied mythology, as portrayed, for instance, on Moche and Nazca ceramics.

In this context, however, we are concerned with Inca rather than pan-Andean myths, though, according to Demarest's account, Viracocha's cult is virtually inseparable from that of the pre-Inca coastal deity Pachacama.[12] In this Demarest differs from Rowe, who insists that the events of the basic Inca legend all take place around Lake Titicaca. Rowe thereby deduces that the Incas borrowed their creation saga from the Aymara peoples of that region, implying that this myth was a fairly late compilation based in part on the tale of the Aymara thunder god Thunapa and subsequently revamped by the ruler Pachacutec.[13]

Mircea Eliade, in affirming that myths generally tend to tell how something came into existence, attaches great significance to the foundation of cities.[14] But in Inca mythology, in contrast to that of many cultures, most versions suggest that man had been created *before* the narration begins; in some accounts the creator sends his son and daughter to civilize and teach beings who already exist. Similarly, for most chroniclers Cuzco was not "founded" by the Incas but was already inhabited when they arrived upon the scene and only later absorbed, together with the surrounding valley, by their early rulers. An exception to this version is Garcilasco, who tells how the son and daughter of the creator founded Cuzco after first sinking their magic staff into the earth.[15]

Regardless of how far one accepts Rowe's contention that the Viracocha creation saga was a borrowed version, he may be right in suggesting that much of Inca legend was contrived by the ruler Pachacutec at a later date. In this instance it seems that we are faced not with primordial mythology but with myth manipulated and modified to serve the ends of state and empire. This alteration was achieved in part by refurbishing the tale of the first Incas who settled in Cuzco but also in part by stressing the semidivine genius of the alleged architect of the city's true greatness, Pachacutec. As Jean Puhvel writes, myth may serve to bring a sacred past to bear preemptively on the present and, inferentially, on the future. At the next level of transmission, "The sacred narrative has already been secularized, myth has been turned into saga, sacred time into heroic past, gods into heroes, and mythical action into 'historical' plot."[16]

In this context, Franklyn Pease writes of the reign of Pachacutec as literally "a new primordial age, identifiable with the origin of the state."[17] In terms of comparative mythology, this phenomenon, which will be further considered in the following chapter, conforms more to Georges Dumézil's description not of fictitious creation myths but of another type of saga. Stories of this type are drawn from authentic events and real actors, though presented in more or less stylized fashion, duly embellished, and set forth as an example to emulate. They adorn a remote past or future, performing in inaccessible zones where gods, giants, and demons have their sport.[18] Dumézil, in his many studies of the common Indo-European heritage, points out that every people has its own epic history based on the acts of its heroes and underlying traditional philosophy.[19]

Hence, in assessing Inca mythology, perhaps better regarded as Inca narrative saga, the original stress is laid upon the Viracocha legend centered on the Lake Titicaca region. But, as we shall also see later in more detail, the Viracocha cult, originally related in part to that of the thunder god Illapa, becomes progressively "solarized." The main ceremonies are dedicated to Inti, the sun god, and it is Inti who personifies the imperial cultand is imposed as the supreme symbol of Inca rule on the many conquered peoples.

THE ROAD TO CUZCO

Inca creation (or postcreation) mythology may serve as a preface to their early history, which embraces the reigns of the first seven rulers. The story is told by many chroniclers; on certain matters they generally concur, whereas on others they differ. The great Pachacutec, the ninth ruler, in establishing the households, or *panacas*, of the first seven rulers, in effect formalized a kind of official history that served as a background for the different accounts of early Cuzco. Hence, the chroniclers generally agree as to the names of these first seven Inca rulers, who preceded Viracocha, father of the great Pachacutec. As spelled in Rowe's account, they are as follows:

1. Manco Capac
2. Sinchi Roca
3. Lloqui Yupanqui
4. Mayta Capac
5. Capac Yupanqui
6. Inca Roca
7. Yahuar Huaca[20]

A variant on this theme is the version of Montesinos, who, not content with an enlarged succession of Inca rulers, names a bewildering array of supposedly pre-Inca kings. This list, now generally discounted, achieved a short-lived credibility in the work of Clements Markham, *The Incas of Peru*. Philip Ainsworth Means, whose *Ancient Civilizations of the Andes* was published in 1931, accepted the orthodox list of seven rulers given above but, largely following Garcilasco's account, stretched the Inca chronology and credited these earlier rulers with spectacular triumphs, starting with the conquest of the Lake Titicaca basin in about A.D. 1200. According to this Garcilascan version, the third Inca, Lloqui Yupanqui, advanced into Collao and conquered the province of Chucuito; the fourth, Mayta Capac, occupied the ancient site of Tihuanaco and thereafter proceeded to subdue the Arequipa region; his successor, Capac Yupanqui, had scarcely ascended the throne before he embarked on a long-range campaign of conquest.[21] Rowe helps to clarify the issue by listing both the chroniclers who credited the early rulers with such conquests and those who denied that such conquests occurred.[22] But the shorter list of those who follow the Garcilasco line and favor early conquests includes chroniclers such as Murúa and Huaman Poma, whose data are of lesser historical significance.

Many accounts exist of the arrival of the first Incas in the Cuzco Valley. Cieza de León states that he based his account of their coming on what he learned from Cayo Tupac, son of Sayri Tupac, heir to the post-Conquest

Inca rebel Manco and hence a descendant of Huayna Capac. Cieza and other chroniclers offer a fairly uniform version of these early happenings, which can be summarized as follows. Proceeding from the Lake Titicaca region, the Incas reached Paucartambo, lying to the southeast of Cuzco. Their leader, Manco, was accompanied by three brothers (in some versions by two), each of whom had a sister-wife. From Paucartambo they proceeded to the hill of Huanacauri, some eight miles from Cuzco; here one brother, Ayar Cachi, was turned to stone. Ayar Cachi was an almost god-like figure of prodigious strength. He could throw boulders that would level whole hills; sometimes those cast by his sling flew so high that they rose above the clouds. He entered a cave, and his brothers blocked the entrance. He was then turned into a *huaca,* or sacred stone, which became one of the most holy objects in Inca ritual. The second brother, Ayar Uchu, was transformed into a winged being and thereafter was changed into a stone at Matahua on the slopes of Huanacauri. The third brother, Ayar Auca, reportedly flew on ahead of Manco to Cuzco; when he alighted there he became the community stone, called Cuzco Huanca, the Field of Cuzco.[23]

Having rid himself of his brothers, Manco, accompanied by his wife, Mama Ocllo, reached Cuzco. There, according to Cieza and others, he built the first Coricancha temple. Manco, according to Sarmiento, found Cuzco already inhabited and fought battles against nearby peoples variously named Huallas and Alcavizas.[24]

Though certain sources, in particular Cieza, Cobo, Sarmiento, and Cabello de Balboa, offer some details of each of the early reigns, others, such as Betanzos, say little about them. Certain specific events are common to these sources, though at times the chroniclers disagree as to the reign in which they occurred. For instance, Cieza states that the fourth ruler, Mayta Capac, married a princess from Oma, about five miles from Cuzco, whereas Cobo says that it was his predecessor, Lloqui Yupanqui, who married the daughter of the ruler of Oma.[25] The war against the Ayarmacas is attributed by Cieza to Inca Roca but by Sarmiento to Inca Roca's successor, Yahuar Huaca.[26]

In certain instances the sources differ sharply. For instance, for Sarmiento the second Inca, Sinchi Roca, was not a man of war, whereas for Murúa he was a great military leader. Equally, Sarmiento describes Lloqui Yupanqui as an indolent monarch, whereas Cobo states that he subdued many local lords and fought battles against the Ayarmacas.[27] Often they differ concerning marriages: Cieza maintains that Sinchi Roca married his sister, but Cobo states that he wedded the daughter of a neighboring chief.[28] (In reality the practice of marrying a sister was probably a late introduction into Inca custom.) Cieza also writes that the sixth ruler, Inca Roca, married his sister, though this is denied by other sources.[29]

Nonetheless, a curious kind of common thread does seem to run through these rather conflicting accounts of early Cuzco, as if they were based at least in part on some single standard or official version. For instance, Cieza, Cobo, Sarmiento, and Cabello agree in mentioning the Incas' arrival at Paucartambo and their proceeding thence to Huanacauri; all give the same information as to the distances of these two places from Cuzco itself (seven and four leagues, respectively). All agree that Mayta Capac succeeded to the throne when he was still very young and, equally, that this prince fought against the Alcavizas. To Capac Yupanqui some southward excursion into Condesuyu is generally ascribed. To the sixth ruler, Inca Roca, is almost invariably attributed the division of the capital into Hurin (lower) and Hanan (upper) Cuzco; he is stated to have been the first ruler to govern from Hanan Cuzco, whereas his predecessors had lived in Hurin, in Coricancha. Hence, accounts do seem to have some common, if cryptic, background, to which each chronicler adds his own embellishments.

The fullest accounts of the first six reigns are those of Sarmiento and Cabello de Balboa. Though they wrote their chronicles in 1572 and 1586, respectively, they seem to have obtained virtually the same data from a single version of events. Much of this information is not included, for instance, in Cieza's earlier work. The two writers tell a very similar story, mixing the obviously fabulous with the ostensibly factual, though differing on lesser details. Their stories of the deeds of the last two rulers before the Conquest, Tupac Inca and Huayna Capac, have so many items in common, including textually identical passages, that they seem to derive to a considerable degree from some common source (as we shall later see in detail).

To cite a specific instance of their record of the early rulers: In describing Mayta Capac, the fourth king, both start by telling of confrontations between the Incas on the one hand and Alcavizas and Culunchimas on the other. The latter are described as "natives of Cuzco," implying that the Inca presence in that place was as yet not very firmly established. Both then tell a confused story of how the Incas' adversaries sent "ten Indians" with the intention of killing Mayta Capac and his father, Lloqui Yupanqui (who was still reigning), in their abode in the temple of the sun. Sarmiento states that the prince Mayta Capac killed one of the ten by hurling a ball with which he was playing; the others fled. Cabello merely differs in stating that two of the invaders were killed.

In both versions the Alcavizas attack Cuzco and reach the walls of Coricancha; Lloqui Yupanqui is panic-stricken but is told by his advisers (*ayllus* in Sarmiento and "priests" in Cabello) to place full reliance on his son, Mayta Capac. A magic hailstorm, rather than Mayta's prowess, puts the Alcavizas to flight. After this event, Mayta Capac ascends the throne and reportedly rules peacefully, fighting no more wars. Both chroniclers give details of his marriage to Mama Tacucaray and name the same three sons. Cobo, incidentally, also names the same wife and two of the sons of the marriage.[30]

To mention one further example, other sources concur that the sixth ruler, Inca Roca, was the first to divide Cuzco into Hanan (upper) and Hurin (lower) Cuzco. To this brief tale Sarmiento and Cabello add further parallel details; for instance, Roca conquers Muina, said to be four leagues distant from Cuzco by Sarmiento, and then captures or kills the leaders of the pueblos of Muina and Huamantupa.[31]

Any such convergence of these two leading chroniclers' accounts comes to be a factor of major significance in judging the provenance of their data regarding the conquests of later reigns. Gary Urton points out that the Incas had come to be identified with, or "concretized to," the town of Paucartambo but points to the disconcerting fact that no certainty exists as to the location of a site of that name between the mid-1530s and early 1570s. The Paucartambo that exists today, about eighteen miles southeast of Cuzco, came into existence, according to documentary evidence, in 1571, one year prior to the completion of Sarmiento's history; Urton questions whether Sarmiento might not have prodded his informants to get them to identify the original place in concrete geographical terms.

Urton further comments on the phenomenon of the existence of two series of origin myths, one centered upon Lake Titicaca and the other recording the Inca emergence from the cave of Paucartambo. Given the overall significance of the historical traditions of the Aymara kingdoms around Lake Titicaca, it is not surprising that the Incas might have sought such associations as a legitimate mandate for their rule; however, it is surely harder to justify a myth centered upon Paucartambo, then as now something of a political and cultural backwater.[32]

ALTERNATIVE APPROACHES

Rowe was among the first scholars to pose the question of whether the rulers before Viracocha made real conquests. He concludes that the triumphs attributed to these kings were mere raids and that the same places had to be reconquered again in subsequent reigns. This conclusion would appear logical in the absence of evidence to the contrary. One is, however, left with the impression that even if their hold on the surrounding region was tenuous, the rulers that preceded Viracocha Inca may at least have begun to achieve a certain primacy over their late neighbors, though perhaps not to the extent of exacting regular tribute.

Rowe has suggested that the period of the first eight Inca rulers, including Viracocha, lasted from about A.D. 1200 until 1438, the date he gives (following the Cabello de Balboa chronology) for the accession of Pachacutec. He further mentions pre-Inca remains in four sites in the Valley of Cuzco belonging to what he calls the Chanapata culture; their pottery is well made and abundant, metal objects are lacking, and very few remains of buildings can be identified. For the early Inca period, the pottery is classified within the Killke series, named from a site near Cuzco where Rowe first identified this ware. In the three sites named, one of which lies literally within the great fortress of Sacsahuaman, metal continues to be rare, and bone tools are common. Wall foundations are of uncut field stones. Killke is described as a carelessly executed ware whose designs are linear and geometric; it displays some relationship to the contemporary Collao black-on-red common in the region of Puno and to some of the characteristic motives used by Late Inca potters.[33] González Corrales, giving more data on Killke pottery, also mentions a Killke wall.[34]

Based on much more recent investigations of Killke pottery, Brian Bauer in effect suggests that the Incas were not invaders of the Cuzco Valley but had lived there already for many centuries; he proposes that the incipient Inca state was not localized within the city of Cuzco but incorporated a much broader region. He cites Huaman Poma as stating that Incas — i.e., those with ear perforations — came from a fairly extensive area around the city, having already become Incas by privilege *(Incas de privilegio)* at a comparatively early date.[35]

Bauer thus associates the birth of the Inca state with much of the Killke period, which on the basis of radiocarbon dating he believes to have started as early as A.D. 1000, after the abandonment of the Huari site of Pikillacta, rather than about A.D. 1200, as previously proposed by Rowe. Bauer in effect expands the views of Moseley, who argues that the origins of Cuzco may derive from Killke times; though Cuzco's expansion during that era is not well understood, such expansion might have begun much earlier than Inca lore would suggest.[36]

Admittedly, evidence for the association of the Incas with Killke pottery seems to be somewhat tenuous at present, but the notion that they were basically native to the Valley of Cuzco nonetheless merits serious consideration. To cite a parallel instance, I myself, though not altogether accepting Bauer's tendency to disparage "event-based" history, have consistently proposed, in agreement with Rudolf van Zantwijk and others, that the Mexica (later to become known as Aztecs) were not predominately nomads but people who had resided for several centuries in the Valley of Mexico and who later merged with a smaller nomad group from the north; hence, the story of their wanderings from Aztlan might therefore be at least partly mythical.[37]

Rowe includes this period of the seven rulers in what he calls the "more or less historic time." Brundage goes somewhat further and devotes a full chapter of his *Empire of the Inca* to the first seven rulers, narrating events of each reign. In view of contradictions between certain chroniclers on these early rulers, however, this kind of history must rely on individual judgment as to which of several accounts can more logically be woven into a coherent story.

Alfred Métraux, writing in 1961 in his *History of the Incas*, already sounded a warning note about the reliability of such accounts of the deeds of the earlier Incas:

> At first sight the precision with which their reigns are numbered, and the stories they tell us, inspire confidence. On closer examination this favourable impression is found to be illusory. Behind a superabundance of often insignificant detail the big historical events grow blurred, and, in spite of their apparent exactitude, are found to amount to very little. It is naturally in the more distant periods that the line dividing myth from history is most difficult to trace. If on the whole the chroniclers agree in their account of events, these are not always attributed to the same Inca. It is not uncommon for some events to have a double use and to be told in the same manner about two sep-

> arate reigns. The dynastic lists do not always agree, and father, son and grandson are sometimes mistaken for one another.[38]

Métraux aptly describes the uncertainties that beset the accounts of early Cuzco. Zuidema goes much further in seeking to demonstrate that myths relating to Inca Roca and even to Pachacutec were also attached in certain accounts to the later kings, Tupac Yupanqui and Huayna Capac, still remembered by certain informants of the Spanish chroniclers. Because mythical elements are present in accounts of events up to the time of the Spanish Conquest, Zuidema asks: "How do we distinguish historicized myth that sounds reasonable in terms of history from real history, even where it concerns the last kings? We do not have to doubt that the persons existed, but there is every reason to be critical in accepting events in the generational sequence as given." According to Zuidema, chroniclers writing after Molina and Polo de Ondegardo further modified this scheme to make it more and more "reasonable to Western understanding." Zuidema adds that the same confusion applies to our knowledge of Inca social organization. The relationship between the panacas and ayllus is obscure and only achieves a more logical sense when related to a cosmological structure, although an understanding of this relationship is basic to Inca political institutions and history.[39]

In another context Zuidema further stresses the mythological content of Inca history: "Inca 'history,' then, integrates religious, calendrically ritual and remembered facts into one ideological system, which was hierarchical in terms of space and time. This Inca hierarchical ideology should not be confused with the Western linear conception of history imposed by the Spanish."[40] Zuidema suggests that a historical chronology up to the Spanish Conquest could perhaps only be provided by archaeology. This task might seem hard to achieve in the immediate future, although archaeological research has indeed made impressive additions to our knowledge of the range of Inca conquest and, to a more limited extent, of the sequence in which those conquests might have taken place.

Descriptions of Inca history as largely mythological might be treated by some investigators as overstated or exaggerated if taken out of context. However, the basic message conveyed by such conclusions — the belief that in the Inca chroniclers an element of myth is seldom wholly absent — is surely not without a certain validity.

It may be tempting, though not necessarily accurate, to dismiss the story of the first seven rulers as pure fiction, but such labels can hardly be applied to Pachacutec or even to his father, Viracocha Inca. As noted above, a kind of common thread seems to connect the principal chroniclers' accounts of early rulers, a thread that might be seen as based on something more solid than mere invention. Moreover, in the final instance the historian cannot escape the fact that, if these monarchs were expunged from the record as totally fictitious, then wholly anonymous leaders would simply have to be credited with the same achievements — namely, the feat of acquiring over a few generations at least a certain control over part of the Valley of Cuzco. Without some such preponderance, Pachacutec's spectacular defeat of the Chancas, as described by the chroniclers, would have been surely unattainable. The Alban king list, which by a most curious coincidence also consists of seven shadowy monarchs who ruled before the foundation of Rome, might be viewed in a comparable light. Few today believe the list to amount to much more than a fiction, but any suggestion that there are insufficient grounds to give it any credence are apt to be greeted with outraged cries of "hypercriticism." The whole justification for these kings lies in their function of bridging the gap between the fall of Troy and the foundation of Rome, regardless of whether the actual names are correct.

Given the vagueness of the written evidence concerning the first seven Inca kings, it would surely be hard to dispel the cloud of uncertainty by any attempt to describe this era reign by reign. Possibly this initial period, whose length we really ignore, might best be divided simply into early and late. The early phase, beginning with the "founder," Manco Capac, is rich in elements of pure myth involving the elimination of his brothers, turned into stone huacas or even into birds. Of his successor, Sinchi Roca, almost nothing of note is reported, and the third ruler, Lloqui Yupanqui, is generally described as pacific or inactive. In the earliest of these pre-Pachacutec reigns, the Incas may have strengthened their hold on most of what became the city of Cuzco, leading to inevitable conflict with other peoples who occupied the region, in particular the Alcavizas, mentioned by many sources.

In the later portion of this era of the seven kings, embracing perhaps the fourth, fifth, sixth, and even seventh reigns, the Incas may have tightened their grip on the site of Cuzco and even ventured farther afield on forays that scarcely deserve to rank as conquests. In contrast to the reportedly passive third ruler, the fourth, Mayta Capac, is said to have led victories over the Alcavizas and clashes with Ayarmacas. The sixth, Roca, is generally credited, as we have seen, with the division of the city into upper (Hanan) and lower (Hurin) Cuzco and with the relocation of the leading dynasty in Hanan Cuzco. The latter is itself an event of great importance, implying the complete domination at least of the elongated triangle between the two rivers, later to become the core of urban Cuzco. Cabello reports that Inca Roca advanced farther from Cuzco than his predecessor, but the mention by certain sources of expeditions to Condesuyu, lying to the southwest, or to places on the road to Collao, to the southeast, should not be taken to imply long-range conquests. Only the Garcilascan school pretends that at this stage the Incas advanced deep into Collao.

Two Kings or One?

Even such a brief and tentative review of the early Inca monarchy poses certain questions worthy of comment as relevant to the future course of events.

First, a basic feature of the historic Cuzco was its division into two moieties, Hurin and Hanan. This step is attributed by some to Manco Capac but more generally associated with the sixth ruler, Inca Roca. Rostworowski suggests that the division of Andean cities into upper and lower halves stems from a remote past.[41] In this respect, it may be worth noting that Michael Moseley raises the possibility that moiety organization and dual role prevailed in the pre-Inca kingdom of Chimor. He presents the last four *ciudadelas*, or palaces, of Chanchan as being built in pairs, with the principal ruler residing in the eastern palace and his "segunda persona" occupying a more modest structure in the Western moiety.[42] Rostworowski, however, questions whether in fact duality was not first imposed by the Incas when they conquered the region.[43]

Rostworowski further demonstrates that the practice was almost universal, existing in polities as distant one from another as Puno on Lake Titicaca, the Cañari region of Ecuador, the coastal Yungas, and certain settlements of the high Andes. Sarmiento even relates that the Chancas, the Incas' implacable foes, were divided into Hurin and Hanan Chanca, each with its own ruler, the latter being the more powerful of the two.[44] Among the more notable examples of dual rule are the Lupaqa, of which we have an eyewitness account in the 1567 *visita* of Garci Díez de San Miguel. At the time of this visita, the Lupaqa were still divided into Hanansaya and

Hurinsaya, governed, respectively, by Don Martín Cari and Don Martín Cusi. Cari and Cusi had been the traditional names of the rulers of the two moieties.[45] Murra questions whether this dual monarchy could not have been imposed on the Lupaqa by the Incas, a suggestion that might imply some kind of dual government in Cuzco itself involving not only a division into two halves but also the presence of two kings.[46] The *Relaciones Geográficas* in some instances do mention the Incas' involvement in imposing a dual division on others. The Soras, who lived in the vicinity of Huamanga, were divided into two groups, Hanansora and Hurinsora. The *Relaciones* attribute this dual division to a system implanted by the Incas when they first conquered the land.[47]

The division of Cuzco, in conformity with so many other places, into two halves lies at the very root of the system of control of the city and of its future empire. With respect to certain parts of the Incas' domain, the question remains somewhat open as to how far the Hurin/Hanan duality existed already or was introduced by the conquerors. Another question raised by certain authors is whether the two Cuzcos, upper and lower, might have been ruled not by one but two dynasties, as occurred, for instance, in Collao.

Rostworowski elaborates on this theme but agrees that any suggestion of dual government is purely a hypothesis, almost impossible to prove in practice. She writes of the possibility that the first Incas to approach Cuzco might have had two rulers and cites Sarmiento, Cabello, and Betanzos as stating that a second of the original four "brothers," Ayar Auca, settled in Cuzco in addition to Ayar Manco, the founder mentioned by all sources. (Manco's other two brothers had already been converted into huacas.) The sources unite in stating that Coricancha was the residence of the Hurin rulers, whereas those of Hanan built their own palaces. If Manco belonged to the Hurin moiety, conceivably Ayar Auca was the progenitor of the Hanan Incas, who installed themselves in the upper part of the settlement. The name Auca indicates that its possessor was principally a warrior, in conformity with the prevailing notion of Hanan as the more warlike and hence more powerful moiety. The consensus is that the Hanan dynasty launched the great territorial expansion, whereas Hurin reportedly prevailed in matters of religion.[48]

Zuidema, in writing of the same problem, quotes Polo de Ondegardo as treating the Hurin and Hanan dynasties, both descended from Manco, the first ruler, as contemporary halves of a dual kingship. In Zuidema's reconstruction of Polo's data, Manco heads the king list as sole ruler; the second place on the list features two kings, Sinchi Roca as ruler of Hanan and Inca Roca as ruler of Hurin; the fourth place is jointly occupied by Mayta Capac as ruler of Hurin and Pachacutec as contemporary Hanan ruler. Like Rostworowski, Zuidema agrees that any supposition concerning a dual dynasty remains unproven: "Some will trust certain facts or dates of the Inca as historical, whereas others consider as more important how Inca concepts of their past might help to clarify Inca culture in general. . . . Even if a dual Inca dynasty might be preferred, comparing it to other Andean institutions outside Cuzco, we do not know whether or how such a dynasty really did exist in Cuzco."[49] Zuidema further suggests, as already proposed in his earlier work, *The Ceque System of Cuzco*, that the Hurin/Hanan split reveals itself as a division into right and left sides (facing upriver) of the Huatanay River. Fortresses and military installations are all to be found on the right side of the Huatanay.[50]

Pierre Duviols is among the leading exponents of the theory of a dual monarchy, as expressed in his 1979 paper, "The Dynasty of the Incas: Monarchy or Duarchy?" His initial scheme also derives from Polo, and, in agreement with Zuidema's analysis, identifies Mayta Capac as the fourth Hurin sub-ruler, paired with Pachacutec; only Pachacutec's successors become sole leaders, without any Hurin co-ruler (again in agreement with Zuidema). Duviols reproduces Zuidema's parallel list of rulers but attributes the roster more to Acosta, though it needs to be borne in mind that, according to Acosta himself, much of the material on Peru in his "Historia Natural y Moral de las Indias" was derived (or perhaps copied) from Polo.[51] Duviols cites certain documents as avoiding any reference to the existence of Hurin rulers prior to those of Hanan, but his sources include chroniclers such as López de Gómara (whose information, as we have seen, tended to reflect his Mexican experiences) and Montesinos (described by Wedin as practically useless in providing information on the Incas).[52]

More relevant perhaps is Duviols's reference to a statement by Cieza de Léon, who indeed mentions Indian reports to the effect that one Inca leader had to be from one moiety and the other from the other moiety (though not necessarily reigning at the same time). Cieza, however, goes on to say that he gives little credit to this report, which differs from what the nobles had told him.[53] Duviols also cites another chronicler, Cristóbal de Molina, known as "el Cuzqueno," whose *Fábulas y Ritos de los Incas*, dated 1575, was the product of careful inquiry among survivors of the clergy of the native religion. De Molina recalls that the Inca, on his accession, would name an important relative to take charge of certain affairs and that this "second person" was connected with the priests of the sun. But this assertion implies the presence not of a co-ruler in the fullest sense but rather of a kind of coadjutor chosen specifically from Hurin Cuzco, where the Temple of the Sun was situated. Duviols, moreover, cites Santillán as writing of a "secretary" who was informed of all the affairs of state.[54] Even the later Inca rulers seem to have had a kind of alter ego; Huayna Capac had an adviser, Auqui Topa, who was always with him. Sarmiento also notes that de la Bandera describes Auqui Topa as Huayna Capac's secretary.[55] Cabello even states that Pachacutec named Apo Mayta, his brother, "second person" in military operations.[56] Huaman Poma de Ayala, however, portrays his own grandfather, Guaman Chinchay Suyu, as Huayna Capac's "second person." Described also as "captain general," he conquered the province of Quito.[57]

Duviols rightly points to the inability of the Spaniards to conceive of any type of monarchy except their own, noting also the Incas' lack of interest in explaining their system to their conquerors. But for Duviols, as for others, the notion of a dual monarchy is basically a hypothesis, even though he describes the legend of the change of dynasty from Hurin to Hanan as absurd. The existence of a kind of special assistant from the sacerdotal class of Hurin is not incompatible with a single monarchy based on Hanan and might be a vestige from earlier times of some kind of dual rule, a system that continued in Collao, whose influence on Inca culture is undeniable. Moreover, Duviols's reference to the possible selection by each Inca ruler of his own Hurin-based coadjutor, whose office would terminate on that ruler's death, would eliminate the objection that a neat dual king list is hard to conceive because the reign of a given Hanan king could hardly coincide exactly with that of a Hurin colleague (i.e., a single long-lived ruler of one dynasty might have outlived successive kings of the other).

The story of the first seven rulers is so fragmentary that the possibility that they might have in certain cases reigned simultaneously is not to be excluded. A further possibility arises, though it is seldom proposed. Until the time of the sixth ruler, Inca Roca, the Incas — who according to all accounts faced many hostile neighbors — might have controlled only part of Cuzco, the sector of the city centered upon Coricancha and lying nearest to the confluence of the two rivers. The Alcavizas still lived in Cuzco at the time of the fourth Inca. It would then have been natural for Roca to install his government in the upper part, newly secured, and henceforth Hanan would have taken precedence in temporal affairs over Hurin, which preserved its significance more as a religious center. If from the time of their arrival the Incas had also occupied Hanan, then Hanan, in accordance with traditional Andean norms, surely would have been predominant over Hurin and over the dynasty generally described as installed in Coricancha.

Dualism is an ever-present factor in human society in one form or another. In Persia, Zoroastrianism was a religion impregnated with the principle of dualism, and in China the *yin-yang* precept served as the ethical basis of society. The division of cities into two, or four, distinct sectors, each with a distinct role, is also a common practice throughout the world. For instance, in India ancient cities were divided into four parts; the most high-ranking class of citizens, the Brahmans, lived in the northern, or upper, sector, which thus became predominant.[58] Examples of dual political control are not hard to find, whether in the form of two kings in Sparta or of two consuls in Rome. However, in early imperial times Rome came to be governed by one ruler; moreover, it is hard to imagine that a system of divided control would have been well suited to the phase of expansion set in motion by Pachacutec and to the conquest of the immense Inca realm. Fundamental to this process of conquest was the imperial solar cult, imposed on the provinces as the essential symbol of Inca control; this cult was clearly based on the godlike status of a single monarch, not of two.

The Immortal Kings

One of the strangest facets of Inca kingship requires mention at this point, as it came to involve the more shadowy early rulers as well as their better-documented successors. In Cuzco the descendants of each Inca, excluding the reigning monarch, constituted a group known as a panaca. This group's mission was to conserve the dead ruler's mummy and to immortalize his life and achievements with the help of chants and rituals performed on ceremonial occasions in the presence of the reigning king and the mummies of other dead Incas. These rites were passed on from generation to generation. Each panaca possessed lands, worked by numerous slaves or servants known as *yana*. The royal panacas formed the elite of

Cuzco, and doubtless their differences contributed to a chronic instability marked by periodic plots against reigning monarchs and in particular by confrontations over the succession when a ruler died.

Rostworowski suggests that the panacas might be an early phenomenon in Inca history and that the adherents of Ayar Manco and Ayar Auca might have used this term to denote their followers.[59] But even if the system had such ancient roots, it was revitalized by Pachacutec. Sarmiento, for instance, tells how Pachacutec disinterred the bodies of the first seven Incas, situated in the Temple of the Sun.[60] Betanzos even states that Pachacutec was responsible for the fashioning of mortuary bundles of the remains of these seven rulers, which were then set on thrones beside that of his own father; he adds that it was Pachacutec who provided the lands and servants for the lavish maintenance of the panacas, which henceforth played such a leading role in Cuzco.[61] After the death of Huayna Capac, shortly before the Spanish invasion, there were eleven such mummies. On ceremonial occasions, that of Huayna Capac was flanked on one side by those of the Hurin rulers and on the other by the five, including his father, Tupac, of the Hanan dynasty. Matters were somewhat complicated by the existence of five additional panacas, two belonging to Hanan and three to Hurin.

Also present in Cuzco was the institution of the ayllu, a kingship group that still exists in present-day Peru. The possibility arises that originally the terms *panaca* and *ayllu* might have been synonymous; however, they developed on somewhat different lines. A probable difference between them was that the ayllu was patrilineal and the panaca matrilineal.[62] The Cuzco ayllu system embraced not only the royal ayllus, of which there were at the time of the Conquest eleven (six in Hanan and five in Hurin), but also those of the Incas by privilege *(por privilegio)*, formed not by nobles of Inca descent but by leaders of neighboring peoples who had been granted this title. The original Incas, often kin of the ruler, were called *orejones*, thus named because their ears were pierced with unusually large holes.

Rowe gives perhaps the best description of the ayllu. The earliest modern writers insisted that it was a clan, but chroniclers' accounts fail to clarify the precise role of the ancient ayllu because of the looseness of Quechua terminology. Rowe rejects the description of the ayllu as a clan, as it was not a totemic group derived from some animal ancestor. He defines the ayllu as a kin group with theoretical endogamy, with descent in the male line, and without totemism.[63] Its most important function was the ownership of a well-defined territory, within which each married couple cultivated a parcel of land sufficient for their support. Zuidema also views the ayllu as being related to a shared territory; the land could not be sold, but members of one ayllu could also hold land in another in which they did not live.[64] However, both men and women belonged, and may still belong today, to the ayllu in which they reside and in which they possess the right and eventual obligation to occupy an office in the political and religious hierarchies.

Problems involving the status of the ayllus and panacas are inseparable from the *ceque* system in Cuzco. Both in Cuzco and in the surrounding country, numerous sanctuaries and huacas, many connected with the royal panacas, were situated on ceques, or imaginary lines. Ceques were divided into four sections, or quarters, as defined by the principal roads radiating from the capital in the direction of the four quarters of Cuzco and of Tahuantinsuyu, the Inca Empire. These quarters were called Chinchasuyu, Antisuyu, Collasuyu, and Condesuyu (occasionally written Cuntisuyu). This complicated ceque system was an ancient institution, found both among Quechua- and Aymara-speaking peoples.[65]

Zuidema made an extensive study, *The Ceque System of Cuzco*, published in 1964. He stresses both the antiquity of the system in Andean civilization and its extreme complexity.[66] In all there were 41 ceques radiating from the Temple of the Sun, and on these were situated 328 huacas in and around the city, together with a number of sanctuaries. The ceques played an important part in the calendrical system and in Inca religion in general, including such aspects as child sacrifice. The most puzzling aspect of the system is the association of the ceques with the royal panacas; a seemingly arbitrary number of royal sanctuaries is connected with each. In general terms, earlier rulers such as Sinchi Roca and Lloqui Yupanqui had only one sanctuary or one huaca situated on a ceque. By contrast, Pachacutec's panaca was more generously endowed, but his successor, Tupac, also had only one huaca situated on a ceque. Although sanctuaries can be identified with certain panacas, the data leave us confused as to the association of political divisions with groups of ceques. Zuidema, in his most valuable, if involved, description, lays much emphasis on the importance of ceques not only for religious ritual in general but also for the related task of astronomical observation. In a more recent work, Zuidema writes of certain specific ceques, in particular the first ceque of Antisuyu, which was important in relation to Pachacutec.[67]

AYARMACAS AND OTHERS

The Incas found various peoples already established in the Cuzco region, groups frequently mentioned by the sources. Their identity is more important than might appear at first sight; by all accounts the Inca themselves were limited in number, and it was these neighbors, once subdued, who came to form a large proportion of the inhabitants of the core region of the Empire. Their elite, granted the title of Inca by privilege, played an important role in the Inca state.

The sources' accounts of these pre-Inca inhabitants scarcely permit a coherent analysis of their respective roles or even of the order in which their confrontations with the Incas occurred. Groups reportedly encountered by the first three Inca rulers include the Huallas and the Sausirays. In particular the first ruler, Manco Capac, is credited with victories over these two peoples. Cabello de Balboa describes the Hualla ruler, Copalimayta, as the "Señor Natural de Cuzco."[68] However, Sarmiento goes so far as to affirm that Manco killed the entire Hualla population, taking special care to eliminate pregnant women and their embryo offspring in order to ensure that no trace of them should survive.[69]

This chronicler states that Manco also defeated the Sausirays, then located in the crucial triangle between the two rivers. Brundage cites evidence to the effect that the Sausirays, who had arrived in the Cuzco Valley later than the Huallas, controlled the important crossing over the Tullumayo River, whereas another newly arrived group, the Alcavizas, who had also crossed over into the triangle, dominated the equally important passage over the Huatanay River.[70] In particular, the *Informaciones* of the Viceroy Toledo, always anxious to depict the Incas as usurpers, treat the Sausirays and Huallas as the earliest inhabitants and state that the ayllu of the Sausirays, which still existed when he wrote, had occupied the part of Cuzco where Coricancha was later built.[71] Somewhat more formidable were the Alcavizas, mentioned by Cieza, Sarmiento, and Cabello as having been routed by the fourth Inca, Mayta Capac.[72] Toledo, presumably drawing his conclusions from a common tradition confirmed by the many informants that he gathered, concurs that it was Mayta Capac who subdued the Alcavizas and drove them from the central part of Cuzco. He mentions that they still lived very near to Cuzco in his time.[73]

Outstanding among the early adversaries of the Incas were the Ayarmacas. In a detailed study, Rostworowski notes the significance of the fact that the four Inca brothers who traditionally set forth from their legendary home were themselves named Ayar Cache, Ayar Uchu, Ayar Auca, and Ayar Manco.[74] She cites Murúa and Garcilasco as affirming that the Ayarmacas occupied a fairly extensive territory that stretched toward the Vilcanota River (about ten miles north of Cuzco) but also embraced eighteen villages south of Cuzco. Her account includes a map of areas still occupied by Ayarmacas in the eighteenth century, naming in particular various ayllus in the Pucyura area, about twelve miles northwest of Cuzco.[75] The same author points out that Tocay Capac and Pinahua Capac are generic names of the two Ayarmaca chiefs, as reported in many sixteenth-century manuscripts; possibly these corresponded to Hurin and Hanan moieties, suggestive of a dual rulership of the kind mentioned above.

Most reports of Inca hostilities against the Ayarmacas belong to the reign of the sixth ruler, Inca Roca. These are linked to the legend related by certain sources (though omitted by others) of the kidnapping by the Ayarmacas of Roca's son, who became the seventh ruler, Yahuar Huaca. The latter, when still a child, was reportedly consigned to the people of Huayllacan, who concealed his whereabouts by making him serve as a simple herdsman in the mountains for a whole year. After a hard-fought battle, the prince was liberated, and the rift between Incas and Ayarmacas was at least temporarily healed by a double marriage between their ruling houses.[76] According to Sarmiento, further hostilities ensued in the reign of Viracocha, and the Ayarmacas were finally subjugated by Pachacutec, following his epic struggle against the Chancas. After the Chanca defeat, the Ayarmacas were the first to face the victorious ruler; the Tocay Capac of the time reportedly refused to submit, considering himself a leading potentate in his own right. He assembled a large force but was defeated; many of his subjects were massacred, and he was taken to Cuzco, where he died as a captive.[77] The Ayarmacas did not play a leading role in the expanding Inca Empire but did retain a place in the Cuzco ceque system; the eighth of the nine ceques corresponding to Antisuyu was named Ayarmaca.

Uncertain Premises

As we have seen, it is hard to offer a very coherent picture of Inca society, let alone a chronology of events, prior to the initial phase of imperial conquest. Not only chroniclers but also modern authors disagree. For some of the latter, the early rulers are historical personalities, almost comparable, say, to some early medieval kings; for others, they are pure legend.

Many scholars accept Rowe's summing up as a fair appraisal of the problem. According to Rowe, reports that depict Cuzco as little more than a village until the mid-fifteenth century are probably correct. He observes that the more credible sources write only of very limited conquests before the reign of Pachacutec, conquests so inconclusive that this ruler had to reconquer the same places.[78] In another context Rowe aptly sums up the situation:

> In early times, neither the Inca nor any of their neighbours thought of organizing their conquests as a permanent domain. A defeated village was looted, and perhaps a tribute was imposed on it, but otherwise it was left alone until it recovered sufficient strength to be a menace again. Down to the reign of Pachacutec, towns very near to Cuzco preserved complete freedom of action and raided one another's territory whenever there seemed to be a good opportunity for plunder. Yahuar Huaca and Viracocha were probably responsible for the first attempts to organize conquered territory, at least around the capital itself, and their successful campaigns gave the Inca state a political importance it had entirely lacked in earlier times.[79]

The last sentence of this passage is significant. Surely at least the credit for certain achievements must be conceded to Pachacutec's immediate predecessors, as his spectacular career is hardly conceivable if at the outset he could claim nothing but disputed control over a single village. Rostworowski asks whether Cuzco was not first dominated by some fairly powerful non-Inca ruler. It is difficult to see how it ever rose to prominence if the ruler or rulers lacked power and means.[80]

It is far from clear to what extent the Incas themselves were native to the Cuzco region. Sources write of the first rulers of Cuzco as emerging from Paucartambo, a mere eighteen miles distant. But in Inca religion and mythology some kind of connection with the Lake Titicaca region is undeniable, in view of the presence in the Inca pantheon of Viracocha, the creator divinity whose cult by all accounts originated in Collao. As Pease writes, modern archaeologists agree with the early chroniclers in maintaining that at the time immediately prior to the formation of Tahuantinsuyu, a significant relationship existed between the region of Cuzco and that of Lake Titicaca.[81] The existence of some Collao connection is thus hardly in dispute, even if the extent to which Viracocha should be regarded as an early introduction into the Inca pantheon is, as we have seen, more open to question.

Hence, no consensus exists as to how far this pantheon may serve as proof of early links with the Collao region. Many peoples cherish their myths of early migration from an earlier sacred place of origin, though archaeologists nowadays tend to question migration legends as overall explanations of the historical record. For myself, as for certain other authors, the Mexicas, the builders of the Aztec Empire, consisted of a blend between the legendary group of migrants from afar and other groups local to the Valley of Mexico. Similarly, it is not inconceivable that the Incas represented a unique blend arising from a merging of migrants from the Lake Titicaca area with peoples native to the Cuzco region. Such a mingling might serve to account both for the oft-repeated stories of a migration from Collao and for the alternative tale of the emergence of the founding fathers from the cave at Paucartambo, so near to Cuzco.

CHAPTER 3

The Era of Pachacutec

A New Era

The reigns of Viracocha, successor to Yahuar Huaca, and of Viracocha's heir, most commonly known as Pachacutec, mark the dawning of an era generally accepted as historical. By contrast, some scholars treat Viracocha's predecessors as authentic rulers, whereas for others they belong more to the realm of fiction.

In writing of this new era, the available data present certain problems. Foremost among these is the relationship of Pachacutec to his father and predecessor, Viracocha. Pachacutec is alternatively portrayed by sources as a legitimate successor on Viracocha's death, as co-ruler with his father for a substantial period, or as a mere usurper whom Viracocha sought to kill. Moreover, in writing of Pachacutec we are concerned not just with a great ruler but with the primordial cultural hero, creator of both city and empire. In conformity with this role, Pachacutec even revamped the Inca past, to a point that at times he himself becomes as much a figure of legend as of history. A wealth of information about Pachacutec survives, on which Maria Rostworowski in 1953 based a lengthy biography. With the help of a careful appraisement of the sources, she offers a meaningful study of the traditional founder and creator of the Inca Empire. While considering these sources, however, it should be borne in mind that certain scholars now tend to question how far the overall Inca achievement can spring from the achievements of a single ruler, a point that will be further considered at the conclusion of this chapter.

In writing of the career of Pachacutec, the investigator still faces the basic division of the sources into two categories: those who say there was a rapid expansion by the last three rulers before the conquest and those, of whom the principal exponent is Garcilasco de la Vega, who credit earlier rulers with major conquests and accordingly maintain that Viracocha inherited an extensive realm. Garcilasco further confuses the story by insisting that Viracocha, not his heir (as reported by others), vanquished the Chancas, thus unleashing the forces of Inca expansion, and by stating that Viracocha then made conquests up to a distance of about six hundred miles from Cuzco.

Whereas earlier writers, such as Means, tend to endorse the Garcilascan account of Viracocha as heir to an empire, which he then greatly extended, Rostworowski and subsequent authors mainly reject this version. Rostworowski goes so far as to describe Garcilasco's work as little more than a historical novel, a story that in effect advances the course of history by one reign, denying to Pachacutec his epic role in vanquishing the Chanca foe but, in turn, crediting him with distant conquests more probably made by his son, Tupac.[1]

For the reign of Pachacutec, as for the shadowy early rulers, the four sources most often cited — Sarmiento, Cabello de Balboa, Cieza de León, and Cobo — at times concur and at times differ. The Garcilasco version of events is so dissimilar from these four accounts that it becomes more convenient to consider it separately. In addition to these four chroniclers, Betanzos offers much information on the reign of Pachacutec. He generally agrees with the four major sources on certain events of Viracocha's reign, such as his eventual withdrawal from Cuzco and his preference for Urco as his successor, though most state that the latter was an illegitimate son. Particularly in such matters of genealogy the sources tend to agree, a tendency that might imply the existence of some single standard and accessible version of royal lineage. All concur in naming the wives of Pachacutec's father, Viracocha, and of his grandfather, Yahuar Huaca; all describe Pachacutec as a legitimate son; and most name his brothers — Roca, Mayta, and Vicaquirao — and record their active role in his support.

Sarmiento and Cabello, whose accounts of the events of the early kings have much in common, diverge somewhat in reporting the actions of Viracocha and the initial stages of Pachacutec's career; Cabello, for unknown reasons, gives only a very brief report of this period. However, the two chroniclers' versions of later events in this monarch's reign once more run closely parallel; they describe in very similar terms the final flight of the remaining Chancas across the Andes, together with the expedition to Cajamarca led by Capac Yupanqui and his subsequent execution. As we shall see in the following chapter, the accounts of Sarmiento and Cabello are beyond all doubt closely linked for the reigns of Pachacutec's successors. Our most detailed information on the achievements of Tupac and

Huayna Capac comes from these two writers and is plainly based in part upon some common source that lists in more detail the events of these two reigns (see Appendix A).

Though chroniclers generally concur in treating Pachacutec as the virtual founder of the Inca Empire, some at times reveal a marked animosity toward this cultural hero. Sarmiento writes of his cruelty, citing as an example the killing of two brothers who had commanded the expedition to Chinchasuyu. The chronicler further accuses Pachacutec of extreme brutality against his enemies, in particular the Collas, two of whose leaders he threw to the wild beasts.[2] Cabello de Balboa writes that Pachacutec was so hated after the wanton killing of his brother that all longed for him to die.[3] Such statements might reflect certain grudges on the part of descendants of rival *panacas;* moreover, it should be recalled that Sarmiento's long history was commissioned by the Viceroy Toledo, who had instructed the author to demonstrate that the Incas were usurpers rather than rightful rulers.

In contrast, for other authors, such as Cieza and Betanzos, Pachacutec is basically virtuous. Cobo describes him as the most valiant, warlike, wise, and statesmanlike of all the Inca rulers; he injected order and reason into everything. As part of his recording of Inca rites, Pachacutec himself composed many elegant prayers and was most diligent in matters pertaining to the temporal welfare of his subjects.[4]

VIRACOCHA

Before examining the circumstances of Pachacutec's rise to power, the reign of his predecessor, Viracocha, must first be considered. Rostworowski cites sources that imply that Viracocha's accession to the throne was disputed after the heir originally named by Yahuar Huaca, the former monarch, was assassinated.[5] Cieza in particular describes a division of opinion among the Inca nobles before they eventually chose Viracocha as Inca. According to Cieza's version, Yahuar Huaca (whom Cieza calls Inca Yupanqui) was murdered, together with many of his wives, by rebellious generals after taking refuge in a temple.[6] In writing of his disputed succession, however, Cieza denies reports that Viracocha was not the son of his predecessor but rather was brought to Cuzco from outside.[7] Disputed successions, sometimes following the violent death of a ruler, were all too frequent, though exactly how a decision was then reached (except for the all-out civil war witnessed by the first Spaniards) is not always clear.

The course of events during Viracocha's reign is somewhat obscure, to a point that Rostworowski in a more recent work even questions whether he existed at all, raising the possibility that Pachacutec and Viracocha might have been one and the same person.[8] Nonetheless, this ruler appears extensively in the more relevant sources, quite apart from Garcilasco, whose account will be considered separately and who credits Viracocha with many of the triumphs more generally ascribed to Pachacutec.

Sarmiento describes Viracocha as the third legitimate son of Yahuar Huaca and writes of his conquests of places in the vicinity of Cuzco that had been occupied by earlier rulers and later abandoned after they had rebelled. Viracocha not only consolidated Inca control of Cuzco itself but also made conquests farther afield than those of his predecessor.[9] Cobo even credits him with the conquest of the town of Cacha, eighteen leagues from Cuzco.[10] Cieza implies that this ruler was the first to impose formal payment of tribute on conquered peoples. Cobo, perhaps following Garcilasco, with whose writings he was familiar, reports that Viracocha, before he had ascended the throne, defeated the Chancas (a triumph generally ascribed to Pachacutec) at a point situated only one league distant from Cuzco. His namesake, the god Viracocha, who had previously appeared to the prince in the guise of a bearded white man, assured his victory by sending reinforcements.[11] This account, as well as others (perhaps including Cieza's report of a kind of bloodless occupation of Collao), might suggest that Viracocha, as father of Pachacutec, was indeed a historical personage but that his reign is described in terms that savor of legend as much as of fact. Cieza, in describing Viracocha's expedition to Collao, somewhat unconvincingly maintains that the Incas fought no battles but merely witnessed a civil war between two Collao rulers, after which the victor, Cari, took possession of Chucuito. The triumphant ruler then proceeded to make a pact with Viracocha that acknowledged the latter not only as friend but as his *señor,* or lord, after which Viracocha returned peacefully to Cuzco.[12]

PACHACUTEC'S ACCESSION

Sources vary in describing Pachacutec as either the oldest or youngest son of his father, a point that counted more for Spanish chroniclers than for pre-Hispanic Incas. Some originally refer to Pachacutec as Titu Cusi Yupanqui, and certain chroniclers continue to call him Inca Yupanqui rather than Pachacutec, a name that he may have only adopted later. Sarmiento states that he came to be known by this title after his great victory over the Incas.

Cabello de Balboa describes Pachacutec as the eldest son and therefore "legitimate heir," though he names the illegitimate Urco as Viracocha's favorite child. Cabello, who tends to portray Pachacutec in unflattering terms, relates that after his victory over the Chancas he wickedly usurped the throne and subjected the "good youth" *(buen mozo)* Urco to a cruel death. Sarmiento differs somewhat in describing Pachacutec as his father's fourth son but concurs in stating that he usurped his father's throne, also implying that he killed Urco.[13] Murúa, like Cabello, describes Pachacutec as Viracocha's eldest son and therefore, according to Spanish notions, the "legitimate" heir; Murúa, however, confuses the whole story by subsequently describing Urco as a "great captain" and credits him with the most improbable feat of conquering distant Quito.[14] Cobo agrees with Cabello in stating that Pachacutec arranged to have Urco killed. He sent for Urco and pretended to honor him by offering him the command of a military expedition, then secretly ordered his captains to kill his rival in the heat of battle.[15]

These sources concur that Pachacutec was a legitimate son of the previous ruler, whereas Urco was his preferred heir, though illegitimate. Cieza, however, names Urco as rightful heir. According to him, Viracocha went to Collao and left Urco as governor of Cuzco, a privilege that in Cieza's history is invariably accorded to the ruler's most trusted relative. When the Chanca peril arose Viracocha retired from the scene but delivered the royal insignia to Urco; this drunken and feckless prince thereupon also resolved to abandon Cuzco. After the defeat of the Chancas, Cieza relates, the principal *orejones* decided that Urco could not return but should cease to be Inca and surrender his crown to Pachacutec, described as the second son of Viracocha; the latter thereafter died.[16]

As Rostworowski rightly remarks, the existence of Urco as a son of Viracocha is almost undeniable; to suppress him would be to suppress history itself. She lists no less than five sources that mention Urco as actual ruler and eleven others that describe him as son of Viracocha.[17] The possibility arises that, in the absence of firm rules of succession, additional Inca rulers such as Urco may at times have enjoyed a brief, if contested, reign;

but such ephemeral claimants would not then be accepted by the official record as true rulers or be endowed with a panaca. For instance, Cieza implies that Urco actually reigned for a short time but nonetheless names Pachacutec as ninth ruler, following Viracocha, because "the Indians only treat matters concerning Urco as a joke" *(los indios no tratan de sus cosas si no es para reir).*[18] In other words, his reign was not accorded historical recognition. The story of Pachacutec's accession to the throne does little to clarify the process whereby one pretender prevailed over another. Cieza in one instance writes that "those of Cuzco" *(los de Cuzco)* decided that Urco should lose his crown.[19] In another passage he states more specifically that the orejones, together with other native leaders, opposed Urco.[20]

The identity is not disclosed of those orejones who favored certain rulers and opposed others; as we shall later see, the role of any formal council of nobles is hard to identify. A dominant feature, common to most accounts, is the incapacity of the authors to escape from the fixed, Spanish notion of primogeniture. This bias helps explain why native informants were reluctant to discuss the fundamentals of the Inca monarchy, preferring simply to pander to the preconceived notions of their new masters.

The Chancas

The defeat of the Chancas constitutes the dramatic turning point in Inca history. The question then arises: Who were the Chancas, and what were their origins?

The Inca claim to statehood might be dated to the early fifteenth century, after their expedition to Collao (reportedly before Pachacutec's reign), though this campaign did not directly result in any formal conquest. For Schaedel, the important Chanca confederation was originally separated from the Cuzco region by a buffer Quechua chiefdom to the north. This territory was eventually overrun by the Chancas, located in the Andahuaylas region, lying to the west of Cuzco. This author, along with various other sources, also writes of the long cold war between Incas and Chancas, beginning well before Pachacutec's crushing of these adversaries. So little is known of the Chancas that one can only speculate about their population and extent. Relying on examination of the present-day potential of the region, Schaedel adds that one would suppose they were in an even smaller and less productive macroniche than the Cuzco basin and that their southward expansion may have been due to this very factor — namely, a thrust for *lebensraum*.[21]

Rostworowski attributes the origins of the Inca-Chanca rivalry to the reign of Inca Roca. This conclusion remains rather speculative, however, because the report derives mainly from Garcilasco, as repeated by Cobo. For Rostworowski, the Chanca nation was formed by the Pocras of Ayacucho together with the Rucanas and Soras of the province of Andahuaylas, the occupation of the latter having brought the Chancas to within striking distance of the Cuzco Valley.[22] The original language of the Soras was not Quechua but Aymara.[23] Certain accounts, such as Cobo's, maintain that the Chancas were natives of Andahuaylas, but Cieza implicitly differs by describing the Chanca conquest of that province.[24] In any event, at a moment when Cuzco was already an expanding chiefdom, the Chancas clearly had formed an important and aggressive confederation, and the Cuzco region was an obvious target for its further extension.

In a monograph on the Chancas, Lumbreras points out that confusion has arisen from Julio Tello's use of this name to designate a people associated with a style of pottery denominated as early as 1927 as Nazca B; its makers occupied an extensive territory stretching as far as the Pacific coast and embracing the lands of the Sora and Rucana groups.[25] But Lumbreras insists that Tello did not mean to associate this people, whom he linked to Nazca, with the bellicose Chancas who fought the Incas. The same author does acknowledge that archaeological sites, which he lists from the region of Vilcashuaman, owe their origins to the latter-day Chancas of the Inca period. One of these sites is actually called Willca Chanca. However, information remains scanty on this area, and although Lumbreras describes the Chanca question as basically archaeological, much remains to be done to clarify the problem.[26]

The Chanca War

Though accounts may differ as to the details of the Chanca war, a virtual consensus of historical sources views the Inca victory as the springboard for the explosive territorial expansion that followed. In the more standard versions of the story, the Chancas, by then a powerful confederation, had absorbed the Quechua buffer-state between Chancas and Incas during the early part of Viracocha's reign. They did not, however, penetrate to the Cuzco Valley itself until Viracocha was already an old man. The threat was so grave that many Incas, including Urco, the appointed heir to the crown, believed resistance was impossible. Viracocha, also convinced that the cause was hopeless, abandoned Cuzco and took refuge in Xaquixahuana, a fortress situated above Calca.

The events that followed are aptly summarized by Rowe. Pachacutec and his brother, Roca, backed by two able generals and a group of important nobles, refused to leave Cuzco and organized a last-ditch defense. Every inducement was used to secure allies. The Chancas tried to storm the city, but the Incas resisted heroically. At this crucial juncture the tide of fortune turned, as the very stones were transformed by the gods into warrior bands at Pachacutec's behest. After the attack was repulsed, the stones were collected and placed in the principal shrines of the city. In further encounters the Chancas were crushed, and as a consequence the Incas became the paramount power of the region.[27]

This version of events is amplified by several basic sources. Cieza reports that the Chancas defeated the Quechuas and occupied the province of Andahuaylas and that Viracocha left Pachacutec in charge when the Chancas advanced on Cuzco while he and Urco beat an ignominious retreat. Pachacutec called on neighboring rulers (possibly already in part subject to the Incas) for support and, after a hard-fought war, defeated the Chancas. Following this victory the leading orejones proclaimed Pachacutec ruler, and Viracocha died soon after.[28] The story of the stones that rose from the ground and transformed into warriors is dramatically told by Santacruz Pachacuti (who, incidentally, attributes the victory to Inca Viracocha). Sarmiento and Betanzos relate that the god Viracocha appeared in a vision to Pachacutec before the battle and promised that he would send reinforcements to ensure victory; the prince received from the god a mirror in which were reflected all the provinces he was destined to conquer.[29]

According to Betanzos, Pachacutec brought the Chanca insignia to Viracocha, but the latter, consumed with envy of his triumphant son, made an unsuccessful attempt to kill him, though he eventually abdicated in his favor.[30] Sarmiento agrees with this version, stating that Pachacutec deposed Viracocha and took the crown for himself.[31] As an example of the kind of confusion that can arise over names and events, Betanzos refers to the fallen Chanca leader as Uscovilca; Sarmiento reports that the Chancas bore with them on their campaign as a *huaca* a statue of Uscovilca, a *former* chieftain, and instead names as the *present* Chanca commanders Astu Huaraca and Tumay Huaraca, names repeated by Cabello and Cieza.[32] These two chiefs were killed in a second encounter, after the Chancas had rallied their forces and retreated from Cuzco itself. Sarmiento states that their heads were displayed on lances, and Cabello relates that their skulls were made into drinking cups.[33]

The Garcilasco Version

The sources cited above may differ over details, but at least they concur that Pachacutec rescued his city, obstructed more than aided by his father, who thereafter yielded the throne or died. Quite a different version of events is offered by Garcilasco; his account, partly based on that of Blas Valera, runs as follows. When Yahuar Huaca was still alive, it was his heir, Viracocha, rather than Pachacutec, who saw a vision of the god Viracocha. The latter appeared as a bearded man and in the name of the sun commanded him to undertake extensive conquests.[34] The god ordered the prince to assume his own name, Viracocha, stating that he himself was the brother of Manco (the first ruler). At this point in Yahuar Huaca's reign the Chancas appeared, coming from Andahuaylas, forty leagues distant. Three principal Chanca leaders are named who had established a powerful confederacy and engaged in prolonged hostilities against the peoples of the Cuzco Valley. Interestingly, the names of two of these Chanca leaders coincide with those given by Cieza, Sarmiento, and Cabello for Chanca chiefs. Events are, in effect, simply transposed backwards in time from Viracocha's reign to that of his father; like Viracocha in other accounts, Yahuar Huaca abandons the city in cowardly fashion, whereas Viracocha becomes the gallant defender and defeats the invaders.[35]

Yahuar Huaca in other respects is accorded the role assigned to Viracocha by many chroniclers, including the invidious treatment of his son after the latter's triumph over the Chancas. However, Garcilasco's Viracocha, as victor over the Chancas, respects his father's wish to continue to share the throne. Following this, Viracocha, not Pachacutec, launches ambitious campaigns leading to the acquisition of a vast empire, conquering such remote provinces as Tucumán (a feat more commonly attributed to Pachacutec's son, Tupac).[36]

Garcilasco is at times anti-Pachacutec, belittling his role as founder of the Empire. Nonetheless, he hotly denies the assertions of earlier chroniclers that Pachacutec forcibly deposed his father and insists that these reports are distorted. For Garcilasco, Pachacutec is the legitimate heir and the beneficiary of his father's achievements. Moreover, Garcilasco is not alone in giving a different story and in attributing certain triumphs to Viracocha. Cobo follows Garcilasco rather than earlier chroniclers in stating that Viracocha defeated the Chancas after a vision in which he was promised victory by a bearded and white-faced man in long robes. However, this battle was not decisive, and the Chancas were finally crushed by Pachacutec.[37]

Cobo also credits Viracocha with certain victories and conquests *after* the Chanca war. However, unlike Garcilasco, who contends that Viracocha then went on to conquer a huge domain, Cobo writes of more local triumphs, the farthest of which was the town of Cacha, eighteen leagues from Cuzco.[38] One other source, the *Declaración de los Quipocamayos*, refers to distant conquests made by Viracocha, including the great kingdom of Chimor, which dominated much of the northwestern coast of present-day Peru.[39] But apart from this account, few except Garcilasco credit Viracocha with more than limited conquests; most unite in describing Pachacutec not only as the true victor over the Chancas but also as the creative genius who inspired the Inca quest for imperial glory.

Pachacutec and the Inca State

Pachacutec, whether as co-ruler or ruler, seemingly enjoyed full control in the period after the Chanca defeat, during which he presided in person over the transformation of Cuzco into a resplendent city. At the same time he transformed its established religion into a dynamic force, the spiritual expression of the Inca will to conquer. By all accounts Pachacutec enjoyed a comparatively long reign, during the latter part of which his sons, first Amaru and subsequently Tupac, served as co-rulers. Rowe, on the basis of the Cabello de Balboa chronology, states that he reigned from 1438 to 1471.[40] Rowe describes this chronology, used only by Cabello, as "the most plausible yet proposed," but, as he himself implicitly agrees, no proven Inca system of dating exists.

Pachacutec's internal reconstruction was basic to the imperial expansion initiated in his reign. Vital to the process was the volume of material resources available to the king in the early stages of empire building.

Rostworowski insists that a *curaca*, or chieftain, could hardly begin to confront other powers without complete control over the resources and manpower of his late neighbors. She describes this as the key to the aggrandizement of the ruler of Cuzco and further suggests that the haul of booty snatched from his triumphs over the Chancas enabled Pachacutec to offer lavish rewards to local potentates; previously more or less independent, they now became subject to his rule.[41] Andean notions of reciprocity involved the bestowal of lavish gifts by major rulers upon lesser neighbors, presents symbolizing their obligation to serve his interests. According to such notions, the true sign of wealth was an ample reserve of foodstuffs and sumptuary goods. These could be amassed in storage facilities stocked with all that the land could produce and that human labor could fashion. Hence the economic factor, in the form of an imposing store of riches, might have served as a springboard for the conquests that followed.[42]

The sources unite in telling how Pachacutec inspired the building of the new Cuzco. Even Garcilasco, who attributes the feats of Pachacutec to Viracocha, affirms that it was the latter's son who re-created the city. Garcilasco further portrays Pachacutec as a reformer and legislator who promulgated many new laws and promoted many changes in Inca ceremonial and ritual.

The rebuilding in Hurin Cuzco of Coricancha, the great shrine of the sun (formerly also the residence of the ruler), was a major task. Under Pachacutec's successors this complex, the very heart of the imperial cult, was continually embellished. But Pachacutec gave Coricancha a very special aura by endowing it with resplendent golden statues of former rulers, elaborately clothed and fully armed. New chants were composed and special sacrificial rituals devised to honor their memory. As an expression of his reverence for the sun, Pachacutec ordered that numerous children, both boys and girls, should be buried alive in front of the main solar image. Betanzos tells how Pachacutec adorned the sun temple with a second statue, the image of a boy cast in pure gold, that recalled a figure that had appeared to him the night before his second battle with the Chancas, in which the enemy chief was killed. When the king prayed before this statue, it reportedly spoke with him. Only the greatest nobles were allowed to venerate this image.[43]

The continuous accumulation of precious metal in Cuzco must have been prodigious, as attested by the inventory of its trophies that Hernando Pizarro took to Seville.[44] Not content with the treasures of Coricancha itself, the Incas, Garcilasco writes, created a surrounding garden adorned with gold and silver. In this garden many exotic plants were cultivated for use in the temple rites. In the temple enclosure there were five imposing fountains with basins made of gold or silver in which sacrificial victims were cleansed. Garcilasco himself only saw one of these fountains, which served to provide water for the garden; at the time of his visit no more water flowed, and the plants were desiccated.[45]

Pachacutec, using labor provided by local curacas, launched an ambitious program of public works, including the canalization of the two rivers, whose flooding in the rainy season constantly menaced the city. Betanzos describes in some detail this laborious task, which even required the construction of protective works several leagues from the capital. In order to complete the undertaking, Pachacutec summoned many local curacas, explained the problem in detail, and commanded them to build a barrier upstream from the city; the barrier was to be made of rough stones held together with clay mortar.[46]

Apart from temples, imposing palaces now adorned the city, including that of Pachacutec himself. Its exact location is hard to identify. The palace called Casana is attributed to Pachacutec by Garcilasco, but other sources, including Pedro Pizarro, state that this was the palace of Huayna Capac. The dimensions of Sacsahuaman, the huge fortress that dominates the city, suggest that it was the work of several sovereigns, but both Cieza and Cobo state that construction was started by Pachacutec. Cieza writes that the fortress was originally called the House of the Sun and required twenty thousand men to build. Four thousand of these broke the stones, six thousand bore them to the site, and others dug the foundations. The workers were housed in nearby buildings, the ruins of which were still visible in Cieza's time. Sacsahuaman served as the city's main storehouse for arms and clothing as well as for massive quantities of jewels, gold, and silver.[47]

The first long-range conquests undertaken by Pachacutec implied at least an embryo version of the Inca road system, later to attain such spectacular proportions. Archaeological evidence cited by Hyslop indicates that in the Huari period roads were already built, perhaps for military purposes.[48] But the Inca system enjoyed a unique symbolism of its own, with its four principal roads radiating from the central square of Cuzco toward the four *suyus*. The city thus became the very navel of its nascent empire, being itself also divided into four sectors by these roads.

Pachacutec did not confine himself to rebuilding the city and renovating its infrastructure; his impact on the whole social fabric of the community was profound. Schaedel affirms that Pachacutec not only created a truly regal court and a centralized government but also introduced the corvée system to meet the immense demands for human labor. Both the use of *yana* serfs and of *mitimae* groups were fundamental to the establishment of an imperial capital.[49] Rostworowski, using hitherto unpublished documents, writes of the role of mitimaes, or contingents of people moved from conquered lands, as a major source of labor and also notes the use of yanaconas in irrigation work in Cuzco and in cultivation of the lands of the panacas.[50] As we shall later see, the mitimaes and the yanas were basic to the social structure, though the status of the latter is hard to define.

The creative process even transformed the social structure. The need arose because the members of the hereditary aristocracy belonging to the eleven royal *ayllus*, the original Incas linked by blood ties, were too few in number for the administration of a rapidly expanding state. To remedy the situation Pachacutec relied on the additional class of Incas by privilege. According to Rowe, these apparently came to form ten further ayllus, five from Hurin and five from Hanan Cuzco. These ayllus became an essential part of the Cuzco elite. Rowe cites evidence to show that the appellation "Inca by privilege" was extended to all those drawn from the surrounding region who spoke Quechua. Many were later settled as mitimaes in distant parts of the Empire, and they are often simply called Incas by the chroniclers.[51]

To make room in Cuzco for the great holdings and palaces of the growing aristocracy, Pachacutec removed the remaining inhabitants from the city. In particular the Ayarmacas, former adversaries of the Incas, were expelled. Rostworowski names the various localities in which they were then settled; in particular, eighteen Ayarmaca villages on the road to Collasuyu are mentioned by Garcilasco.[52]

Pachacutec's Pantheon

Basic to Pachacutec's achievement was his impact on the Inca state religion; it was now transformed into a powerful instrument that served to legitimize the process of conquest. However, opinions differ as to the precise orientation of certain religious changes. The sun, totem of the Andean tribes, was transformed into the official cult of empire, whereas the ancient deity, Viracocha, creator of the world and of man, continued to represent a more abstract, or higher, notion of religion. Pachacutec invoked the help of Viracocha when facing the Chanca menace, and after his victory this deity's status was further consolidated as the universal godhead, forming a triad with Inti, the sun, and Illapa, the thunder god. Pachacutec built a shrine dedicated to Viracocha in Quishuarcancha, and in the Temple of the Sun, Coricancha, the main altar contained the symbol of Viracocha. In Coricancha the effigies of past rulers were placed on golden thrones in order of antiquity. These faced toward the center of the temple, and it was only later that the emperor Huayna Capac ordered that his own image should face the solar disc. These effigies were statues of the rulers rather than mummified remains, which were jealously preserved by their panacas.[53]

Rowe argues that it was Pachacutec who promoted Inca creator worship in the form of the cult of Viracocha (whom, as we have seen, Rowe considers a product of the Lake Titicaca region). He states that this cult, which became fundamental to Inca religion, began with Pachacutec's great reforms. Hence, he views it as a vital but unquestionably late development, as the Incas only became familiar with the Lake Titicaca region in Pachacutec's time. Writes Rowe: "Inca creator worship began, as the Incas said it did, with the great religious reforms instituted by Pachakuti Inca Yupanqui. The religious reforms were a necessary part of the effort made by the great organizer to provide new and coherent central institutions which might integrate the diverse peoples over whom Pachakuti had recently extended imperial rule. . . . Secondary details were then added from a variety of traditional sources."[54]

Demarest, however, has pointed out that Rowe assumes a degree of isolationism that probably never existed in the Andean area and is certainly an inappropriate characterization of the post-Huari Andean world.[55] Archaeological research has now provided a plethora of data on the Huari and post-Huari periods and on the many aspects of Inca culture that were inherited from these earlier peoples and states. Demarest further describes as implausible the denial of any influence on Inca religion of the coastal cult of Pachacamac (which possessed a similar creation myth) and concludes that creator worship as a general cult, but particularly associated with Viracocha, was thus a basic element in the Inca pantheon rather than a later addition.

Demarest stresses that although the dichotomy between Inti and Viracocha as part of a general sky complex may be rather artificial, the enhanced role of Inti as dynastic ancestor, generally reported by the chroniclers, is fundamental to the development of the Inca religious system. He presents a range of arguments to the effect that Pachacutec succeeded in establishing the virtual supremacy not of Viracocha, the creator, but of Inti, the sun god: "Clearly the most recurrent contradiction between the creator and the sun concerns their roles and relative importance. Viracocha had no name, no endowment and no direct power, yet we hear repeatedly that he is the foremost deity. The largest ceremonies seem to be in honor of the sun. The presiding priest at all important rituals is the priest of Inti."[56] As further evidence of solar domination, Demarest cites the fact that the royal panacas trace their ancestry to the sun, not to the creator. The interwoven identity of the two gods is reflected in details of ceremonies, which frequently involve prayers and sacrifices to Viracocha in the name of the sun. The Inca himself confessed his sins not to Viracocha but directly to the sun, secretly asking the sun to be his intercessor with Viracocha.

One may concede that the issue tends to be confused by the identity of the figure in Pachacutec's famous vision, in which a bearded, white-faced god promised him victory. The importance of this figure cannot be exaggerated, regardless of the fact that certain sources attribute the vision to Pachacutec's predecessor. The deity in question, according to Demarest, is both the inspirational force behind the imperial ideal and the major idol of the state cult; yet, shockingly, the chroniclers themselves are divided as to whether this figure was the sun or Viracocha. As Demarest points out, Betanzos offers perhaps the most ambiguous version of all, explaining in some detail how Viracocha appeared before Pachacutec, who then proceeded to build temples to Inti, the sun.[57] The chronicler suggests that the resplendent nature of the vision misled the Inca into believing that this god was not Viracocha but the sun.

Many doubts thus beset our understanding of the fundamentals of the Inca religion, not only as to its origins but also as to the relative status of the leading gods. In truth, the respective rank of these chief deities was probably ill-defined. The notion of one supreme god as arbiter of the universe is a Judaeo-Christian concept that did not apply in pre-Hispanic America, where the specific standing of the various deities was not defined in precise terms and where no single god was necessarily regarded as supreme. The functions of the gods often overlap, and they cannot be pigeonholed and thus limited to a single specific role. This phenomenon is particularly notable in Mesoamerica, with its plethora of deities.

Any search for clarity may become even more blurred by the presence of a third deity, the weather, or thunder god, Illapa. Demarest cites ample evidence from the sources as to the importance not only of Viracocha and Inti but also of Illapa in forming the familiar trio of deities and stresses the rather bewildering tendency for their functions to merge.[58] Illapa is the Inca version of the archetypal Andean high god, the storm, sky, and creator deity Thunapa. Cobo even mentions Pachacutec's special veneration of a golden image of Inti Illapa.

The emphasis on the solar aspect of this intertwined trinity seems to be a unique Inca phenomenon, defined by Pease as the solarization of the state religion.[59] Such solarization was surely furthered by Pachacutec as promotor of the imperial cult.

Pachacutec the Conqueror

The tendency of chroniclers to name specific campaigns of conquest against a given adversary but to ascribe such conquests to different rulers makes it hard to define the territorial gains made by Pachacutec and to determine the limits of empire at the time of his death. Garcilasco is one of few sources to include Viracocha among the long-range conquerors. Others, such as Cieza, mention expeditions that were undertaken by this ruler but that were not necessarily conquests in the stricter sense. The records generally imply that, regardless of any longer-range incursions, Viracocha's own conquests were confined to places lying only a few leagues from Cuzco, in most cases within the range mentioned by Cobo, eighteen leagues. Viracocha thus at least appears to have subjected certain neighbors who had retained a degree of independence before his time.

Once the Chanca menace was removed, Pachacutec was free to embark on a much more ambitious career of expansion. His first aim was to complete the conquest — or reconquest — of the Valley of Cuzco and the surrounding region, in which the Incas were now the paramount power. Sarmiento mentions many centers subdued in the early stages, such as Cugma and Guata, four leagues from Cuzco, and the slightly more distant Ollantaytambo, lying six leagues to the northwest. As in subsequent campaigns, Pachacutec relied heavily on his generals, in particular on his brother, Inca Roca (namesake of the sixth Inca ruler).[60]

Leading chroniclers unite in attributing certain other major conquests to the reign of Pachacutec, though certain differences arise as to the order in which they occurred. The principal accounts of military operations continue to be those of Cieza, Sarmiento, and Cabello, together with the very divergent story of Garcilasco; Cobo, as an even later source, occasionally concurs with the latter but more often coincides with the former three chroniclers.

Except for Garcilasco, the sources agree in stating that, proceeding somewhat farther afield, Pachacutec next conquered the territory of the Soras, forty leagues distant from Cuzco and centered upon Huamanga; the Soras had previously been Chanca vassals. Following this campaign, several sources say, there was an expedition to Collao, led by Pachacutec in person. Sarmiento gives a fairly detailed account of Pachacutec's expedition against the important Colla center of Hatunqolla, wherein he took the defeated ruler, Chuchi Capac, back to Cuzco and had him beheaded, an incident repeated in Cabello's briefer account. Pachacutec's victory against this Colla ruler followed a long and hard-fought battle; the outcome remained uncertain until the Inca chided his troops for their failure to conquer an enemy so inferior in training and armaments. Chuchi Capac ruled a large domain centered on the Lake Titicaca region but also embracing land a mere twenty leagues from Cuzco and stretching as far as Arequipa.[61]

Cieza mentions incursions by Pachacutec into Collao in which he encountered the peoples of the Lake Titicaca region.[62] Cobo, in a fuller account, contrasts the conduct of the ruler of Collao, identified as Colla Capac (the name also given by Cabello for this ruler), with that of the Lupaqa Indians of Chucuito. The former led a fierce resistance, whereas the latter, who were just as powerful, received the Inca in peace and voluntarily surrendered their state. After these encounters, Pachacutec proceeded to subdue all the cities and peoples surrounding Lake Titicaca. He visited the great ruins of Tihuanaco and was amazed by the fine stonework, taking careful note of the method of construction, with a view to his own rebuilding of Cuzco. He thereafter went to the important shrine of Copacabana.[63]

The lack of reports of hostilities between the Lupaqas and Incas leads John Hyslop to ask whether an alliance between the two peoples might have existed before Pachacutec's campaign (perhaps forged following Viracocha's reported visit). Hyslop also refers to the great Colla revolt just before or after the death of Pachacutec and notes that only Cieza suggests active Lupaqa participation.[64] The same author nonetheless stresses the eventual impact of Inca penetration upon the Lupaqa region; archaeology demonstrates the abandonment of the earlier practice of living in high, fortified settlements and the establishment of new villages in the plains below as a result of the Inca presence.

The last major campaign undertaken during Pachacutec's reign, before his son Tupac Inca either succeeded as sole monarch or became co-ruler, was directed toward the northwest in the direction of Huánuco and led to the conquest of parts of the mountainous interior of present-day Peru. Commanded by Pachacutec's brother, Capac Yupanqui (namesake of the fifth Inca ruler), the expedition had as its primary objectives the valleys of Xauxa and Bonbón. Accounts differ as to whether this campaign preceded or followed the war against Collasuyu.

As was now their custom, the Incas enlisted in their army large contingents from previously conquered peoples, including in this instance the Chancas. In one of the first battles of the campaign, fought, according to Sarmiento, in the vicinity of Huamanga, these Chancas made a more notable contribution to the hard-won victory than the Incas themselves. This led to such a state of friction that the Incas took fright; Pachacutec sent a message to his general, Capac Yupanqui, ordering him to have all the Chancas massacred and telling him that if he failed in this task, he himself would be killed. The content of this order was leaked to the wife of Capac Yupanqui, who was the sister of the Chanca commander. Apprised of this threat, the Chanca force fled far inland. After crossing the cordillera in the area between Huánuco and Chachapoyas, they established themselves on the farther side of the Andean slopes.[65] In this instance, Cieza's account is closer to the Sarmiento and Cabello versions than is his description of Collao campaigns. Like the two other chroniclers, he states that the Chancas passed between Huánuco and Chachapoyas in their flight over the Andes; he even mentions the same Chanca leader, Anca Ayllo.[66]

According to Sarmiento and Cabello, Capac Yupanqui then advanced yet farther, reaching Cajamarca, where he was victorious in spite of help sent to that city by the ruler of Chimor. But in proceeding so far afield, Pachacutec's general had far exceeded his instructions, and, notwithstanding his triumphs, he was executed on his return to the capital.[67]

The sources thus generally agree as to Pachacutec's subjection of much of Collao and of territory to the northwest of Cuzco as far as Xauxa and

Bonbón; they also concur on the expedition to Cajamarca, which did not at this stage involve permanent conquest. From this point onward, Pachacutec in effect fades from the scene, and both the reins of government and the military command are assumed by his son, Tupac Inca. Cobo and Cieza actually state that Pachacutec felt too old to reign and surrendered the crown to Tupac.[68] Cabello, by contrast, writes that Pachacutec handed over the military command to Tupac before the latter's spectacular Chinchasuyu campaign to distant Ecuador but retained the title of co-ruler until his death, which according to this chronicler occurred in A.D. 1473.[69] Sarmiento states that before the same Chinchasuyu expedition, Pachacutec set aside his original heir apparent, Amaru Tupac, and ordered a series of great ceremonies to witness his surrender of power to Tupac Inca. As co-ruler he made a peaceful tour of inspection of many provinces before he fell ill and died.[70]

The accounts of Cabello and Sarmiento in effect treat a major portion of Tupac's conquests, notably his subjection of the coastal kingdom of Chimor and his campaign in Ecuador, as taking place during this co-reign of Tupac and his father. Hence, scholars at times credit Pachacutec with conquests ranging as far as Quito. However, Pachacutec's rescue and reconstruction of both city and state, followed by the subjection of a large territory, are feats prodigious enough in themselves. It surely is open to question whether he was also an active participant in those boundless additions to the realm usually associated with Tupac, embracing Ecuador in the north and Chile in the south. It seems more logical to suppose that Pachacutec had by then either died, rich in achievement, or abdicated.

Pachacutec, Man and Legend

The sources present Pachacutec in a dual role, part history and part legend. In particular, the story of the Chanca war blends myth with fact; in one instance the very stones of the field of battle are transformed into warriors visible only to Pachacutec. He is both legitimate ruler and cultural hero, recalling perhaps the status of Tlacaelel in the Aztec saga. Though his role as creator is indeed outstanding, his image may tend to be further enhanced by the feats more accurately attributable to his predecessor or successor; as in the case of Tlacaelel, his life is prolonged to include victories probably gained after he had passed from the scene.

As Friedrich Katz writes, Pachacutec's deeds are so intermingled with legends and religious representations that it is hard to define the historical personality. Though he is said to have laid the foundations of institutions basic to the Incas' control of a huge empire, doubts remain as to whether all such institutions really owe their origin to one ruler. It has been proposed, for instance, that the Incas adopted certain aspects of the political system of Chimor, which was only conquered at the end of — or after — the reign of Pachacutec. But even if exaggerations in the record are taken into account, much evidence remains that the fundamental institutions of the Empire can be traced back to his initiative. When he became ruler, the Incas formed only a modest village community; at his death they were the mightiest empire of South America.[71] Nonetheless, Murra questions whether Pachacutec really invented all the administrative devices that made the state function. After examining information dredged from *quipu* records, Murra finds it hard to fully accept this bureaucrats' culture-hero as a historical figure. He adds that quipu knot recording predated Pachacutec and probably originated before the Inca period;[72] quipulike string devices have been found in Middle Horizon burials.[73]

Certain achievements, such as the transformation of Cuzco, are attributed to Pachacutec even by such chroniclers as Cabello, who insists that this ruler was cruel and at times unpopular. The respective roles of Viracocha and Pachacutec in the creation of the Inca state remain hard to unravel. Garcilasco confuses the whole picture by ascribing the deeds traditionally credited to Viracocha to his predecessor and by transferring the events of the early part of Pachacutec's reign to that of Viracocha. However, other accounts also give some credit to Pachacutec's predecessor. Though he does not accept the whole Garcilascan story, Cobo writes of battles against the Chancas early in Viracocha's reign.[74] Cieza, together with other sources, describes Viracocha's expedition to Collao, though not in terms of a war of conquest.[75] Various sources, as we have seen, credit Viracocha with important, if short-range, conquests, and it is hard to see how Pachacutec could have faced the Chanca invasion if he controlled Cuzco alone, then little more than a village, rather than at least some sort of confederation, however limited in size.

Pachacutec's valiant defense of Cuzco against the Chancas may be accepted as basically historical, as the chroniclers' accounts differ enough to suggest that they do not derive all their data from a single source. This early triumph sets in a heroic perspective the life of the king whose subsequent career was so spectacular. However, the contemptible nature of Viracocha's demeanor in face of this crisis is perhaps more open to question; his dereliction of kingly duties might have been grafted onto the record as a means of enhancing, by way of comparison, the courageous qualities of his son. It rather strains credulity to assert that Viracocha, after certain successes in the earlier part of his reign, should later have acted as a craven coward, bolting into a safe haven and abandoning his capital to the advancing Chancas; even less plausible is the report that his appointed heir, Urco, not yet burdened with age, should have behaved in a like manner. If the Chancas had been allowed to take Cuzco, surely they would have been quick to track down Viracocha and Urco, whose chances of dignified survival would then have been slim. The various accounts of the petulant, if not capricious, conduct of his father even after Pachacutec's victory form part of the official legend. Any reluctance to accept them as historical in no sense detracts from the achievement of Pachacutec in defeating the Chancas.

Baudin hardly exaggerates in writing that Pachacutec's personality dominates pre-Columbian Peruvian history. Chroniclers unite in lauding his achievements; even Garcilasco, who tends to set certain limits to the ruler's triumphs (attributing his noblest feat to his father), nonetheless affirms that Pachacutec remodeled the Empire, refurbishing its religious rites as well as its social customs.[76] Rostworowski, in her biography of Pachacutec, is ready to admit that he made errors, in particular the endowment of the royal panacas with too much power and wealth. The importance of the panacas is almost beyond the power of the modern mind to conceive. The individual acquired his identity through association with his panaca, and the many sons of a ruler might belong to a different panaca in accordance with the genealogy of their mother.[77] However, some equivalent institution may well have existed many centuries before the Incas in Peru, where the cult of the dead has such profound roots and where mummification was an ancient practice.

Attaining a balanced assessment of the Viracocha-Pachacutec era is hard; though it unleashed a process of mass conquest, its recorded history is interwoven with legend. Murra is surely right to assume that such an explosive expansion must have involved new institutional form and a new ideology and that it is therefore ipso facto correct to treat Pachacutec as not merely a military genius but also a builder and reformer of social and religious conditions.[78]

Murra, as we have seen, hesitates to accept as historical every achievement the sources attribute to Pachacutec. Zuidema, in accord with his overall view of Andean ethnohistory, goes much further. He maintains that the Chanca war plays a key role in the purely mythical sequence of events to which the Incas attributed the formation of their Empire; thus, in effect, he places this epic struggle within a basically legendary framework. The very name Pachacutec ("he who changes the world") shows that the Incas viewed this war more in cosmological terms. Zuidema cites Sarmiento as stating that Pachacutec worshipped the god of thunder (also the god of war) as his personal deity; in contrast, his son Tupac Inca was linked more closely with the sun god. In such terms Pachacutec could be viewed as fulfilling the intermediate role of preparing the way for his son, a role comparable to that played by the thunder god between the two principal deities: the sun and Viracocha, the creator.[79]

Zuidema even suggests that the Chanca war was crucial to Inca history not because, chronologically and historically, Pachacutec had fought such an enemy but because in his symbolic role he had to reflect the actions of the thunder god.[80] In addition to citing certain incidents of the Chanca war, Zuidema points out another mythical event in Pachacutec's reign: During a severe drought only the lands of Pachacutec's son Amaru Tupac were protected by clouds, whereas in other parts of the valley crops were burned by the sun.[81]

Zuidema's assessment may be challenging and guard against any overcomplacent acceptance of the more orthodox interpretations. Nonetheless, it leaves us with a problem: If Pachacutec belongs more to myth than to history or was even a kind of huaca (a phrase also used by Zuidema in this context), then some other dynamic leader presumably launched the process of conquest. Archaeology points to a rapid expansion; thus, if we dismiss the highly personalized hero, Pachacutec, as the founder, we must explain the same story but merely attribute the historical creation to some kind of anonymous superman. Admittedly, some of those who treat Pachacutec as a fully historical figure are reluctant to place his father, Viracocha, in the same category.

Rowe and Rostworowski, and even earlier writers such as Means and Markham, also tend to make a basic distinction between Manco Capac, viewed as mainly legendary, and Pachacutec, treated as more strictly historical, albeit with certain legends attached to his name. Pease, though paying tribute to the value of Rowe's standard version of Andean history (written as early as 1946), at the same time opines that, starting with the publication of the *Visita de Chucuito* by Garci Díez de San Miguel, subsequent events have shed new light on the problem. Such studies, together with information presented in the *Relaciones Geográficas de Indias*, suggest that the chroniclers tended to present an idealized perspective of the history of Tahuantinsuyu. Pease even questions whether their description of its conquests might correspond to a kind of ritual sequence, starting with the south and then, after the Chanca victory, continuing first westward and then to the north.[82]

The standard sources present Manco Capac as a primordial archetype; he is followed by seven rulers, the last of which bears the name of the most ancient creator deity. Sources even refer metaphorically to Pachacutec as "son" of Manco Capac.[83] As such, he lends added luster to the sun god, Inti, and reduces the creator, Viracocha, to a role more comparable to that of the "otiose" god as described by Mircea Eliade.[84] Pachacutec thus appears as a new archetype, now solar, who creates, or re-creates, Cuzco. As Pease signifies, after the Empire was destroyed by the Spanish god, the Inca himself assumed the mantle of a creator divinity who might one day bring about a new rebirth, returning to a past time when misery and hunger were unknown. The Inca has the personal power to transform the face of the earth, turning stones into soldiers.[85] Pachacutec even repeats the feat of the god Viracocha, who had previously divided the world into four sectors.[86]

Wedin also expresses reservations about Inca dynastic history; he is reluctant to accept what Sverker Arnoldsson calls "the great man theory" as applied to pre-Columbian civilizations, as it is basically a European concept.[87] Wedin stresses that Inca conquests may have begun before the Chanca war and cites the *Relaciones Geográficas* and Polo de Ondegardo as mentioning that both Tupac and Huayna Capac continued to be involved in hostile encounters with the Chancas.[88] The *Relaciones* mention Pachacutec only once as conqueror of a given territory, but this is probably because the main informants' memories did not stretch back to his time.[89] I agree with Wedin about the difficulty of determining the extent of the conquests of the later Inca rulers but nonetheless believe that by almost any standards, European or other, both Pachacutec and Tupac would merit the term *great*. One has only to look at the map to conclude that the conquest and organization of such a boundless realm in two reigns were the feat of great rather than ordinary men.

Moreover, though I accept Wedin's assertion that the "great man theory" has served as a conceptual basis for much of European historical writing, it is harder for me to agree that it is only valid for Europe and is inapplicable elsewhere. On the contrary, it is precisely in polities at whose apex stands a divine or semidivine kingship that the precept becomes particularly relevant. Marshall Sahlins, in writing of New Zealand, quotes J. Prytz Johansen as stating that the Maori chief "lives the life of a whole tribe" and "gathers the relationship to other tribes in his person." Sahlins writes that although history is much more than the doings of great men and is always also concerned with the life of communities, in heroic polities the king is the embodiment of the possibility of the community.[90]

In writing of the Incas and their empire, no modern-day scholar would neglect to study the life of the whole community, as far as that can be identified. Indeed, Murra and others have made notable progress in that respect. But it is equally undeniable that the Incas did form a "heroic polity" in the sense that the Inca ruler was elevated to a semidivine status as the symbol and standard-bearer of the imperial cult of the sun, Inti. And in such a polity, in view of their unique achievements of conquest and organization, both Pachacutec and Tupac are surely rulers cast in a heroic mold.

CHAPTER 4

The Last Conquerors

This chapter is concerned with the process of long-range conquest attributed to Tupac Inca and his successor, Huayna Capac. The available evidence will be presented as to the extent of their domains and the order in which they were occupied. Such matters as the administration and impressive infrastructure of these conquered provinces will be discussed in subsequent chapters.

The most coherent sources of information on Inca conquests subsequent to those made by Pachacutec are Cieza, Sarmiento, and Cabello, together with the much later version of Cobo. Contemporary archaeological research offers important data as to the final extent of Inca domination. The conquests assigned by two of these leading sources to a co-reign of Pachacutec and Tupac probably were in fact made by the latter at a time when Pachacutec was either dead or too old to be much involved; Pachacutec's own long-range expeditions were likely confined to Collao and the highland regions of central Peru.

Tupac Inca, though never attaining the status of his father as founder and creator, both human and divine, was nonetheless an accomplished leader. In Inca tradition his fame was legendary. His range of conquests stretched for nearly two thousand miles, from northern Ecuador to central Chile; hence, his achievement bears comparison with that of Alexander the Great, whose farthest penetration into India, reached with the decisive aid of horses, brought him to a distance of some 2,500 miles as the crow flies from his home base in Macedon. In considering the course of these expeditions, one point must constantly be borne in mind: The importance of the *mitimae* system as a means of consolidation cannot be exaggerated; without it, the expansion of the Empire would have served little purpose.

Tables 1 and 2 offer a summary of the main events in the military careers of Tupac and Huayna Capac as given by the four chroniclers mentioned above. What they offer is far from a complete record of what occurred but rather a kind of résumé of such data as survived decades after the Empire collapsed. The earliest account, that of Cieza, was written in about 1553; the last, Cobo, is dated exactly a century later. At this point we are concerned simply with what each source relates on the sequence of conquest; the absorption of specific regions, such as Chile, Ecuador, and Chimor, will subsequently be considered. Finally, some consideration as to how the chroniclers might have obtained their information becomes essential in order to assess the validity of these documents.

For the reigns of Tupac and his successor, the link between Sarmiento's account (1572) and that of Cabello (1586) is even closer than for earlier events. Of the two, Cabello generally offers more names of people and places, particularly in Ecuador, but Sarmiento provides material not included in the Cabello version. The information of the two chroniclers on both reigns can be compared with that of Cieza and Cobo in Tables 1 and 2. Certain episodes are described in much more detail in Appendix A, which omits the Cieza and Cobo versions of events. (Appendix A simply serves to demonstrate beyond any doubt that a large proportion of the historical data provided by the most informative historical sources, Sarmiento and Cabello, derive from some common source.)

Table 1 summarizes the main events reported for the reign of Tupac, including the period when, according to two versions, an aging Pachacutec still survived as co-ruler. (Because the table gives page references for each event, these are not included in the text that follows.) In this table, certain series of place-names that appear to belong to a single campaign have been somewhat arbitrarily bracketed together and labeled "A" through "E." As can be seen from the table, such campaigns do not necessarily follow each other in the same order in each version. For the interlinked accounts of Sarmiento and Cabello, the order is almost the same; for the other two chroniclers, the sequence differs more widely. At this stage, a short examination of the four sources may help to clarify their similarities and differences.

Taking first the Sarmiento and Cabello versions, the campaign designated "A1" starts in Cuzco and takes the "road to Chinchasuyu," leading to the "Province of the Quechuas." As may be noted in Table 1, the principal places mentioned largely concur. From the comparative list of these two versions given in Appendix A it can be seen, for instance, that in each of the provinces of the Quechuas and in the province of Angaraes three identically named forts are occupied, together with the capture of one chief called Chuquisguaman; the chroniclers then report an initial assault

Table 1
THE CAMPAIGNS OF TUPAC INCA
Four Versions

Sarmiento de Gamboa (1572)

pp. 117–118	Tupac named successor to Pachacutec	
pp. 118–121	Expedition to Chinchasuyu	
	Province of Quechuas	A_1
	Angaraes	
	Xauxa	
	Chachapoyas	
	First assault on Chimor	
	Tumebamba	
	Quito	
pp. 123–125	Campaign from Quito to Huancavilcas	A_2
	Manta	
	Tumbez	
	Puná	
	Conquers Chimor	
p. 126	Pachacutec dies	
pp. 128–130	War against Antisuyu	B
	Conquers four great nations, including Opataris, Chunchos	
p. 131	Campaign in Collao	C
	Conquers four forts; two chiefs skinned	
	Charcas	
	Reaches Coquimbo and Río Maule in Chile	
p. 132	Chachapoyas rising suppressed; many provinces visited	D
pp. 133–134	Visits Yanacayo	E
p. 137	Tupac dies	

TABLE 1
THE CAMPAIGNS OF TUPAC INCA
FOUR VERSIONS

CABELLO DE BALBOA (1586)

p. 318	Tupac named heir to Pachacutec	
pp. 318–321	Takes road to Chinchasuyu	A_1
	Province of Quechuas	
	Angaraes	
	Xauxa	
	Cajamarca	
	Sends force against Chimor	
	Chachapoyas	
	Tumebamba	
	Quito	
pp. 322–334	Campaign from Quito to Huancavilcas	A_2
	Xixipa	
	Manta	
	Tumbez	
	Conquers Chimor	
pp. 334–335	Attacks four provinces — Chunchos, Opataris, etc.	B
pp. 335–336	Collao expedition	C
	Conquers four forts; two chiefs skinned	
	Takes Coquimbo in Chile	
p. 337	Pachacutec dies	
pp. 337–338	Tupac goes to Xauxa, sends captains to Pachacamac	D
	Nazca	
	Ica	
	Then goes to Cajamarca and Chachapoyas	
pp. 347-348	Visits Yanacayo	E
p. 356	Tupac dies	

TABLE 1
THE CAMPAIGNS OF TUPAC INCA
FOUR VERSIONS

CIEZA DE LEÓN (1553)

p. 190	Pachacutec yields government to Tupac	
pp. 192–194	Collao expedition	C
	Chucuito	
p. 195	"Sends messengers to" (i.e., makes war on)	
	Condesuyu and the Andes	B
pp. 196–201	Sets out on road to Chinchasuyu	A_1
	Proceeds to Bonbón	
	Xauxa	
	Cajamarca	
	Chachapoyas	
	Bracamoros	
	Huancabamba	
	Caxas	
	Ayavaca	
	Lacatunga	
	Quito	
pp. 202–203	Puerto Viejo	A_2
	Tumbez	
	Conquers Chimor	
	Visits Pachacamac and returns to Cuzco	
pp. 210–211	Expedition to Chincha	D
	Nazca	
	War against Huarco	
pp. 214–215	Collasuyu	C
	Chucuito, Charcas	
	Chile up to Río Maule	
p. 217	Tupac dies	

Table 1
THE CAMPAIGNS OF TUPAC INCA
Four Versions

Bernabé Cobo (1653)

p. 142	Pachacutec hands over power to Tupac	
p. 142	Expedition to Antisuyu, Chunchos, Mojos	B
p. 143	Campaign to Collao; two chiefs skinned	C
p. 143	Expedition to Chinchasuyu and on to Quito	A_1
	Fights Chachapoyas and Cañaris (Tumebamba)	
pp. 144–146	Collao, again	C
	Chucuito	
	Tihuanaco	
	Cochabamba	
	Charcas	
	Tucumán	
	Coquimbo in Chile and Río Maule	
pp. 149–150	Goes to Chinchasuyu	D, E
	Visits Yanacayo	
	Proceeds to coast and conquers all the valleys up to Tumbez	A_2
p. 151	Tupac dies	

on the kingdom of Chimor, the Pacsamayo River or Pacsamayo Valley being mentioned in each instance.

In both accounts, campaign A1 involves the subjection of Tumebamba and ends in Quito. The role of Quito in the conquests of Tupac, as we shall later see, is probably much exaggerated by the two chroniclers. Both then report that Tupac, without returning to Cuzco, descended to the Ecuadorian coastal province of Huancavilcas (campaign A2) and, proceeding via Tumbez, undertook a conquest of Chimor. Cabello (but not Sarmiento) states that its ruler was sent to Cuzco. He also includes a long and valuable account of the dynasty of Lambayeque, Chimor's neighbor.

According to the same two chroniclers, campaign B was directed against a region lying east and southeast of Cuzco that formed part of Antisuyu and on whose mountain slopes lived many primitive peoples. Both accounts note that the Inca army encountered four nations, or provinces; the names of these as given in Appendix A — the Opataris, Manosuyos, Chunchos, and Chiponahuas (who were subsequently attacked) — approximately coincide, and both sources identify the same chieftains as being captured. Though victories are reported, the campaign apparently achieved little, and in the hot and damp climate (to which they were unaccustomed) the Incas suffered heavy losses.

The campaign designated "C" is described most succinctly by Cabello and Sarmiento in spite of its vast extent. It starts in Collao, where both mention the taking of the same four forts (see Appendix A) and the capture of the same two leaders, who are skinned and made into drums. The campaign ends in Chile, preceded in Sarmiento's version by Charcas. Both accounts mention the taking of Coquimbo in Chile. Sarmiento names the Chilean chieftain Michimalongo and describes the Río Maule as the southernmost limit of the campaign.

Campaign D in Sarmiento consists of a briefly mentioned expedition against Chachapoyas (northeast of Cajamarca). The two sources then make passing reference to operations in the coastal region of Condesuyu and note a visit to "many provinces." Cabello concurs that Tupac marched in a northwesterly direction as far as Xauxa, finally reaching Cajamarca and Chachapoyas; he adds that "captains" were sent from Cuzco to the coast, where the Chinchas resisted but others, such as the Nazca and Ica, yielded peacefully. Finally, both texts tell of a visit to Yanacayo, where a group of rebels were ceremoniously pardoned, followed by the death of Tupac.

The much earlier report of Cieza de León is informative but somewhat more brief; many names differ from those mentioned above. The account begins with an expedition to Collao after Pachacutec handed over power to Tupac. This incident might be identified with Sarmiento's mention of a campaign carried out in Collasuyu by Pachacutec just before he named Tupac heir and co-ruler; Cieza reports Chucuito in Chile as the site of Tupac's last campaign. He then states that Tupac sent messengers to Condesuyu and to "the Andes" (i.e., Antisuyu). Various sources describe the sending of messengers as a standard preliminary to the dispatch of a military expedition; hence, this mention of messengers may legitimately be taken as Cieza's sole reference to Sarmiento and Cabello's campaign B. (Cabello also makes an oblique reference to Condesuyu in this context.) Cieza next mentions an expedition that proceeded via Bonbón and Xauxa to the province of Huaylas, also named by Sarmiento and Cabello. The latter's campaign A1 is thus in effect reported by Cieza, who merely alters the sequence and adds to the list of objectives Bracamoros, Ayahuaca (near the present-day border between Peru and Ecuador), and Lacatunga (in Ecuador).

Exactly as in Sarmiento and Cabello's campaign A2, Cieza reports an advance to the coast starting from Quito, without mention of any prior return to Cuzco. After Tumbez was taken, Chimor was duly defeated, though again only the very briefest description is given of this momentous event. Tupac then returned to Cuzco before mounting a new expedition to the coastal region south of Pachacamac (corresponding in part to campaign D), where Nazcas and Chinchas both yielded without a struggle. Against Huarco a bitter war was fought that lasted three years. (Huarco is also mentioned by Cabello.) Finally, Cieza reports an expedition against Collasuyu and Chile that would appear to relate to Sarmiento and Cabello's campaign C because of the mention of Charcas and the Río Maule in Chile.

Cobo's account of Tupac's conquests bears a very distinct resemblance to those of Sarmiento and Cabello, but the order of events is rather different. Antisuyu (campaign B) comes first, with specific mention of the same peoples, Chunchos and Mojos. Part of the Collasuyu campaign (C) comes next and includes the same story of the two Colla chiefs made into drums, followed by an abbreviated version of the Chinchasuyu expedition (A1), with a much shorter list of place-names on the route. Cobo thereafter reports a second installment of the Collasuyu campaign, ending in Chile; he mentions Coquimbo and Charcas, as does Sarmiento, but adds Tihuanaco and Tucumán, omitted from the other lists. The story continues with Yanacayo (campaign E in the other versions) and ends with a journey to Quito and down to Tumbez (reflecting for a second time campaigns A1 and A2 of Sarmiento and Cabello).

To these accounts may be added that of Garcilasco, who tells a somewhat different tale. His story is diffuse and confused, to the point that it becomes hard to compare it with other sources. His version of Tupac's reign mentions approximately the same conquests as the others. A campaign against Chachapoyas is described, followed by a descent upon Huancabamba and Ayavaca. Numerous place-names are included, and Tupac finally reaches Quito, descends to the sea, and conquers Chimor.[1]

Betanzos gives interesting accounts of Tupac's construction of Sacsahuaman as well as a fort in the Yucay Valley, but he offers relatively few place-names that relate to campaigns; indeed, it is hardly feasible to make of such names another column in Tables 1 and 2. Betanzos mentions two campaigns against Antisuyu but offers data on local modes of dress and methods of cultivation rather than on people or places. Nonetheless, in writing of an expedition to Collao, he does name three of the four forts Sarmiento described as captured: Asillo, Arapa, and Pucarane (sic).[2] In short, Tupac is credited with the conquest of most of what we know as the Inca Empire. In the north he penetrated far into Ecuador; in the south he went beyond Collao and subdued large areas of Bolivia, Argentina, and Chile. It may be worth noting that Huaman Poma attributes the conquest of Chile to a relative identified as Apo Capac, as well as other distinguished leaders.[3]

Huayna Capac

In discussing the conquests of Huayna Capac, Tupac's successor, the fullest accounts are again those of Sarmiento and Cabello, and again they follow each other so closely that they can conveniently be taken together. They differ in a few respects, as can be seen in some detail in Appendix A; in general terms, Cabello names many more places and people than Sarmiento does in describing the Ecuadorian campaigns.

For Huayna Capac's military expeditions, the story can in effect be reduced to two sections, designated in Table 1 as parts A and B. Part C is a mere prolongation of part B. According to both Sarmiento and Cabello, the Inca, after a lightning excursion northward to defeat the rebellious

Chachapoyas beyond Cajamarca, returned to Cuzco and then headed southward. As described by Cabello, after passing through Collao, Huayna Capac fought hard battles against the savage Mojos and Chiriguanos on the eastern frontier of the Empire. Sarmiento makes a passing reference to Antisuyu. According to both chroniclers, Huayna Capac then proceeded to Cochabamba, where he settled many mitimaes, then went on to Pocona, and returned to Cuzco after a pilgrimage to the shrine of Copacabana on Lake Titicaca. Sarmiento (but not Cabello) interposes a campaign in Chile between the battle with the Chiriguanos and the visit to Cochabamba.

Certain details listed in Appendix A, such as the building of the palace of Casana by Sinchi Roca (who was appointed governor of Cuzco in the ruler's absence) and the reconstruction of the frontier fortress of Pocona (built by the Inca's father), demonstrate the continued interconnection between the two accounts. The link is established even more precisely by the comments the two sources give on the Urus. According to both versions, Huayna Capac instructed them as to how they should live and in what parts of the lake they should fish. Cabello's statement, "Having given to the Uru Indians orders as to how they should live in that lagoon and defining the boundaries of the area where they should fish," compares with that of Sarmiento: "Gave orders as to how the Urus should live, and gave them their boundary, defining the part in which each of their villages should fish in the lagoon."

The remainder of Huayna Capac's wars are described in very similar terms in the two accounts, as can be clearly seen in Table 2. Specific aspects of the prolonged struggle against the tribes of Ecuador will be considered later. In effect, the rest of Huayna Capac's life is said to be dedicated to these northern wars. One of the Inca campaigns in other parts of the Empire that receives mention is a second expedition against the Chiriguanos, in which the ruler did not personally take part. At the end of his reign, he visited the island of Puná, returned to Quito, and died.

Cobo's data for this reign obviously derive from virtually the same sources as those used by Sarmiento and Cabello. The first part, likewise designated A, includes basically the same places referred to by the other two chroniclers; it differs mainly in adding a visit to Quito to the account of the Chachapoyas expedition, placing this before rather than after the first part of the southward expedition. Thus, the ruler supposedly headed south to Collao, then north all the way to Quito, and once more south-

Table 2
THE CAMPAIGNS OF HUAYNA CAPAC
Four Versions

Sarmiento de Gamboa (1572)

p. 140	Huyna Capac becomes ruler	
p. 141	Expedition against Chachapoyas	A
	Returns to Cuzco	
p. 142	Campaign via Collao to Charcas and Chile — Coquimbo and Copiapo	
	Visits Antisuyu, Cochabamba, rebuilds Pocona fort	
	Visits Ticci Viracocha shrine on Lake Titicaca	
pp. 143–144	Goes straight to Quito	B
	Defeats Pastos	
	Returns to Tumebamba	
	Descends to Tumbez	
pp. 145–146	Fights Caranquis and Cayambis, who kill his brother, Auqui Topa	
	War against Cayambis; final victory at Yahuarcocha	
p. 147	More fighting against Cayambis	
	Chief Pinto captured and made into drum	
p. 148	Huayna Capac returns to Cuzco	
	Sends Yasca to fight Chiriguanos	
p. 149	Returns to Quito and campaigns up to Río Angasamayo, which he establishes as a border	C
pp. 149–150	Sets out toward the ocean after severe fighting and much hardship; goes back to Quito and dies	

Table 2
THE CAMPAIGNS OF HUAYNA CAPAC
Four Versions

Cabello de Balboa (1586)

p. 356	Huayna Capac succeeds	
p. 361	Expedition to Chachapoyas	A
pp. 362–363	Leaves Cuzco for Collao	
	Abortive campaign against Mojos and Chiriguanos	
	Visits Cochabamba	
	Rebuilds Pocona fort and visits Ticci Viracocha shrine on Lake Titicaca	
	Returns to Cuzco	
pp. 364–378	Goes via Tumebamba to Quito	B
	Defeats Pastos	
	Returns to Tumebamba	
	Fights Caranquis (long account)	
	Auqui Topa killed	
pp. 380–382	Further conflict with Caranquis, victory at Yahuarcocha	
p. 383	Further Caranqui resistance	
	Pinto taken and made into drum	
p. 384	Returns to Cuzco	
	Sends Yasca to fight Chiriguanos	
p. 384	Returns to Quito	C
	Advances northward and sets border at Río Angasamayo	
p. 393	More fierce fighting	
	After almost dying of thirst, Huayna Capac returns to Quito and dies	

Table 2
THE CAMPAIGNS OF HUAYNA CAPAC
Four Versions

Cieza de León (1553)

p. 217	Huayna Capac is crowned	
p. 222	Campaign to Collao, Charcas, and Tucumán	A
	Sends expedition against Chiriguanos	
	Spends one year fighting in Chile	
	Returns to Cuzo	
pp. 226–228	Proceeds to Xauxa	B
	Bonbón	
	Cajamarca	
	Attacks Chachapoyas	
	Cajas	
	Ayahuaca	
	Huancabamba	
	Defeated by Bracamoros	
p. 229	Sends expedition to Guayaquil and Collique	
	Tumebamba	
	Los Puruaes	
	Lacatunga	
	Quito	
pp. 232–234	Descends to Puerto Viejo	
	Guayaquil	
	Tumbez	
	Chimor	
	Lima	
	Pachacamac	
	Returns to Cuzco (or Quito?)	
pp. 236–239	Defeat near Quito	
	War against Cayambis, Cochisquis, Pastos	
	Victory of Yahuarcocha	
p. 243	Huayna Capac dies in Quito	

Table 2
THE CAMPAIGNS OF HUAYNA CAPAC
Four Versions

Bernabé Cobo (1653)

p. 152	Huayna Capac succeeds to the throne	
p. 153	Campaign to Collao, Tucumán, and Chile	A
	Returns to Cuzco	
p. 153	After subduing Chachapoyas, proceeds via Cajamarca to Quito and returns to Cuzco	B
p. 154	Again to Collasuyu	A
	Then to Antisuyu	
	Fights Mojos and Chiriguanos	
	Leaves Andes via Cochabamba	
	Goes to Pocona and rebuilds fort	
	Returns to Chucuito and Cuzco	
pp. 155–158	Goes to Tumebamba and conquers Pastos	B
	War with Cayambis	
	Auqui Topa killed	
pp. 159–160	Descends to Tumbez	
	Returns to Quito, spends ten years pacifying the region, then dies	

ward to Collasuyu. The last part of the A series speaks of Mojos and Chiriguanos, exactly as in Cabello's version, and recounts the reconstruction of the fortress of Pocona, again described as having originally been built by Huayna Capac's father. The remainder of Cobo's account, designated part B, is little more than a résumé of Sarmiento and Cabello, giving, for example, the same names for generals involved in the Pastos campaign and briefly describing the same massacre at Yahuarcocha. Cobo includes a visit to the coastal region toward the end of the reign, an event also mentioned by Cabello and Sarmiento.

Cieza de León's much earlier account presents certain problems. In many respects, Cieza agrees with the other sources. Like them, he writes of an initial phase in Huayna Capac's reign involving a southward campaign via Collao as far as Chile and a defeat by the Chiriguanos. Following this, the Inca proceeded to Cajamarca and (as at the beginning of the reign in the Cabello version) attacked the Chachapoyas, suffering two defeats before finally prevailing. Cieza then describes a visit to the coast, and the remainder of his catalogue of places resembles closely that of part B of the Sarmiento-Cabello account, including the Yahuarcocha episode and the Pastos war.

At this stage, however, a most curious aspect of Cieza's reports needs to be considered. With the exception of the last part (B in Table 2), which basically coincides with the Sarmiento-Cabello version, much of his account of Huayna Capac's reign amounts to little more than a repetition of what he himself tells of Tupac. In both reigns, as Cieza has it, the ruler first visited Collasuyu; Tupac then merely sent messengers (i.e., made plans for war) against Antisuyu, whereas Huayna Capac actually attacked the wild Chiriguanos. Following this the two rulers pursued an identical route: Xauxa, Bonbón, Cajamarca, Chachapoyas, Bracamoros, Caxas, Ayahuaca, Huancabamba, Tumebamba, Puruaes, Lacatunga, Quito. In the accounts of each reign a few additional names are included in the northern march to Quito; for example, Tiquizambi follows Tumebamba in the first, and Ríobamba is mentioned in the second. The order of places named also differs, but only slightly.

Unlike the other chroniclers, Cieza reports attacks by both rulers on the savage Bracamoros, whom he described in another context as living in the mountains east of the town of Ayahuaca near the present-day border between Peru and Ecuador. But the setbacks reportedly suffered both by Tupac and by Huayna Capac are described in *identical* words: "He entered and turned in flight" *(entró y volvió huyendo)*. In the first instance the defeat is attributed to the harsh terrain and in the second, to the ferocity of the inhabitants. Cieza's memoir of his own visit to southern Ecuador is far more detailed than his historical report on conquests, and in this account also he writes of the Bracamoros and tells how the Inca ruler (in this case Huayna Capac) "turned and fled" *(volvió huyendo)* after his encounter with these savages.

The uncanny resemblance between descriptions of the two rulers' campaigns in Cieza's relatively early account raises a fundamental problem. Spanish chroniclers at this stage might have been able to obtain from informants reasonably accurate historical data on Huayna Capac, then still of recent memory, whereas the deeds of Tupac were already at least partly forgotten. Hence, informants might in certain cases have attributed to Tupac feats that were in fact carried out by his successor, only omitting those wars in northern Ecuador known by all to have been fought by Huayna Capac rather than by Tupac.

Garcilasco also recounts at length the triumphs of Huayna Capac, offering a version that has much in common with others but placing events in a different order. Here the Inca first conquered the province of Quito, including tribes farther to the north. He descended thence to the coast, and a long description follows of his confrontation with the people at Tumbez and other places. He then undertook an expedition to Charcas and Chile before returning to the north where, among other events, a massacre of his enemies occurred at Yahuarcocha.[4]

Betanzos writes in rather general terms of a visit to Collao by Huayna Capac, who then continued to Cochabamba. His version of this reign includes only a fairly brief report on the northern campaigns, mentioning Yahuarcocha but omitting many other accounts of battles against local tribes.[5]

The Long and the Short

Having reviewed the principal reports of the different campaigns of the last two emperors before the arrival of the Spaniards, I would like to add a few comments on the chroniclers' treatment of the conquest of specific regions before considering the archaeological evidence as to the fullest extent of such conquests.

Their reports, particularly the more detailed versions of Sarmiento and Cabello, offer long accounts of wars in the Andean region of Ecuador and northern Peru, whereas their writings on yet more extensive conquests in the south are short. Though this emphasis may be appropriate for the reign of Huayna Capac, who made of Tumebamba a second capital and clearly spent much of his life in Ecuador, it can hardly constitute a very comprehensive account of the achievements of Tupac, who reportedly conquered a vast territory south of Cuzco comprising parts of Bolivia, northwestern Argentina, and Chile, regions in which the depth and extent of the Inca penetration are becoming more closely defined by archaeological research. Equally, the extreme brevity of the chroniclers' mention of the conquest of the great kingdom of Chimor serves as a reminder of the rather selective nature of their record of Inca military history.

ANDEAN ECUADOR

Some confusion over Ecuadorian conquests arises from the widespread tradition to the effect that Tupac was the conqueror not only of Quito but also of much of the far northern empire. Cieza even credits him with originating the establishment of a new Cuzco in Quito, although the great temples and palaces that Cieza himself saw were in Tumebanba.[6] Salomon accordingly contrasts the high ideological pretensions of the Incaic city with the small quantity of Inca remains that have been unearthed in Quito.[7]

Tumebamba, presumably first conquered by Tupac, became Huayna Capac's principal base in Ecuador. Much of the surrounding region had already been absorbed in Tupac's reign, but, as Larrea points out, we do not really know how far Tupac conquered beyond Tumebamba.[8] Cabello states that it was Huayna Capac who spent ten years in the conquest of the territory between Quito and the present-day northern frontier of Ecuador. Plaza Schuller cites a local source, Hieronimo Puento, as making the same statement, which is also repeated by Pedro Pizarro.[9] Puento, whose work dates from 1586, was himself a chieftain of the Cayambi people, whose traditions so vividly recalled their struggles against the Incas. Plaza Schuller expresses the conviction that Tupac's incursions into the Quito region were mainly exploratory and that Huayna Capac was the real conqueror; he also cites Alonso de Borregán to that effect.

Reports differ as to the final extent of Huayna Capac's northern conquests. The available evidence suggests a rather loose frontier more or less following the present-day border between Colombia and Ecuador. Cobo states that Huayna Capac had extended his rule beyond the town of Pasto, some fifty miles inside that border, and that the Incas were in the process of conquering the province of Popayan at the time of the Spanish invasion.[10] Many chroniclers report that the northern borders of the Empire coincided with a river called the Río Angasamayo. Romoli de Avery identifies the Río Angasamayo (sometimes confused with the Río Mayo) with either the present-day Río Carchi or the Río Guaitaira. The Carchi would seem to be the more correct identification, as it does run east-west on a line approximately coinciding with a stretch of the Colombian-Ecuadorian border. The same author points out that any notion that southwestern Colombia was conquered by the Incas may arise from the presence of Pasto tribes on both sides of the present-day border; those of Ecuador were indeed conquered, but those living on the northern side of that border were not.[11] Murra also writes of Pastos living on both sides of the Colombian-Ecuadorian border.[12]

Cabello makes what seems to be a reasonable appraisal. He states that Huayna Capac contemplated the conquest of the more northerly Pastos; he reached the fortress of Rumichaca (near the border town of Ipiales) and sent his captains to explore the territory. But the inhabitants were so poor and so savage that the ruler decided to proceed no farther than the Río Angasamayo.[13] Though the Incas perhaps made forays into southwestern Colombia, the absence of Inca sites and pottery confirms the impression that they never controlled the region.[14]

By far the liveliest account, as well as the fullest, of Huayna Capac's Ecuadorian wars is given by Cabello. The same events are recorded by Sarmiento, but Cabello adds colorful details and offers a blow-by-blow description of a prolonged and hard-fought campaign. He himself spent several years in Quito before he wrote his book in 1586, and the author knew descendants of local chieftains, who surely still cherished certain traditions of battles fought by their forbears in the early part of the century.

A point stressed by Cabello and other chroniclers is the frequency with which the Incas, in fighting these ferocious tribes, suffered stunning defeats before they finally triumphed. They were initially repulsed by the Pastos, but among their most inveterate foes were the Caranquis. On their first encounter with this tribe, the *orejones* were driven back with huge losses, and the ruler was himself thrown to the ground and had to be rescued by his guard. In another attack on a Caranqui fort, Auqui Topa, the Inca's brother, was killed.

The description of the final and most dramatic event in the war serves as a good example of Cabello's lively narrative. For five whole days the Incas attacked a fort defended by the Caranquis (Cayambis in Sarmiento's version) but were unable to breach its defenses. Before the fifth attack, Huayna Capac ordered two generals, commanding a substantial force, to remain at a certain distance from the fort and to occupy a strategic point from which they could see how the attack fared. Thereafter an assault followed, but this was only a feigned attack, and after it had seemingly failed the ruler ordered a retreat. The unsuspecting Caranquis duly sallied forth from their stronghold in hot pursuit. Meanwhile, the second Inca force, commanded by the two generals, was able to penetrate the now unguarded fort with part of its strength while the remainder, together with the soldiers under the ruler's direct command, fell upon the Caranquis who had made the sally. Surrounded on all sides, the defenders floundered in a nearby marsh of reeds, where they either drowned or were slaughtered. The locality was henceforth known as Yahuarcocha, the Lake of Blood.[15]

The Coast

Cieza, and to an even greater extent Garcilasco, enlarges upon Inca wars of conquest against the coast of Ecuador and the Tumbez region, across the present-day Peruvian border. Accounts of these expeditions, which were usually launched from Quito or Tumebamba, engendered the notion that this region became a province of the Inca Empire; however, as early as 1946 Murra denied that the Incas controlled the area, and Hyslop stresses that there is no good archaeological evidence of any such control.[16]

The absence of Inca sites or even pottery on the Ecuadorian coast serves to establish that the incursions of Tupac and his successor did not lead to outright control. In addition, though the chroniclers state that the Incas fought wars and won victories, their reports leave somewhat open the question of whether the Ecuadorian coast was truly conquered. Cieza merely states that Huayna Capac sent expeditions in order to try to subject the natives of Guayaquil and Porto Viejo; the Incas fought battles and won some victories but also suffered defeats.[17] In describing his own visit to that region, Cieza states that he found no Inca sites or storehouses; some of the natives told him that they were never conquered, but others refuted this statement.[18] Cabello writes that at the end of his reign Huayna Capac visited the island of Puná and was well received, but this is hardly the description of a conquest.[19] Cobo reports that the ruler fought against the people of Puná but that after he left the latter massacred the Inca garrison.[20]

In contrast to the chroniclers' ample digressions on expeditions to the Tumbez region, their descriptions of the conquest of the rich kingdom of Chimor are extremely meager, notwithstanding the importance of this extensive realm. Cieza in a mere paragraph mentions fierce Chimu resistance to an Inca attack made from the direction of Tumbez. Sarmiento suggests in an even briefer passage that Tupac himself did not lead this attack on Chimor. Cabello, after reporting an initial assault on Chimor from Tupac's base in Cajamarca, writes of a final conquest by an army proceeding from Tumbez, after which the defeated ruler was carried off to Cuzco; all accounts stress the immense store of treasure found in the capital, Chanchan.

The sources generally mention the conquest of the southern part of the Peruvian coast. Cieza, for instance, reports that Tupac, after the assault on Chimor, visited the great shrine of Pachacamac, where he consulted the oracle; he then proceeded to establish control over major principalities such as Nazca and Chincha. At first sight, the notion that principalities with a long tradition of independence should surrender their freedom with little or no resistance might seem far-fetched. However, such reports acquire a certain credibility in view of the Inca commanders' ability to mobilize subject peoples and hence to achieve such a crushing superiority in numbers as to render resistance almost futile. In addition, in desert regions on the coast, the invaders could deal the defenders a deadly blow and even force their submission by cutting off the irrigation canals on which they depended for their food supply. Such vital intakes, of which some but not all were protected by fortresses and walls, were naturally vulnerable. Those of the Lima and Lurin valleys lacked any such defenses.[21]

Collao and Beyond

For the key province of Collao, reports of expeditions by Tupac and his successor tend to be brief. As we have already seen, the absorption of the principal centers of the Colla — who, according to some, had been initially as much allies as subjects — had reportedly occurred before Pachacutec delegated the military command to Tupac. Cieza mentions a war against Cari, ruler of Chucuito, early in Tupac's reign; in the Sarmiento and Cabello versions a campaign against the Collas occurs at a later stage. Both accounts mention enemy fortresses with similar names, as well as the same two leaders, skinned and made into drums. One of these forts, simply called Pucara, is also mentioned by Cieza.

Beyond Collao lay rich and fertile provinces of the Empire, but information on how they were acquired is minimal. Cieza, Sarmiento, and Cobo mention briefly that Tupac campaigned in Charcas, a region situated to the southwest of Cochabamba, after which he went on to Chile. Visits to Cochabamba itself are described by Sarmiento and Cabello as occurring early in the reign of Huayna Capac, followed by a visit to Pocona (between Cochabamba and Charcas), where the ruler rebuilt the fortress.

In contrast to their meager reports on conquests beyond Collao, the sources write extensively about rather abortive attacks on certain savage mountain tribes of Antisuyu, on the eastern frontier of the Empire. According to Sarmiento and Cabello, Tupac first campaigned against these peoples after his Ecuadorian expedition, though Cobo maintains that this assault occurred at the beginning of Tupac's reign. Initially the Chunchos were attacked; Casevitz places this tribe (mentioned in the Sarmiento and Cabello accounts, as listed in Appendix A) some distance to the east of Cuzco.[22] Cabello also reports an abortive campaign conducted by Huayna Capac against the Mojos before he reached Pocona. Saignes argues that Chuncho and Mojo are more generic terms than names of specific tribes; the name Mojo he considers to be of Aymara origin.[23] Huayna Capac, in addition to battling the Mojos, also reportedly fought the Chiriguanos, situated farther to the southeast. According to Cieza, the latter attack ended in a disastrous defeat.

Farther to the south, however, ethnohistorical material on Inca penetration of northwest Argentina is almost nonexistent, though as we shall later see in discussing imperial boundaries, archaeological research of frontier fortresses helps us define the limits of Inca rule, both in southern Bolivia and Argentina. The four sources of Tables 1 and 2 state, probably correctly, that Tupac conquered northern Chile, but details are scarce. Sarmiento devotes a few lines to Huayna Capac's expedition to Chile after restating that part of Chile was conquered by Tupac; repeating the names of the two principal chiefs, Michimalongo and Antalongo, he writes of the occupation of Coquimbo, about one hundred miles north of Santiago, and Copiapo. Cabello also mentions Tupac's conquest of Coquimbo.[24] Cieza, after describing Huayna Capac's occupation of Tucumán in northwestern Argentina, states that this ruler passed a year fighting the Chilean tribes, building numerous fortresses and abducting many inhabitants.[25]

The discoveries of Inca remains, whether cemeteries, roads, or fortresses, together with studies of regional documents, demonstrate that the conquest of Chile was not a once-and-for-all event accomplished by a single ruler in one campaign. Although Tucumán apparently offered less opposition than other provinces, according to the historical record the invaders encountered total rejection in Chile and had to fight battles in valley after valley.[26] Leonardo León cites sources that tell of the stiff resistance encountered in Chile; Inca expansion probably continued in Huayna Capac's reign, but such conquests may be attributed more to the Inca's generals than to the ruler himself.[27]

Bounds of Empire

Up to this point, the process and extent of Inca conquest have been reviewed as they are described by the traditional chroniclers. In certain cases, comments by purely local chroniclers also offer some additional information. But in recent times, much has been added to our knowledge both of the extent of Inca conquest and of the intensity of their cultural penetration by archaeological research.

The degree to which Inca culture was imposed on a region clearly varied, as did the extent to which its inhabitants became loyal subjects or remained recalcitrant rebels. The natives' disposition depended partly on the length of time since a given region had first been invaded. Even in the case of the Cañaris, reportedly subjugated by Tupac, loyalty remained divided until Huayna Capac's reign. Jaime Idrovo cites evidence that although Tupac dominated the central Cañari region, tribes to the north of the Cuenca Valley recovered their independence and had to be reconquered by his successor.[28]

Some of the results of contemporary research were discussed in a symposium on Inca frontiers held in Bogotá in 1985.[29] The overall summary of the border problem offered by John Hyslop at the symposium may serve as the basis for a few relevant comments.[30] Hyslop, in referring to a renewed interest in this Inca frontier problem, stresses the need to combine the archaeological evidence with an intensified use of early legal and administrative documents and with a more critical evaluation of the "classical" chroniclers. In the past, Inca borders have been defined mainly through evidence in the early written sources. However, after nearly seventy years of archaeology it is now becoming evident that Inca pottery, wherever found in any quantity, is a clear indicator of the presence of the Inca state. Far less well studied, but of great potential utility for the definition of boundaries, are Inca forts. As more of these are located and investigated, they help to define (for some areas) the outermost Inca boundary as well as earlier boundaries achieved before subsequent expansions.

Hence, archaeology may be expected to play an ever-increasing role, as much can be learned simply by mapping the points where Inca pottery has been located. If we find Inca pottery present in a given site but absent from a place, say, ten kilometers south, then in that instance a border can sometimes, but not always, be established. Much remains to be done in this and other respects. On the basis of information now available, large sectors of the frontier still remain poorly defined, particularly in northern Peru and in southern Bolivia. Existing maps of an Inca presence in these regions may contain major errors and tend to conflict with the latest findings.[31]

The extreme northern frontier in Ecuador has been discussed above, with the view that it approximately coincided with the present Ecuadorian-Colombian border. Hyslop concludes that Inca incursions into southern Colombia probably did occur, even if they did not result in outright conquest. Reports of such conquest may arise, as previously mentioned, from the presence of Pastos on both sides of this border. Equally, as already stressed, the inclination to treat coastal Ecuador as an Inca province is no longer acceptable because of the scarcity of archaeological evidence of an Inca presence and the tendency of some chroniclers to describe expeditions by Inca rulers to Tumbez, Porto Viejo, and other sites as incursions rather than as conquests. Inca pottery is notable by its absence in these places.

Vast stretches of the Inca frontiers in Bolivia and Peru still defy precise demarcation. Not one frontier fortress has been located in present-day Peru; the *visita* of Ortiz de Zúñiga mentions three or four forts east of Huánuco, garrisoned by mitimae settlers from Cuzco. These have not been located, but the report suggests that at least part of this eastern border was fortified.[32] However, here again, if forts are eventually located, they cannot necessarily be taken as marking the final limits of the Empire. They may have been constructed well behind the ultimate bounds of expansion. Alternatively, as surely occurred in Ecuador, some might be the strongholds of their adversaries rather than those of the Incas themselves.

Leading chroniclers, though virtually ignoring the long border stretching from southern Bolivia to far-off Chile, lend a certain prominence to Inca campaigns against the mysterious Mojos and Chunchos, who lived astride part of the eastern boundary of the Empire. The tribes are usually described as savages, and the Incas, in fighting them, gained few laurels. Saignes, after discussing the uncertain etymology of the names of these tribes, suggests that the Incas had seized control of only part of their territory, which consisted of foothills rich in jungle vegetation and lay between the upper reaches of the Río Madre de Dios and the Río Beni.[33] In general, the sources insist on the Incas' reluctance to absorb "savage" peoples, though Strube among others suspects that they penetrated the Amazonic jungle to a greater extent than is generally admitted.[34]

Most of the remaining frontier in Bolivia, southeast of Cochabamba, is ill-defined. The area to the west of Santa Cruz is now considered to have formed part of the Empire, following the investigation of the site of Samaipata. Yet Rodolfo Raffino describes a whole series of sites farther south, beyond Potosí, most of them lying between latitude 20 and 22, with obvious signs of Inca occupation. The most significant of these is Chipihuayco, where the ruins cover an area of twenty hectares and include a complex irrigation system. Another site, Chuquiago, occupies a comparable area; its location on an imposing hill with a panoramic view in all directions might imply a certain strategic significance. It was supplied with water by a system of aqueducts; an important Inca road crosses the site from north to south.[35] Raffino also lists the different types of Inca pottery found in the various localities.[36] However, it should be noted that these sites stand at some three thousand meters above sea level, and we do not know to what extent the Incas controlled the intermediate territory down toward the foothills of the cordillera.

In northwest Argentina certain more positive indications exist. Archaeologists have identified many Inca sites, often more easy to locate in Argentina than in Bolivia because of their greater proximity to modern highways. In contrast, few historical sources exist for this sector. Early colonial data indicate that Santiago del Estero was a Quechua-speaking zone, which led to an initial assumption that it lay within Inca territory, but this view now tends to be questioned because it has been demonstrated that Quechua was introduced by Spanish missionaries.[37]

Traditional accounts place the extreme southern limit of Inca rule on the Río Maule or even farther south on the Río Bío Bío. Hyslop, however, cites fairly extensive evidence to the effect that the Incas secured firm control only as far as the Río Maipo Valley, south of Santiago. The southernmost Inca remains so far discovered are the cemetery of Nos in San José de Maipo and the fortress of Chena, both situated less than twenty kilometers south of Santiago.[38] The Chilean chronicler Gerónimo de Bibar confirms this viewpoint when he writes of an Inca expedition against the Pomorcaes, who fled to the southern side of the Río Maule; the Incas did not absorb the land of the Pomorcaes, whose northern limit lay seven leagues south of Santiago.[39] Osvaldo Silva Galdames interprets the letters of the Spanish conquistador Pedro de Valdivia as implying that the Incas never conquered beyond the Río Mapocho.[40]

According to Dillehay, there may be a consensus among modern investigators that the strictly political frontier lay somewhere between the Río Maipo and the Río Maule, traditionally described as the southernmost limit of conquest. But in this instance a purely geoeconomic border farther to the south marked another zone not under Inca military control but lying within the Araucanian homeland. To the north of the political frontier Inca forts have been found, indicating full subjection to their rule. Dillehay cites Bibar as stating that he saw gold mines south of this line, and pottery showing clear signs of Inca influence has been located between Temucu and Valdivia, over one hundred miles south of the Río Maipo. Dillehay thus proposes the existence of islands of Inca activity well to the south of the formal frontier; the mines were seemingly worked by Inca *yanas*, as no archaeological or ethnohistorical evidence suggests that the Araucanos ever exploited gold mines.[41]

Hence, though the ferocity of the local resistance and the immensity of the distance from Cuzco may have limited the extent of the Incas' control over present-day Chile, there was a certain economic involvement in Araucano territory, but without full military protection.

Chronological Pitfalls

In considering the Inca process of expansion, another question arises: Though indications do survive as to the places conquered by each Inca, does any reliable method exist of dating either reigns or conquests? An initial obstacle is a tendency for chroniclers to tell a similar story twice over, ascribing similar events to two different reigns — as, for instance, Cieza's word-for-word repetition of the tale of Tupac's abortive attack on the Bracamoros in his account of Huayna Capac's wars. We still do not know whether this rather ignominious setback, described in identical terms, really applies to one reign or to the other. The sources repeatedly refer to attempts, often unsuccessful, to tame savage groups such as the Mojos, Chunchos, and Chachapoyas, but we ignore the question of whether such attempts were repeated in two reigns or whether single onslaughts are reported twice over by the chroniclers.

Early writers on Inca ethnohistory were naturally interested in chronology. Because the Inca *quipus* served to record numbers and statistics, it seemed logical to assume that they would have included among their store of data at least the number of years that each king reigned. However, it later became apparent that the quipus recorded only matters of real concern to the Incas themselves rather than information of more interest to their conquerors. From such concerns, any form of chronology was notably absent.

Among initial studies of the problem may be cited that of Philip A. Means, who dates the Inca conquest of the Lake Titicaca basin to A.D. 1200, of the south coast to A.D. 1300, and of the north coast to A.D. 1400.[42] In his "Biblioteca Andina," Means divides the Spanish chroniclers into two schools: the Garcilascan, postulating a slow process of expansion, and the Toledan, which limits the conquest of empire to the last four reigns. Posing the question of whether territory more than fifty miles from Cuzco had been gained before Pachacutec's reign, he lists thirteen chroniclers who say "no" and eight who say "yes."[43]

Subsequently, Rowe, in a more far-reaching study of the chronology of Inca conquest, expresses the conviction that in general terms the "no" list is the more valid of the two. To the "no" list belong the four principal accounts of conquests: Cieza, Sarmiento, Cabello, and Cobo. Moreover, the "no" list embraces all those who finished their works in the sixteenth century and hence were closer to the Incas than were later writers.[44]

Rowe, who basically accepts the traditional list of twelve rulers, then suggests dates for those who reigned from the death of Viracocha to the accession of Huascar: Pachacutec supposedly ruled from 1438 to 1471, Tupac from 1471 to 1493, and Huayna Capac from 1493 to 1525. These dates are derived from Cabello de Balboa; Rowe simply describes them as so plausible that "they cannot be easily dismissed."[45]

Other writers have also attempted to place certain conquests in a firm chronological framework. For instance, Larrea, though agreeing that it is impossible to establish the date of Huayna Capac's birth, suggests that the reconquest of Quito would have taken place in 1494, whereas the subjugation of northern Ecuador probably may be dated to 1499. On the same basis, he calculates that Tupac established himself in Tumebamba between 1465 and 1470.[46]

Rowe is probably correct in opting for a rapid process of conquest, as opposed to Garcilasco and others, who credit earlier rulers with spectacular triumphs. Though he describes Cabello's dates as generally plausible, Rowe concedes that we will probably never be able to date the Inca reigns exactly because the Incas themselves took no interest in the passage of years.[47]

Cabello, though he wrote as late as 1586, might have been better placed than any other chronicler to evolve some system of dating for the northern part of the Empire because of his contacts with the descendants of the pre-Conquest nobility of Ecuador. Nonetheless, the existence of any real Inca chronology in terms of precise dates for reigns or conquests has continued to be questioned. In particular, Åke Wedin insists that such dates simply cannot be determined. According to this author, such attempts are based on uncertain assumptions; he points out that in realistic terms we don't even know whether the exact date of Pizarro's first landing was 1527 or 1528. Wedin further argues that if it is impossible to fix the dates of the last ruler, then we lack a starting point for a backward count, using the years of reign traditionally ascribed to each monarch. According to Wedin, the Incas simply took no interest in preserving information on the number of years of reign or life of their sovereign. It was possible for them to do so by using the quipus, but they obviously saw no point in it.[48]

In another study, Wedin demonstrates in more detail that we cannot determine the exact date of Huayna Capac's death. According to Francisco de Xerez, whose account was published as early as 1534, Atahualpa in 1532 told his captor, Pizarro, that Huayna Capac had died eight years earlier — i.e., in 1524. But Cieza implies that this monarch died in 1527, whereas Cabello states that his death occurred in 1525.

Though he admits that it is conceivable that Cabello found some Indian who knew the chronology of Inca reigns, Wedin considers the probability of this somewhat remote. The only sure date we possess for Inca history is 1532, the year in which Pizarro took Atahualpa captive and in which Huascar died — in effect, therefore, the year in which the Empire collapsed. Wedin, who also accepts the concept of a fairly rapid process of conquest, nonetheless expresses doubts as to whether, in terms of sheer distance involved, this process might not have been stretched over more than three reigns and therefore might have begun before the episode of the Chanca war.[49]

The question remains as to whether, if we cannot establish their dates, we might at least determine with some assurance the *sequence* in which conquests took place. As can be seen from Tables 1 and 2, the leading chroniclers enable us to make certain deductions for the last two reigns, but they are by no means conclusive.

Moreover, as Salomon points out, mid-sixteenth-century documents recording detailed Spanish field studies made in highland Ecuador and Colombia during the period 1557–1571 for the purpose of fixing tribute quotas do assist in the establishment of an *approximate* overall sequence, region by region, in the case of Ecuador. Salomon offers evidence that the Otavalo region north of Quito was conquered later than Quito itself, whereas the Puruha country farther to the south was subdued sometime before this. He also quotes Waldemar Espinosa as demonstrating that the decisive battle of Yahuarcocha, dated by Cabello at 1492, is not likely to have taken place before 1500; mitimaes stationed near Quito had passed through only two generations of political leadership by 1577, so the colony could hardly have been founded much before 1500.[50]

As another very generalized indication of the sequence of conquest, Meyers points out that although Quito is often described as a second Cuzco (and is reported by sources as already having been occupied by Tupac), this is a claim that existing archaeological evidence cannot support. Quito contains no Inca architectural remains and does not fulfill the conditions necessary to qualify as an imperial capital, as opposed to Tumebamba, originally excavated by Max Uhle. Many of the main surviving Inca sites are concentrated around Cuenca (modern-day Tumebamba) and offer proof of the reported "Incaization" of the Cañaris. Meyers quotes Uhle as stating that Quito did not exist in pre-Inca times and that even its existence as an Inca settlement remains somewhat problematical.[51]

Contrived History

The chroniclers of the 1540s and even the 1550s clearly had access to valuable sources of information. These are described in some detail in Cieza's *Señorio*, with direct references to leading Incas. As related in his *Crónica*, Cieza in his southward journey not only saw the ruins of the great palaces of Tumebamba but actually visited the Lake of Yahuarcocha (still marked on modern maps) and would surely have encountered people, perhaps by then in their sixties, who retained memories of an event as dramatic as a war with the Incas. Cieza conversed with the people of Tumbez about Huayna Capac's visit, discussing such details as the presentation to the ruler of a gift of wild animals; he also cites local reports of the treachery of the chieftain of the island of Puná, who plied the ruler with gifts but later killed many of his orejones.[52]

In studying Cieza's information, however, we must explain the rather disconcerting similarity between his descriptions of certain campaigns of Tupac and Huayna Capac. It was suggested above that at least some events attributed to Tupac, such as the conquest of Quito, were really a kind of anticipation of the deeds of Huayna Capac; at the time when the earlier chroniclers wrote, not only *cantares* but also personal recollections of some events of this reign could still have survived, whereas memories of many of the feats of Tupac might have become blurred. Tupac's expeditions tend to be presented as an almost continuous campaign carried to the four quarters of the Empire. As Pease points out, the sources at times appear to relate these conquests in a kind of ritual context.[53] To quote Salomon: "In the authors hospitable to an early version of conquest chronology, there are recurrent motives so regular as to suggest that events have been cast in the mold of ideal normative structures. Northern conquests are almost always told in a stereotyped form in which Tupac Inca the father conquers the northern barbarians but is then betrayed by them, after which Huayna Capac the son must reconquer the 'rebellious' native lords. It is likely that such sequences did occur."[54] It thus seems that for conquests prior to those of Huayna Capac we possess a corpus of data based in historical fact but at times presented in somewhat ritualized form and with a tendency for the-account of earlier events in Inca history to reflect those of more recent times.

Such ambiguities have naturally perplexed contemporary ethnohistorians, though their views may be hard to categorize. On this question one may cite Brian Bauer, with whose opinions I am not wholly in discord on such matters as the time depth of Inca settlement in the Cuzco Valley or even on the historical, as opposed to the legendary, role of Pachacutec in the Inca history. However, I find it harder to accept Bauer's rather cursory division of scholars into three groups. In the first group he places those "who accept the traditional interpretations of Inca history," a category that somewhat paradoxically includes John Rowe, who is often described as the pioneer of modern investigation of the sources and whose archaeological studies of Cuzco are of significant value. The second group views the Inca state "as developed through time as the result of transformations of social, economic and religious institutions," a definition that, in plainer language, presumably refers to those who treat the sources as historical but insist on the need for caution in their interpretation. Bauer's third category comprises researchers who deny to the chroniclers any role "as direct or literal interpretations of the past."[55]

Only Tom Zuidema and Pierre Duviols are cited as scholars who fit into the third category. But it is surely worth recalling that the hypothesis of a dual Inca monarchy, as described in Chapter 2, derives from the detailed study by Zuidema and Duviols of the very chroniclers whose role as interpreters of past events they supposedly deny. In a more recent work Zuidema writes more constructively of "compressed history," a concept applied by Geoffrey Conrad to the dynastic list of the kings of Chimor, in which certain rulers are suppressed. Zuidema suggests that the same principle may have applied to the Inca king list. He points out that the more recent and complete version of the chronicle of Betanzos implies that there was a king between Pachacutec and Tupac Inca.[56]

Bauer commends those scholars who challenge the validity of literal interpretations of the chronicles. But those who accept the more literal interpretations of Inca history are almost an extinct species. The great majority of scholars, whether ethnohistorians or archaeologists, surely adhere to Bauer's second group, to which I might also be said to belong (though I do not reject his third group outright).

Far from denying Zuidema's notion of compressed history — see my discussion in Chapter 3 of the possible suppression of the reign of Urco —

one might suggest that this concept could entail the elimination not only of *rulers* but also of certain *events* from the record. To quote a single specific instance: The long and glorious history of the kingdom of Chimor is amply portrayed in Michael Moseley and Alana Collins's *The Northern Dynasties*. Moreover, in this volume militarism is described by Theresa Lange Topic as an important element in Chimu statecraft, a point confirmed by archaeological research, which offers much data on battles fought and on forts quickly constructed in conquered areas.[57]

Hence, the chroniclers' report that Tupac absorbed this great realm with minimal resistance or, in certain accounts, none at all tends to lack credibility. This could be tentatively interpreted as the possible suppression of an event or series of events in the standard record, notwithstanding the obvious possibility that parts of the Chimu realm, such as Lambayeque, might have welcomed the invaders. The surviving Incas tended to portray themselves to the somewhat credulous Spaniards as people whose forbears bestowed an orderly welfare state on lesser peoples; they were perhaps less eager to tell Viceroy Toledo stories of wars waged to ravage more sophisticated realms, such as Chimor, and forcibly incorporate them into the Inca empire. Hence, Zuidema's notion of compressed history might be extended to embrace the suppression not only of rulers but also of events.

A temptation, therefore, naturally arises to treat all Inca history as contrived, presented merely as a justification for certain episodes rather than as a record of what occurred. But it must equally be borne in mind that the manipulation of history to serve as propaganda (a not unfamiliar characteristic of our own century) was also practiced among *literate* societies of the past, such as Sumer, Babylonia, Vedic India, and even imperial China.

A Common Source?

It may be somewhat easy for investigators to define likely sources of information available to early writers, such as Cieza and Betanzos. However, determining the derivation of the much larger store of campaign data compiled decades later by Sarmiento and Cabello presents more complex problems. The extremely close correspondence between parts of these two accounts, as illustrated in Appendix A, implies that they were based largely on common sources. However, the marked disparities to be found in the texts, in particular Cabello's wholly different spelling and his omission of some of the leaders and places named by Sarmiento (along with the addition of many others), suggest that one author was not simply copied by the other. Some of Cabello's more dramatic passages presumably derived from data gleaned during his stay in Quito.

The major question then arises as to the identity of any such common source or sources. As an initial premise, one may presume that when the Viceroy Toledo commissioned Sarmiento to write his history, it would have become very hard, after an interval of nearly four decades, to compile solely from informants' personal reminiscences a sequence of names and events as detailed and intricate as the one he and Cabello offer. As we shall later see, Sarmiento indeed consulted orejones living in Cuzco, many of royal lineage and married to Spaniards. However, unless one believes that such individuals could have offered, in 1572, memorized data copious enough to provide the substance of Sarmiento's history, so replete with names, one might be tempted to conclude that his account of fairly remote events was little more than ritualized saga enriched by sheer invention. But this conclusion in effect denies basic authenticity to a seemingly serious attempt to retrieve the past (even if, at Toledo's prompting, the attempt was not altogether impartial).

Hence, we should not exclude the possibility that some much earlier written material, now lost, was available in the 1570s and used by Sarmiento and Cabello. Such material could have derived, say, from the early 1550s, just after the time that Cieza and Betanzos completed their own works, and then served as the basis for much of the information later obtained by Sarmiento.

In the early 1570s numerous descendants of Inca rulers still lived in the Cayocache barrio of Cuzco. Unaided by more formal records produced by a previous generation, these surviving Incas could surely have offered Sarmiento and Cabello at least *some* useful data based on local traditions and from what their fathers and grandfathers had told them. Among the more prominent of such orejones was Carlos Inca. Born in 1537, he was the son of Atahualpa's brother Paullu and, like many other Incas, had married a Spaniard. He lived in great splendor and was apparently literate, if we can judge from copies of a letter he sent to the king of Spain in 1571. Cayo Tupac, who had already been consulted by Cieza, was still alive; he was born in about 1502, and his father had been the "second person," or chief assistant, to Huayna Capac and a close confederate of Huascar. A grandson of Atahualpa, Alonso Titu Atauchi, was also consulted by Toledo and Sarmiento.

Both these and other leading Incas were at that time under immense pressure, as Toledo was determined to stamp out the last vestiges of Inca resistance to Spanish control. Carlos himself was arrested by Toledo, whereas Tupac Amaru, son of the rebel emperor, was executed in 1572. Many leading Incas of Cuzco were subsequently exiled to Mexico. Moreover, the Incas of post-Conquest Cuzco, shorn of power, probably led a rather otiose life; perhaps they relieved the tedium of eventless days by reciting the deeds of past heroes, whose names they endlessly recalled. But however desperate the need of this Inca coterie to curry favor with the Spaniards at that moment, one still wonders how they could have produced from memory such a vast compendium of the details of Inca history (a subject in which their interest was at best limited). Even supposing that they *did* perform this prodigious task, a further question remains unresolved: How, if Sarmiento's store of information was a product of sheer memory rather than of recorded data, could it occur that some years later Cabello also extracted these verbal data in so similar a form? As already stressed, Cabello's very different spelling limits the likelihood that he simply copied Sarmiento, if indeed any copy of the latter's work might have been available.

A comparable situation prevails in Mexico, where there is a virtual consensus of ethnohistorians on the probable existence of some lost document or documents, now commonly known as the *Crónica "X,"* recorded much earlier than the most detailed surviving sources. This idea was originally proposed by R. H. Barlow in 1945. He pointed out that though the long works on Aztec history by Fray Diego Durán and Alvarado Tezozómoc are very similar indeed, sufficient differences exist to show that one could not have been copied directly from the other or from another text, known as the *Codex Ramírez*, that is almost a résumé of the work of Durán. Tezozómoc and Durán wrote in the 1580s (i.e., even longer after the arrival of the Spaniards in their country [1519] than the corresponding interval for Sarmiento).

Accordingly, Barlow, for lack of any alternative explanation, tentatively proposed that the histories on which we depend for so much detailed and vivid material on the Aztecs — material lacking in previous accounts — mainly derived from some lost, earlier text, which he called the *Crónica*

"X." He suggested that such a work might have been the work of Fray Juán de Tovar.[58]

Of course, it may be argued that the Mesoamericans' use of a pictographic writing system, together with a means of recording dates in fifty-two-year cycles, would have made it much easier to produce such a document as the *Crónica "X"* in Mexico than in Peru. However, even though copies of pre-Columbian codices that no longer exist today (given the general absence of surviving originals from the Valley of Mexico itself) might in 1580 have offered additional evidence on past events, the chronicles of Tezozómoc and Durán contain many abstract notions, together with detailed accounts of events, that could hardly derive from pictorial codices. Moreover, the two historians' dating of events is sketchy, whereas events in historical codices are commonly linked to specific years of the native calendar; what is more, these chronicles are not principal sources for tentative attempts to reconstruct an Aztec chronology. As in the specific and known instance of Sahagún's twelve volumes, it seems more probable that much of their information originally derived from earlier accounts given verbally by informants and recorded in writing by literate Spaniards.

Had any such "lost" document as the hypothetical *Crónica "X"* existed in Peru, it would logically have been recorded in the early years after the Conquest; Barlow proposes that the *Crónica "X"* dates from not more than twenty years after the conquest of Mexico. It could have been based on one or more historical traditions, including perhaps some that were familiar to Cieza. The latter, in praising the *quipocamayos*, also stresses the role of cantares, which recorded the main events of a king's reign and were to be sung only after his death, thus in effect preserving, at least for one reign, a kind of historical record. But by 1570 any survivors among those charged with reciting cantares of the deeds of Huayna Capac, whose reign may have started some eighty years before that date, could hardly have provided a great deal of information that went unrecorded by earlier chroniclers.

The question logically then arises: If some kind of documentary data was available in Peru, corresponding to the hypothetical *Crónica "X,"* then how and why did this prime source ever come into existence?

The *Declaración de los Quipocamayos* records how the viceroy, Vaca de Castro, who governed from 1541 to 1544, summoned all the older Incas of Cuzco in order to find out about their past history, decades before Viceroy Toledo's famous conference on the same subject. The elders first produced quite different accounts of what had happened but then requested more time to consult together in order to produce a more coherent version.[59] Juán de Betanzos and Francisco de Villacastín served as interpreters for this coordinated account. At this moment, barely a decade after the Conquest, these older Incas of Cuzco could have been well placed to supply vivid recollections of Huayna Capac's campaigns, apart from any information officially memorized in cantares. For instance, at the time of the viceroy's inquiries, the puppet Inca ruler, Paullu Inca — a legitimate son of Huayna Capac — was still alive. (He died in 1549.)

It is surely not illogical to suggest that once a coordinated version of history, based on statements made by older Incas barely ten years after the Conquest, had been produced, it might then have been recorded in writing. But if this indeed occurred, and any *Crónica "X"*–type document came into existence, it would be also reasonable to assume that the text would have been drafted by one or more Spaniards, with the Indians serving as Quechua-speaking informants; at that comparatively early date few if any leading orejones would have been literate. Paullu, for instance, wore Spanish clothes and learned to copy his name but could not read or write Spanish.[60]

Betanzos was, of course, most proficient in Quechua, but now that his complete manuscript has been made available it becomes evident that, particularly for Tupac and Huayna Capac, he tends to focus more upon other aspects of the Inca rulers' reigns than upon the process of conquest, concerning which he supplies relatively few names. Accordingly, although his participation in the compilation of some more specific record of campaigns and battles should not necessarily be ruled out, Francisco de Villacastín and other Spaniards then in Cuzco are perhaps more likely responsible for any record of the viceroy's conference and subsequent inquiries.

In view of the copious information offered by Sarmiento and Cabello, not only on Huayna Capac's campaigns but also on those of Tupac and even Pachacutec, it might be assumed that the editors of any earlier record placed some reliance on oral traditions (much more alive in 1540 than in 1570) and personal recollections. Although certain aspects of accounts of Tupac's achievements tend to bear such an uncanny resemblance to those of his successor, a rich store of oral tradition recalling the deeds and legends associated with the name of the great Pachacutec surely survived for a limited period after the Conquest. Paradoxically, in a few specific aspects, Sarmiento's information is more detailed for Pachacutec's reign than for those of his successors. For instance, only for this reign are the names not only of Inca captains but also of enemy leaders regularly reported.

The Final Version

In 1572, nearly thirty years after Viceroy Vaca de Castro's conference, Viceroy Francisco Toledo summoned the known descendants of Huayna Capac to inquire about Inca history. Few of these individuals can have been closely connected with events occurring so long ago. Of two named as being as many as ninety years old, one was the son of a local *curaca* appointed by Tupac, and the other's father had been a servant of Huayna Capac.[61]

The information recorded by Toledo himself, derived from this Cuzco meeting and other gatherings that took place in provincial centers, is somewhat restricted. However, the viceroy took another step to satisfy his curiosity when he commissioned Sarmiento de Gamboa to probe further into the past. Sarmiento was charged in particular with determining who were the true or rightful owners of the lands dominated by the Incas at the time of the Spanish invasion. Sarmiento was a very important official who had presided over the Royal Council of the Indies prior to Toledo's arrival. His work was certainly the result of the most careful research, supplemented by advice from other learned Spaniards such as Polo de Ondegardo, who had played a leading role in coordinating Toledo's inquiries on the Inca past and held personal consultations with the leading survivors among the orejones of Cuzco. After presenting Sarmiento's work to other Indians, who meekly assented that it was correct, Toledo sent the manuscript, finely bound, to King Philip II. This copy eventually reached the library of the University of Göttingen in 1785 but was not published until 1906!

On the very tentative assumption that some documentary evidence was indeed recorded before the 1570s but later lost, it would seem more plausible to suggest that such detailed information might have been conveyed verbally rather than in writing to Sarmiento, and perhaps later to Cabello, by the Inca princes called by Toledo. More credit was surely to be gained by passing on the information in piecemeal form, as if it were the product of their own ingenuity and knowledge, than by simply handing over any existing written text or texts. Such a method would also help to explain the differences, both in spelling and in content, between the works of Sarmiento and Cabello. The younger and hence more literate Inca princes had been carefully schooled by learned Spaniards such as Juán de Cuellar, "who taught Latin and grammar to the mestizos, sons of noble and rich men."[62] Such princes also could have briefed a few of their non-literate elders on selected items revealed in any document so that they could also play their part and, as if from memory, pass such information on to the Spanish chroniclers.

Cabello, though omitting some of Sarmiento's data, particularly on the reign of Pachacutec, describes in more dramatic detail the major incidents in the Ecuadorian wars of Huayna Capac, such as the massacre at Yahuarcocha and the long and important digression on Lambayeque, no doubt obtained when he was there in 1581. He could have obtained much additional data not recorded by Sarmiento during his period of residence in Quito, where a number of descendants of Inca leaders also resided. In particular he consulted Auqui Francisco Tupac, another son of Atahualpa. From him and from other informants Cabello was doubtless able to glean stories of former wars in which their fathers or grandfathers had fought, together with certain traditions that had survived among those tribes who had fought against the Incas. Cabello was a close friend of Cristóbal de Molina, whose own *Lives of the Emperors* was lost; the latter also knew Sarmiento and had cooperated with Toledo in his inquiries.

THE COST OF CONQUEST

The foregoing suggestions constitute only a tentative attempt to seek plausible origins for much of our available data on Inca history. It is surely fair to imply that, without accepting the existence of some kind of documentary "bridge" between histories of the 1570s and 1580s and events occurring so long before, it becomes harder to concede an adequate degree of credibility to these sources. Obviously, we cannot claim to possess anything approaching a full account of what occurred throughout the empire. Nonetheless, though most, if not all, the recorded data need to be treated with some reservations, it is hardly realistic to go to the opposite extreme and to suggest that accounts of major events, such as the Yahuarcocha massacre (the scene of which was visited by Cieza so soon after the event), were simply invented. In particular for the reign of Huayna Capac, many disasters as well as victories are recorded; it is surely far-fetched to suggest that, however our chroniclers obtained their information, the proud warriors who briefed the Spaniards fabricated so many stories of defeats as well as of victories in their past.

In the final analysis, however abundant the material provided by Cabello and others on the Ecuadorian wars and however scanty their data on many other campaigns, one is left wondering just why the Incas pressed on into such far distant lands at both extremities of their empire, creating an elongated domain of increasingly unmanageable proportions. Waldemar Espinosa suggests that the pacification of the northern extremity of Tahuantinsuyu had literally exhausted the material reserves accumulated by the Incas in that region.[63] All accounts, moreover, refer to the huge losses in manpower incurred in these campaigns. And if the cost was so great, were the rewards in any way commensurate? Few luxury articles were native to Quito and northern Ecuador. Admittedly, pearls and jewels came from the north Ecuadorian coast of Esmeraldas, and so perhaps did the highly prized spondylus shells, but this region was never really subdued. Quito occupied a strategic position in the flow of commodities and was more important in this respect than as a population center.[64]

Moreover, not only the physical but also the political cost of the Ecuadorian expansion was surely immeasurable. As Pease suggests, Huayna Capac, in incorporating the Quito region, imperiled the whole imperial system. Conquests of lands beyond a certain distance from Cuzco made control ever harder. The establishment of Tumebamba as a symbolic replica of Cuzco, involving the absence of the Inca from the capital, encroached upon Cuzco's unique ascendancy. The problem was not exclusively political; the Inca, as "Son of the Sun," bore his divine character wherever he went, and his presence conferred upon Tumebamba an added aura of sanctity — but at the expense of the original capital.[65]

The absorption of Ecuador, which perhaps held forth fewer material rewards than Chile and reportedly offered even fiercer resistance, surely increased the danger of a cleavage in the imperial structure. Equally, the objectives of the various campaigns in Antisuyu, in the large territories occupied by Chunchos, Chiriguanos, and others, are far from clear. Tropical products from the Amazonic jungle were presumably to some extent obtainable without military conquest; the Incas were apparently known to peoples living far beyond the limits of their Empire who might have been suppliers of such products.[66] And if the reports of these campaigns are to be believed, their forces suffered reverses on such a scale that the cost of the operations might have outweighed any material gain. The Spaniards also fought wars against some of these tribes but thereafter chose to abandon territory previously gained by the Incas.[67]

The case of the southern border is somewhat different. Here, too, immense distances from the capital were involved, but at least more tangible rewards may have been present in the form of minerals such as gold, for which Inca appetite was insatiable. One wonders, however, whether even such rewards really justified the effort involved in obtaining them, a point to which we shall return in the concluding chapter.

CHAPTER 5

The Inca State

THE HEART IN THE MIDDLE OF THE BODY

The later Inca rulers exercised control over a vast empire, centered upon the city and valley of Cuzco. But Cuzco was no mere administrative capital. So profound was its religious and spiritual authority that it was revered as a holy city, the very founthead of the cult of the Inca ruler as the cherished descendant of the sun and the model for other Inca centers erected in its image throughout Tahuantinsuyu. To cite Cobo, "In the middle of them (the four quarters of empire) was the royal city of Cuzco, like the heart in the middle of the body."[1]

Spanish descriptions of the general aspect of Cuzco are limited in scope. Pedro Pizarro, among others, concentrates on the treasures amassed in its stores; he is amazed by the variety of gold objects, including gold shoes, shellfish, birds, snakes, and even spiders. In an attempt to conceal this treasure from the conquerors, the Incas buried much of it in remote hillsides; as a further precaution, the Indians who bore it thither were killed.[2]

Coricancha, as reconstructed by Pachacutec, was an enclosure that, according to Cieza, was surrounded by a wall of finely cut stone measuring over four hundred paces in circumference.[3] The Temple of the Sun, plated with gold, took up part of this enclosure and was flanked by other buildings that housed many priests and hundreds of *mamaconas*, the select females (described as "virgins of the sun" by Francisco de Xerez) who attended the principal temples and whose duties included the weaving of the ceremonial textiles. Certain of the many ceremonies that took place in Coricancha involved the sacrifice not only of llamas but also of human victims, including children.[4]

Cobo describes Coricancha as one of the richest shrines that had ever existed in the world. Part of its treasure had been provided by *curacas* and governors, who brought lavish presents of gold, silver, and precious stones

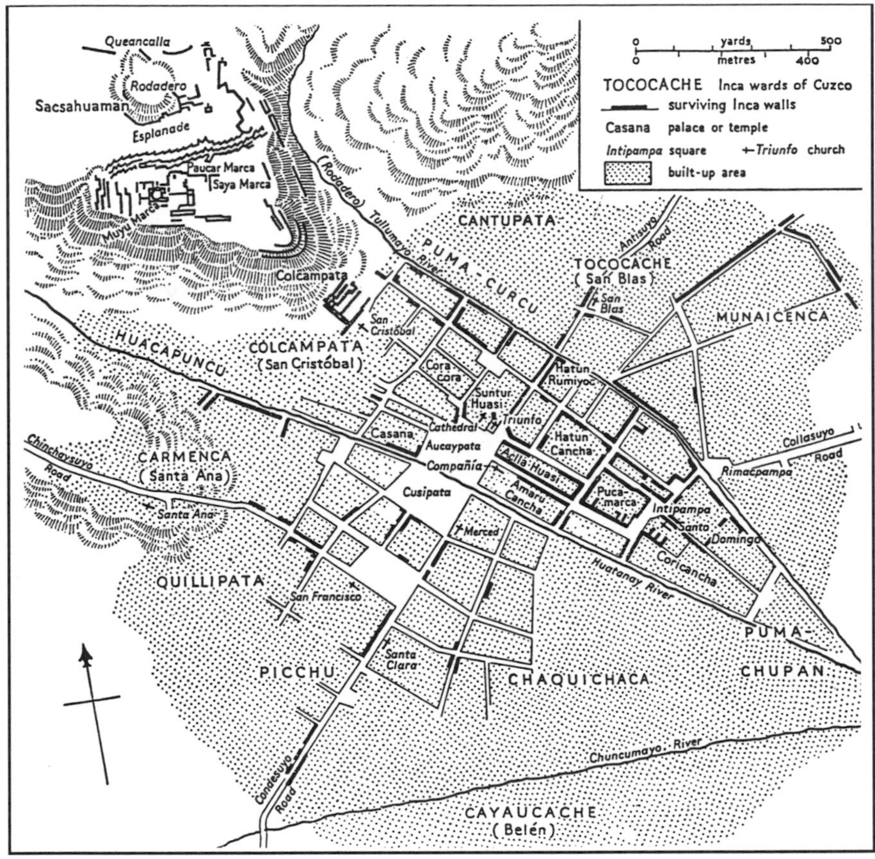

Cuzco at the Time of Conquest. From The Conquest of the Incas *by John Hemming. Macmillan, 1970. Reprinted by permission of John Hemming.*

when they visited Cuzco. Much remained in storage, as few people — only the great nobles — were allowed to use gold and silver adornments. Large amounts of gold and silver also belonged to the *panacas*, the guardians of the riches that former rulers had vied to amass.[5]

Miguel de Estete gives a good overall description of Cuzco in its pre-Conquest state. The main plaza was almost square, neither large nor small. The palace on the square, described as belonging to Atahualpa, had two towers and a portal with silver incrustations. Nearby was a monastery with a hundred dwellings, within whose walls lived innumerable mamaconas; not far distant from this lay the great temple of Coricancha.[6] Four great roads, leading to the four quarters of the Empire, converged on this plaza, within which stood the Ushnu. Zuidema, in a detailed study of the Ushnu (based on an ancient Andean concept), points out that many chroniclers, such as Garcilasco, Betanzos, and Sarmiento, do not mention the Ushnu at all; he cites Molina and Albornoz as the first to describe the Ushnu of Cuzco (others had existed in Huánuco and Tihuanaco).[7] Principally dedicated to the observation and worship of the sun, it was, according to Albornoz, a pillar surmounted by a seat used only by the reigning Inca.[8]

Like Pedro Pizarro, Estete dwells upon the massive hoard of gold, in particular the gold statues in the temples; he also describes the city's spacious residential quarters, lying beyond the more compact center. Another eyewitness, Sancho de la Hoz, writes of the impressive stone houses and the narrow streets, on which two horsemen could barely pass each other. He relates that no poor people lived in central Cuzco. Like many earlier Spanish visitors, he is impressed above all by the towering fortress of Sacsahuaman. De la Hoz relates that Spaniards who had come from Lombardy and other great kingdoms stated that they had seen no citadel of comparable strength. Sacsahuaman commanded a view of the whole valley, filled with houses for a distance of up to one league; he estimated the total number of dwellings at one hundred thousand.[9]

In the Valley of Cuzco certain vestiges of pre-Inca times still survive. Archaeological remains in the vicinity of the city, described by Rowe, have already been mentioned. The valley also contains the Huari-period site of Pikillacta, southeast of Cuzco; its planned structures somewhat recall those of Huari itself in their homogeneity. Gordon McEwan writes of "the overwhelming size and startling layout" of Pikillacta, whose remains cover two square kilometers of ground. He describes this complex as the product of a massive investment of labor, resources, and personnel; the site is among the most striking examples of pure Huari architecture in highland Peru.[10]

Imperial Cuzco was essentially created by Pachacutec, though its splendors were enhanced by later rulers. Before Pachacutec, it was little more than a village. This ruler, as we have seen, built Coricancha, himself tracing with a cord the outlines of the new temple and measuring the stone blocks brought from Salu, five leagues distant. Another basic task was the canalization of the two rivers, performed by labor provided by local curacas and involving the transportation of rough stone of a kind that would resist the ravages of the water. Betanzos, in accordance with other chroniclers, affirms that central Cuzco, situated in the triangle between the two rivers, was the exclusive preserve of the Inca elite. Pachacutec had carved this city into four *suyus*, divided by the roads that led to the four corners of his nascent empire, also called suyus. Because of its triangular form, Cuzco was often conceived by its inhabitants, perhaps in a somewhat metaphorical sense, as being in the guise of a mountain lion lying on its right side, with Sacsahuaman as its head, its back formed by the Tullumayo River, its belly marked by the Huatanay River, and its tail ending where the two streams join. The southwestern extremity of Cuzco was named Pumap Chupan, meaning "lion's tail."[11] Zuidema cites an early Spanish visitor to Cuzco, Juán Ruiz de Arce, as mentioning that the Inca ruler had the decoration of a lion on his golden beakers.[12]

As we shall later see in more detail, Cuzco for the Incas seems to have represented not only a city but a concept; certain provincial centers appear to have reproduced a design based on that of the capital, incorporating the division into four suyus and the apparent integration of symbolic sight lines into their plan of construction. The city, as seen by the Spaniards, was somewhat strange, refined, even awesome, yet it retained a primitive touch. Its temples glittered with gold but were covered by roofs of straw. Cobo asserts that Pachacutec had been influenced by the stone constructions he had seen in Tihuanaco. The grandest buildings, after the temples and shrines, were the palaces. When the Hanan dynasty was established, the rulers no longer lived in Coricancha; instead, each built his own palace. Many stood on the great square of Aucaypata, which lay in the main body of the puma and was where the most imposing ceremonies were performed. The sources differ as to which palace corresponded to each monarch. At the time Francisco Pizarro lodged in the great palace of Casana, it had only one entrance, on each side of which rose two towers built of finely cut stone but surmounted with roofs of straw. When Cuzco was besieged by the rebel Inca Manco II, these roofs caught fire, and the towers collapsed.[13]

In the absence of surviving pictures or plans of Cuzco at the time of the Conquest, a mental image of how it really looked is hard to conceive. Even the central part, though not without a somber splendor, probably lacked true monumentalism in the form of great vistas such as might enhance the grandeur of an imperial city. Notable also for their absence were the teeming markets to be found in most great capitals. The Incas relied on other forms of redistribution.

Ann Kendall stresses that only the nobility, including important officials, enjoyed the right to live in central Cuzco.[14] Chroniclers concur that the Incas by privilege, as opposed to the *orejones*, or original Incas, lived beyond the central triangle between the two rivers. Their dwellings, perhaps modest in comparison with those of the center, were set apart by a belt of open land. According to Santiago Calvo, the barrio that housed these local curacas measured two hundred and eighty-three hectares and was divided into twelve *ayllus*.[15]

Cieza reports that most of the city was inhabited by *mitimaes*; presumably he had in mind a more extended Cuzco, stretching beyond the dwellings of the Incas by privilege and possibly even embracing nearby villages. Cieza in the same context mentions houses made entirely of wood and straw, of a kind he implies did not exist in the center.[16] This greater Cuzco housed not only nobles in and near its center but also countless artisans and technicians in its outer reaches.

Estimates vary widely as to the number of inhabitants. Calvo, cited above, suggests a *total* population of 76,000. Rowe quotes Juán Ruiz de Arce as reporting that before the fire of 1535 Cuzco proper, the central part between the two rivers, contained ten thousand houses. He further cites the estimate of de la Hoz to the effect that there were a hundred thousand buildings in the whole valley.[17] Such a figure might include a fair proportion of dwellings lying even beyond the confines of the extended city and inhabited by the mitimae settlers, among others. Although the center was allegedly the exclusive home of the Incas of royal ayllus, it also housed the *yanas* that served them, as well as many priests. In addition, provincial rulers were obliged to spend part of the year in Cuzco, but it is not very clear where they resided.

THE SON OF THE SUN

The ruler's supremacy was both temporal and spiritual. The solar aspects of the Andean high god, the ancestor of the Inca, were increasingly stressed as the empire expanded. This exaltation of Inti, the sun, was basic to the creation of the imperial cult. Inti became the deified royal progenitor, and his role as dynastic ancestor is described by the chroniclers. Royal ancestryis often traced to Punchao, the young sun. The Incas' solarization of the more generalized sky god may also arise partly from a massive increase in the demand for maize, a relatively low-altitude crop, sensitive to frost and more dependent upon the heat of the sun. Surpluses of maize, easily stored and moved, were needed to feed the imperial armies.[18]

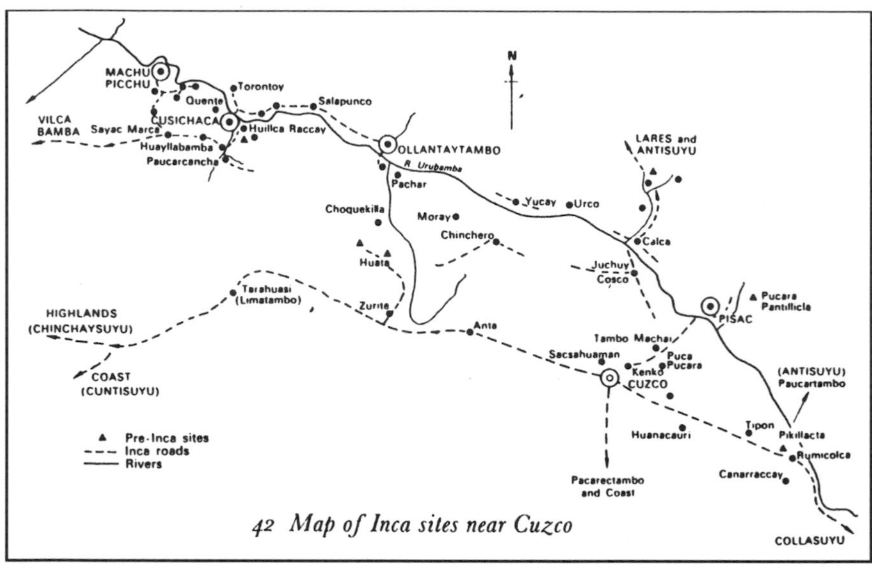

42 Map of Inca sites near Cuzco

Inca Sites Near Cuzco. From Everyday Life of the Incas *by Ann Kendall. Batsford, 1973. Reprinted by permission of Ann Kendall.*

The Incas thus proceeded to add to the traditional religion a new element, the belief that they were the children of the sun. According to Cobo, this fiction became a basic pretext for making war.[19] In each imperial center a temple to Inti was erected, served by special priests. The sources offer ample evidence as to how the role of Inti as dynastic ancestor inspired the ruler's urge to impose his authority on other peoples; hence, this imperial cult reinforced the will to conquer.[20] Veneration of the Inca did not end with his death; his mummy was served by a panaca endowed with great wealth, and his legend was thus retained as a living presence. Once chosen, the reigning Inca in effect was the state, though, as we shall see, even the power of such an exalted being faced certain limitations.

Notwithstanding the unique status of the supreme Inca once chosen, the procedure by which he achieved power is less well defined. The chroniclers, with few exceptions, simply base their ideas on the Spanish monarchy and assert that the choice depended on primogeniture, the ruler's eldest legitimate son thus becoming the rightful heir. Among those who question this accepted notion are Cristóbal de Castro and Diego Ortega Morejón, who report that Huayna Capac had older legitimate brothers.[21]

The Viceroy Toledo came to perceive that the notion of primogeniture did not apply, and in a letter to the king of Spain in 1572 he wrote that the son chosen as imperial successor was not the first-born but rather the son who showed the most capacity to govern.[22] Santillán in effect says the same thing but also stresses the significance of the practice of adoption of a successor by a reigning Inca.[23]

As the Empire expanded, the intrigues and struggles for power marking each succession became a threat to the state. This led to a growing tendency for the number of possible mothers of a legitimate heir to be reduced to one, known as the *coya* (queen); she was the woman the Inca married on the day he received the royal tassel, either as sole king or as an associate monarch. However, some coyas produced no heirs, whereas others had several sons, none of whom possessed a clear right to succeed. In practice, therefore, in the absence of more precise rules, a struggle for power continued to ensue on the death of each king; even formally adopted heirs were far from immune from the challenge of rival claimants.

Some chroniclers state that the ablest of the sovereign's sons was elected; but "ablest" in this context patently implied not only political and military talent but also a certain capacity for intrigue in order to win the greatest support among the royal ayllus making the decision. This tradition of leaving the kingdom to the "ablest" prince inevitably led to plots and even assassinations, with the result that the election was apt to be decided not only by the merits but also by the secret maneuvers of the candidate.[24]

Even after he had achieved the hallowed status of ruler, the new Inca was seldom wholly secure from the threat of would-be usurpers. Apart from the vicissitudes of Viracocha's reign, rumors of dynastic strife stretched into an even more remote past. Details are sketchy, but legend records that during the reign of Viracocha's father, Yahuar Huaca, conspiracies and rebellions were frequent. Cieza relates that Yahuar was eventually murdered.[25] Even Pachacutec was faced with a serious revolt in Cuzco while he was campaigning in Collao, and a disloyal brother tried to dethrone his successor, Tupac Yupanqui, often referred to as Tupac Inca or simply Tupac.

The adoption of an heir as co-ruler during a king's lifetime was intended to reduce strife. But matters were complicated by the tendency of rulers to change their minds and substitute a new co-ruler for their original choice. For instance, Pachacutec initially chose Amaru Yupanqui but later settled on Tupac Yupanqui. Seemingly Amaru was backed by the religious hierarchy but accused of inept conduct as a commander, and he was rejected as heir apparent after a conflict between the religious and military elites. Tupac Yupanqui duly succeeded (serving first as co-ruler according to some sources) but was then confronted with an attempted coup by another royal brother who took advantage of the great responsibilities entrusted to him by the king to revolt in the very city of Cuzco. Defeated, he was condemned to death. Tupac himself declined to name a co-ruler; he was reportedly not very aged at his death. His demise itself is shrouded in mystery, and several sources, including Cabello, even suggest that he might have been murdered.[26]

Tupac's original preference as a successor was withdrawn in favor of Capac Huari, though the latter was never adopted as co-ruler. According to Sarmiento, Tupac changed his mind once more and when he was about to die named as heir Tito Cusi Hualpa, son of his sister-wife, Mama Ocllo. In Cuzco a plot was hatched, partly fomented by female intrigues, to name as ruler Tupac's previous choice, Capac Huari. But with the backing of Tupac's brother, Apoc Achache, the supporters of Tito Cusi prevailed, and he duly ascended the throne, changing his name to Huayna Capac. According to the same chronicler, opinions differ as to whether Capac Huari was then killed or merely exiled.[27]

Cabello de Balboa's account states that Tupac's final choice as heir had been Capac Huari, an illegitimate son, and that the "Lords of the Kingdom" *(Los Grandes del Reino)* made the decision to reject Capac Huari in favor of Huayna Capac, considered the rightful heir because he was the son of the coya, or sister-wife, of the late ruler. But this was not the end of the story; Apoc Hualpaya, an influential noble who was second cousin of Tupac, then secretly plotted to set one of his own sons on the throne. For this purpose he smuggled arms into Cuzco, a step that was discovered by Apoc Achache, who suppressed the uprising and killed the rebels.[28]

Clearly, therefore, disputes over the succession were not confined to the ultimate and disastrous instance, the civil war between Atahualpa and Huascar. If the right to succeed was never clearly defined, such disputes were inevitable. The preference expressed by a reigning monarch was important but not always decisive. The only other device for furthering a more orderly succession, sister marriage, was probably first adopted by Tupac, notwithstanding reports attributing to earlier rulers this practice (which anyway failed to solve the problem, as Huayna Capac's coya produced no son).

The precise identity, or allegiance, of opposing factions in such disputes is seldom clear. Accounts concur in reporting that the orejones were responsible for making the choice, but they do not necessarily state which orejones were involved or on what grounds the decision was made. As Mariusz Ziólkowski affirms in stressing the power of the church, the religious factor also was important in the choice of a successor. According to Murúa, the nomination depended on the tutelary solar deity — in effect, on its priests. But Ziólkowski points out that although at least in theory the choice depended upon the high priest, the "mouthpiece of the Sun," the selection was also influenced by the "señores del Cuzco," or the leading persons in the royal panacas or ayllus, whose exact number and role in the imperial administration are still a matter of controversy. The same author, therefore, basically questions the notion of a divinely inspired election and concedes that the situation of a recently elected ruler was precarious and unstable.[29]

Though matters may have been rather different under the former kings, Pachacutec in effect staged a coup d'état, assuming power by rules that ran counter to former traditions. He transformed the existing ritual-religious system in order to forge a new ideological basis for the nascent empire, introducing special cults, in particular that of Punchao, the young sun. He was able to establish a new priestly hierarchy, headed by the *mayordomo del sol,* who was designated by the Inca himself. Hence, this new high priest, in theory the dignitary best able to influence the choice of a monarch, was in practice chosen by that monarch's predecessor. But, as Ziólkowski concludes, such efforts to install a system that ensured a more or less orderly succession achieved poor results, and the same power struggles continued.[30] This, however, does not signify that a ruler, once established, did not acquire an aura of religious sanctity; the imperial cult of the sun served as the ideological basis for the expansion of the state, and a new ruler's elaborate mystical initiation set him above ordinary mortals, endowed as the god's elect, with unique powers to destroy his enemies.

Problems of succession, and even a proclivity to conspire against the god's elect, are basic to the Inca system of government. In view of the Incas' tendency to re-edit the record, suppressing items unflattering to a new ruler, it is perhaps surprising that the chroniclers learned so much of such dissensions and that by and large their accounts concur in describing them.

The lack of rules to ensure a peaceful succession has served as a destabilizing force in many great empires, of which Rome is an obvious example, but it has seldom destroyed them. The sheer size of the Inca Empire under the later rulers and their prolonged absences from their capital increased the temptation for rival factions to plot against the monarch, however exalted his status. The office rather than the person was paramount, and if a rival could dethrone the incumbent he could claim the absolute submission of those who were now his subjects. One has only to cite the example of the great Pachacutec, who, according to some accounts, virtually usurped the throne from Urco.

The Ruler's Riches

The material, as opposed to the spiritual, strength of the Inca ruler derived from his control of land, the basic measure of wealth, and of mines and herds. Cobo sums up the traditional notion that when the Inca conquered a town or province, the land was divided into three parts; of these he took one for himself, set aside another for the state religion, and left the third for the common use of the people. The proportion assigned to each of the three recipients varied from place to place. Cobo above all stresses that the division of lands showed how absolute was the power of the Inca over everything his vassals possessed. There was no way for them to acquire land except as a gift from the Inca, who would reward individuals for a heroic deed in war or for such services as road or bridge building.[31] Cobo's account is partly based on Polo de Ondegardo, who states that the Inca and the sun had properties in each province.[32]

The Inca may have been the nominal owner of all things, but much property remained in the hands of the traditional local rulers, the curacas. Murra stresses that the respective land rights of the Inca and of the local potentates are hard to determine because of confusion in the sources between traditional holdings and those later granted by the Inca.[33]

Property rights in general will be discussed at greater length in connection with Inca methods of imperial rule. In the present context we are purely concerned with the Inca ruler's personal holdings and the extent to which his riches were material as well as spiritual. As Rostworowski points out, the extent of the Inca's own possessions, accumulated during his lifetime, and the procedure by which all or part of these were transferred after death to his panaca are hard to unravel in the absence of new data from public and private archives. As she further comments, Inca lands throughout the provinces were more state than private property, though the possibility arises that the sovereign personally owned tracts of land in places remote from the capital. Their produce would not have been sent to far-off Cuzco but used locally. Rostworowski cites an unpublished manuscript that mentions Tupac Inca's large provincial properties.[34]

Quite apart from the possibility of royal possessions in more remote provinces, it is far from evident how the ruler obtained private lands nearer home, as the best near Cuzco were mainly held by the royal ayllus. As one alternative, he could confiscate the properties of ayllus unfriendly to him; as a second, he could acquire new land by improved irrigation, a practice mentioned in particular by Cieza and by Garcilasco. By terracing and building new canals, much land could be reclaimed, and cases exist in which rulers did not hesitate to change the course of a river in order to gain additional land. Third, he could send inhabitants of the Valley of Cuzco as mitimaes to other provinces; many examples exist of mitimae groups from Cuzco who settled in other provinces as faithful supporters of Inca rule. Their transfer to other areas served the Inca's personal interest, as he could then confiscate their original holdings.[35]

Perhaps more relevant than the question of mere ownership is the patent fact that the Inca exercised a certain control over the land in conquered provinces. Regardless of whether he, the curaca, or the community was the legal owner, he could determine his own and the state's share of the total resources, whether labor to create local infrastructure or produce to be stored locally or sent to Cuzco.[36]

A similar situation applied to gold and silver mines. In theory, throughout the Empire they belonged to the Inca; in practice, however, the local curacas were clearly also involved in their management. Santillán opines that exploitation could hardly have been very intensified; the Spaniards managed to extract much larger amounts in a much shorter time than the Incas did. Cieza, however, states that great quantities must have been mined in view of the huge stores in Cuzco filled with gold.[37]

The chroniclers also concur that the Inca owned all the herds of llamas. These animals were vital both as a means of transport and as a source of wool, used for the sumptuous clothing of the Inca and his elite; they were also used for sacrifice. However, Murra, who discusses the problem at length, rejected the notion that the Inca was the sole proprietor, dismissing this as an idea that conformed to the ideology of Cuzco but not to basic realities.[38] The *Relaciones Geográficas* cite instances in Collao in which the church, as well as the state, was given herds and grazing grounds by the Inca.[39]

Hence, in a material sense, as the theoretical possessor of all land, mines, and herds, the Inca *was* the state, just as in a spiritual context he personified the state religion as offspring of the solar deity. In practice he may have enjoyed less extensive direct ownership except as pertained to his personal estates, acquired by methods that remain somewhat unclear. Apart from the urge to endow his future panaca, his private needs were perhaps not excessive. Lavish state funds (which in such a society tend to be synonymous with those of the ruler) covered his own expenditures, together with the cost of the huge volume of sumptuary goods that by custom he bestowed on others.

The Social Pyramid

The Inca's own person was thus exalted far above that of the highest dignitaries; the rest of society may, like many others of its kind, be compared to a pyramid in form. At its apex stood the inner elite among the orejones. Betanzos writes that they were all descended from Inca rulers.[40] Their status was unique, enhanced by the fact that the central part of Cuzco, the very heart of the sacred city, was their dwelling place. Though the sources often state that only the orejones lived in central Cuzco, these select few clearly also included the priestly elite, charged with the rituals of Coricancha and the many great temples. The orejones had a special school for their sons (to which Incas by privilege also had access). They alone were entitled to wear sumptuary clothing. Garcilasco even states that they spoke a distinct form of the Quechua language.[41] According to all sources, their position atop the social pyramid was unassailable and immutable. The orejones were exempt from taxes — a concession the Incas by privilege shared. They were supported by the king through his revenues. In practice, though, they had to return part of what they were entitled to receive, as they were not excused from the duty of regaling the king with precious gifts. Because these were "voluntary" and the quantities were not fixed, however, they did not rank as tribute.[42]

On numerous occasions uncles, brothers, and sons were named as being among a ruler's leading commanders. In the case of Pachacutec, his various brothers are credited with playing prominent roles. Inca Roca, Apo Mayta, and Vicaquirao played an important part in the defeat of the Chancas.[43] Equally, Tupac on various occasions put brothers in command of part of his forces.[44] His two sons are also named as leading captains,[45] in the case of Huayna Capac to command an expedition to Chinchasuyu.[46] Close relatives, whether brothers or sons, are also frequently mentioned by the sources as being named governor of Cuzco in the ruler's absence on a military campaign.[47] In accounts of military campaigns, the orejones, often close relatives or even brothers of the reigning monarch, are frequently identified as leading generals, and the sources continually stress their key role as commanders in the field and as provincial administrators. However, in early states and empires, distinctions between the exercise of military leadership and civilian administration are often blurred. As provincial governors, orejones were surely also charged with overseeing the imperial infrastructure, involving irrigation, road construction, and town planning, even if the details were delegated to others, specialists in one field or another.

Information on the true antecedents of the orejones is imprecise. The notion that they were all of royal blood, so widely diffused, is perhaps an oversimplification. Despite plural marriage among the ruling class, in the course of a limited number of generations the rulers alone could scarcely have sired a progeny sufficient to form even the nucleus of a force destined to conquer a huge empire. Kirchhoff wonders whether distinguished commoners could have been added to the ranks of the *orejon* nobility.[48]

The question also arises as to what might have occurred to fledgling nobles conspicuous for a lack of either martial or administrative skills who thereby fell short of the inflexible norms of their caste. In the absence of any flagrant offense, they could hardly have been executed, as reportedly happened to certain orejones guilty of conspiracy and of military disobedience; scant mention occurs of punishment for other failings. But human nature is never wholly conformist, and one can hardly conceive that in any society, ancient or modern, a spartan upbringing will ensure conformity with relentless standards. If some members of the upper class could resort to base treachery, a tendency that is amply documented, others could surely at times have proved to be lazy, mendacious, or simply overindulgent. In this, as in certain other matters, we are perhaps presented with a rather idealized version of Inca society that ignores, among other things, the treatment meted out by the Inca lords to the occasional black sheep among their progeny.

Pachacutec reportedly first enlarged the numbers of those entitled to be called Inca by creating the rank of Inca by privilege. As we have seen, Incas by privilege lived beyond the limits of central Cuzco. Whereas the orejones had their own lands as members of the royal ayllus or received holdings from the ruler, the resources of the Incas by privilege seem to have depended less on land and more on state revenues received from the king. Access to these extensive state revenues formed the basis of their existence.[49]

Clear notions of just how the system of government worked at the very highest level are equally hard to form. The available evidence suggests that the key posts were held by the orejones, though doubtless Incas by privilege also served in the administration of the state. The sources use such phrases as "the highest in the land" when referring to those deciding certain issues, particularly the succession to the throne. Schaedel cites reports of a council of twelve, a supraprovincial consultative body composed of one or more Inca representatives from each Cuzco moiety and one or two representatives from each of the four suyus.[50] Huaman Poma also mentions a council of twelve, of which ten members were representatives of the suyus.[51] Damián de la Bandera states that Tupac Yupanqui named a *capac*, or viceroy, for each of the four suyus; these formed the Inca's principal consultative body, together with a "secretary" who studied the nature of any problem before it was referred to the ruler himself.[52] However, Gibson points out that although Cobo also writes of four *apos*, or heads of the four suyus, these can be taken either as members of a council or simply as local governors who were only concerned with problems and decisions within their own territory.[53] Murúa writes more specifically of four orejones who formed the king's council and who were quite distinct from the four governors of the suyus; the latter, however, had direct access to the council of four in Cuzco.[54]

Moore accepts de la Bandera's assertion that the Inca's council consisted of the four lords, the top administrators of the "four quarters" of the Empire, and writes of the probability that the Inca depended on their advice in making any major decision. They apparently had the power to resolve all but the most difficult questions without even consulting the Inca and played a leading role in deciding when to wage war. These dignitaries could hardly administer the four quarters of the Empire by remaining within the bounds of Cuzco, but if they were located far from the capital it is hard to see how they could confer with the ruler on problems that might suddenly arise, notwithstanding the speed with which verbal messages could be transmitted throughout the Empire's length and breadth.[55]

Basic both to the comfort and status of the orejones living in central Cuzco was the presence of a menial class known as yanas. Their origins are obscure; Murra questions the tendency of chroniclers to classify them as "rebels" or people who had been condemned to death and then pardoned. He suggests that yanas already existed in pre-Inca times. They could marry and have children, and their status was probably hereditary. Murra points to a similar servant class in the Lupaqa region; these servants might have been recruited from the Lupaqa population itself, or they could have derived from a people of lesser standing, the Uru, quite distinct from the Aymara peoples. Among the Lupaqa, highly specialized individuals were surely needed to manage the huge herds, amounting to as many as ten thousand head; Murra proposes that these specialists were yanas and that they came to form a separate social group within the community.[56]

Whatever the pretexts involved, the yanas were basically uprooted people from the provinces brought in to perform services, principally in the capital. Unlike the mitimaes located in the vicinity of Cuzco, the yanas came as individuals. Choy believes they can truly be defined as slaves who might serve temples, the ruler, or even curacas whom the ruler wished to favor. It was not customary to sell yanas but rather to donate them as a reward for services. In general terms, they were less oppressed than slaves in other highly developed societies.[57] Notwithstanding their servile condition, the yanas could attain a certain status. They could become artisans, and their numbers included skilled silversmiths brought to Cuzco from Chincha and other parts of the coast.[58]

THE ADMINISTRATION

In controlling the Inca realm, extended over vast distances, a well-staffed administrative system was indispensable. Writers often refer to this system as a bureaucracy, though the term, derived from the French word for "writing desk," perhaps acquires a rather special sense when applied to a society in which the blessings of conventional paperwork were unknown. Though the Inca elite presumably made the decisions, detailed planning surely required a corps of experts versed in each aspect of administration and able to ensure that decisions, once made, were put into effect.

In a conquest state, the military organization was paramount. In the case of the Incas, the mobilization of armies was complicated by a special factor: Unlike other ancient empires, in which much of the army was recruited from the home base or from nearby regions, the Incas increasingly employed levies drawn from the many loyal and reliable peoples located throughout their Empire. To quote one instance, forces sent from Collao played a conspicuous role in campaigns in Ecuador.[59] The frequent deployment over vast distances of such forces, and their arrival at the right time and at the right place, must have involved military staff work of the highest order.

In this and other matters, communications were paramount. Hyslop describes the roads as an omnipresent symbol of the power and authority of the state; the system was monumental and constitutes South America's largest contiguous archaeological remain. The author, however, remarks that this fact should not detract from other feats of prehistoric Andean civilizations, whose agricultural terraces and irrigation canals may have required even greater labor inputs than did the Inca road system.[60] Hyslop's chapter on Inca bridges amply illustrates the complexity of the technical and administrative problems that affected their construction and maintenance. Bridges of many kinds were built, offering in each case a practical solution, based on the particular problem involved, for crossing rivers. Such solutions were new and amazing to the first Europeans who saw them; curiously, Andean bridges never employed the arch, which had been crucial to Western bridge building for the past two millennia.[61] Technical considerations also affected the siting of the *tampus*, or lodgings; such factors included the supply of water, availability of food, and the avoidance of steep, barren, or marshy terrain.[62]

Such feats of engineering obviously required central planning, as well as a highly integrated communications system to settle questions too important to be decided on a purely provincial level and personnel whose technical qualifications were equal to the task of making plans without the use of writing. The question arises as to whether these plans could be made at all without the use of at least some form of charts or maps, as it seems almost beyond the capacity of the human brain to memorize the whole road system and all the details involved. No such records have survived, however. *Quipus* could at least have recorded certain statistics, such as the quantities of material needed for a given project.

Nonetheless, Craig Morris warns against reliance on models that draw too heavily on principles related to modern states or to tribal societies. Morris accepts that by the time of Pizarro's arrival, some kind of master plan was in place, but one that took fully into account the ecological and cultural diversity of the Empire instead of imposing some set pattern of administrative control. The author stresses the complexity of the process of planning the large-scale movement of whole peoples over long distances under the mitimae system, citing as an example the introduction of no less than fourteen thousand people from different places into the warm lands of Cochabamba to grow maize for the army. In certain cases, not only would peoples be moved thousands of kilometers, but parts of a polity could be detached in situ and assigned to a neighboring polity.[63]

As Murra also observes, the vast Inca territory required a system that could relate the periphery to the center and the coast to the altiplano; this would keep potential rebels under the observation of garrisons and permit the *quipocamayos* to gather the provincial data needed by the central government.[64]

The distinction between decisionmaking and the strictly technical requirements of administration was reflected in the Incas' social organization. The orejones lived in the center of Cuzco, and in most ancient civilizations decisionmaking tended to be exercised by a nucleus of individuals based on the center of the capital rather than on the periphery. The Incas by privilege lived on the outskirts of Cuzco and would thus have less easily formed part of any inner "establishment" that ruled under the Inca and took control in his absence. Occasionally called "administrative Incas," the Incas by privilege may have held important posts and made decisions of a more detailed nature, whereas the orejones, in close accord with the ruler, laid down the overall policy and objectives of the state. The large and important religious hierarchy resided by all accounts in Hurin Cuzco, within the orbit of the orejones who inhabited the central city.

The chroniclers seldom refer to the status of the lower echelons of the administrative machine, whose role was perhaps as much technical as supervisory. Schaedel suggests that the middle and lower levels both of the central and the provincial bureaucracies were staffed mostly by yanas. Though evidence on this point may be incomplete, we know that some yanas did develop skills that raised them far above the level of mere menial workers. Schaedel makes a constructive, if tentative, attempt to outline the Inca system of government. He first draws attention to the eleven panacas, defined as the royal court, created by Pachacutec in an attempt (albeit not altogether successful) to secure the legitimacy of the succession. Next in importance came the royal ayllus, who seem to represent kin groups from which the next potential panaca might be formed. The same author divides the administrative apparatus into "clusters." The judicial cluster included the *tocricoc*, who were responsible for the control of the various provinces and seem to have been traveling representatives as much as permanent residents in any one province. The judicial officials were the *tocoyricoc* (inspectors), specifically assigned to inform on the administration of justice. The treasury cluster included a hierarchy of officials in charge of quipus related to storehouses. The chief of this group may have been the "secretary" of the Inca *(incap cimin quipococ)*, assisted by an accountant general familiar with both the census and revenue totals. The military cluster was the preserve of nobles who served in the field but who also played a role in the civilian government. Each Inca seems to have had his own procedure for selecting, promoting, and demoting — or executing —his generals, most of whom we hear about only in the context of field campaigns or military coups and palace revolts. A further group, the transportation cluster, was most important, as it was responsible for the communications network, roads, bridges, and the system of *chasquis* (messengers).[65]

A key instrument of provincial rule was the decimal system. Inca statistics should not always be interpreted as corresponding exactly to demographic reality, as there could not always be exactly one hundred or one thousand people in each center of population. It has been suggested that the numerical system might have been borrowed from the kingdom of Chimor.[66] This method of counting, like other statistical data at the disposal of the administrators, would surely have been unmanageable without the quipu knots that served to record numbers. Only one known source stems specifically from quipu records, the *Declaración de los Quipocamayos*, so we possess little direct quipu data, and it becomes easy to overlook their crucial role. Sources, however, concur on their importance; statistics for the Empire as a whole simply could not have been retained in Cuzco in officials' heads. Wedin cites Murúa as stating that much of what survived of Inca history was at least based on data recorded in quipus. However, much of this surviving information is really secondhand; certain writers who professed to give facts derived from quipus were in fact relaying the reports of prior sources, from whom they demonstrably copied part of their data. Wedin cites the specific instance of Cabello de Balboa and Murúa. The latter claims that much of his knowledge came from quipus, a source to which Cabello even attributes his "authentic" chronology. Both chroniclers tend to convey the impression of diligence, involving much time spent on interviews with quipocamayos, the ostensible key to Inca historical information. Suspiciously, though, their accounts of how they gleaned information from quipocamayos are couched in almost identical terms![67]

Cieza writes that accountants (described as quipocamayos) resided in each province, recording the tribute that was due. He tells of the curaca of the province of Xauxa, who sent for his quipocamayos in order to show off their talents to Cieza; they were able to state from their meticulous records the exact quantities of everything that had been given to the Spaniards since the arrival of Pizarro, whether gold, silver, textiles, maize, or animals. Cieza was amazed at the precision of their methods. In Cieza's time, quipocamayos were still functioning in each valley and produced reports every four months.[68] Similar skills were surely used to keep track of garrisons, stores, troop movements, and many other aspects of administration, both civil and military. As many sources affirm, the schooling of the quipocamayo was prolonged and laborious. Trainees had to learn to handle the many different colors, strings, and knots and to familiarize themselves with past records. These specialists' skills and feats of memory, as seen by the first European observers, were likely based on long practical experience and a total dedication to their calling.[69]

Ascher's account gives details (complete with diagrams) of how the quipus functioned, depending on the length of the cords as well as on the colors and the number of knots.[70] As he explains, our ignorance of the exact methods derives from the fact that known surviving quipus, having been taken from cemeteries, were buried with dead persons for whom they had a significance in life, but they were without meaning in the absence of a contextual relationship.[71]

Finance and Property

Though information on general administration remains elusive, on specific aspects of the problem data are more copious, in particular on the *mit'a*, the term for services exacted by the state from each individual or community.

On this matter, as on others, accounts differ widely. Murra describes the mit'a as a collective obligation on the part of married males to work for the Inca or the state for a given number of days per annum on such assignments as roads, bridges, and agriculture, as well as public works in the capital. Murra is dealing mainly with the core region of Empire; however, as we shall later see in the case of imperial administration, local curacas in more distant provinces also had claims on the labor of their people but apparently exacted no tribute in kind.[72] The mit'a system was equally used for recruiting purposes, though the proportion of the population drafted for war in this way is hard to quantify. Subsistence needs had to be taken into account, and the ratio of those conscripted must also have varied with the importance of the campaign and the proximity of the community to the battlefield. Not every ethnic group provided its quota; some coastal populations were not considered trustworthy, and their ability to endure combat at an elevation of, say, 3,500 meters may also have been a factor.[73]

Many sources confirm that tribute was normally paid not in goods or produce but in the form of labor used to provide such items as textiles or wood to the state. Santillán, in his fairly explicit account, includes among items produced by mit'a labor articles made of feathers and precious metals; the latter were all sent to Cuzco.[74] Cieza, however, does not hesitate to use the word *tribute,* mentioning among other products huge quantities of maize; peoples of the regions nearest to the capital, however, were used more for construction works in Cuzco. Where goods were sent, they were carefully checked by orejon officials.[75] For the Cuzco region itself, the mit'a was essentially a method of centralizing labor available in the agricultural dead season as part of the overall planning of public works. This massive corvée work force is alleged to have numbered tens of thousands; such levies were used, for instance, in the channeling of the Urubamba River.

As Moore points out, matters tend to be confused by the chroniclers, who were somewhat misled because they themselves saw the laborers rather than their produce, which in effect was a form of tribute.[76] However, if what the Incas levied was in effect tribute in one form or another, considerable evidence shows that they also did much to increase the overall output of those whom they taxed. The description of the Inca tribute as being levied solely in terms of service had a natural appeal for certain writers who were adherents of the labor theory of value and who liked to use the word *socialism* in the Inca context.

The system for mining precious metals for the state was somewhat different, relying more on craftsmen organized by the curacas than on mit'a labor. Miners were local specialists exempt from ordinary forced labor.

When the gold reached its final destination in Cuzco, much was lavished by the Inca on his entourage as a reward for distinguished service. Moreover, the curacas, when they visited the capital, were expected to offer golden gifts to the Inca, who in return loaded them with other presents.

MITIMAES AND YANAS

The notion of a city inhabited exclusively by a noble, or upper, class, together with a quota of yanas to act as servants, is very hard to conceive in practice. Cuzco, taken as a whole, was fairly extensive; the question therefore arises as to what other elements also comprised its population. Rowe cites eyewitnesses as stating that there were no poor people in Cuzco; he agrees that such statements should not be taken as excluding the yanas.[77] But these eyewitnesses were surely concerned with the two moieties of *central* Cuzco, Hurin and Hanan. Their observations hardly account for what lay beyond the fortress of Sacsahuaman, not only the residences of the Incas by privilege but also the outer reaches of "greater Cuzco." This area was inhabited not by patricians but more by plebeians, members of a wide range of social groups.

Early reports describe the large output of the gold- and silversmiths in Cuzco itself, as well as much featherwork and massive quantities of pottery. In addition, building construction in Cuzco and many other forms of public works imply the presence of a skilled labor force. Part of this labor could have been supplied from the subjects of nearby curacas who lived outside the limits of the capital itself. But much of the work force seemingly consisted of mitimaes, people from other regions transported en masse to the Valley of Cuzco. Cieza, writing obviously (as mentioned above) of *outer* Cuzco, states that most of the city was full of "foreigners" (i.e., mitimaes from far away) who had been employed there since the reign of Pachacutec; in Cieza's time people from Ecuador, originally brought in groups as mitimaes, were still present in Cuzco. These migrants were all part of the labor force then available *(todos de industria)*.[78] Cieza also mentions that the Inca's personal herds were attended by mitimaes.

As a form of social engineering, the mitimae system was used on such a scale that it is hard to find a parallel elsewhere in the world. It played a vital role in the process of conquest as a means of pacifying newly acquired lands by removing the more unreliable elements and replacing them with loyal settlers. But the same system also had a major impact on the capital. Espinoza cites documents that show that a large part of the mitimaes settled in Lupaqa territory, in some cases up to 80 percent, actually came from the vicinity of Cuzco; the documents refer to them as "*mitimas inca*" and state that whole ayllus were transported. In turn, Lupaqa groups had been sent over the course of time to more than twenty places, including Cuzco. Garci Díez states that Lupaqas in the Cuzco region served as builders and masons.[79]

The transference of such numbers away from the Cuzco region, moved like pieces on a chessboard, served a dual purpose. First, their lands were vacated and could be either assigned to specialist groups brought from elsewhere or confiscated by the ruler. Such settlers would have included agriculturists skilled in the growing of maize in high altitudes; apart from its use for military supplies, maize had a major ritual significance in Inca culture. The second objective was to settle wholly dependable groups of people from the vicinity of Cuzco itself in other key regions. Such mitimaes from the heartland were compensated with special privileges in their new home. Murra suggests that mitimaes sent from Cuzco occasionally included Incas by privilege and even a few individuals of royal descent; however, the only chronicler quoted in this report is Murúa, and the information he provides is confined to the sanctuaries of the Lake Titicaca region.[80]

Though Cuzco could not have functioned without ample skilled labor, the extent to which it relied on mitimaes for manpower might tend to be exaggerated; the majority of workers could equally have been yanas, and the proportion of each is hard to establish. Any attempt to define the respective roles of mitimaes and yanas in the economy of Cuzco is further obfuscated by the rather fine distinction generally drawn between the status and origin of each. Both are described as descended from "rebels," the difference being that the latter came as individuals, whereas the former were moved in groups. The chroniclers themselves stress the danger of confusing the two categories, and Cieza refers to the error of López de Gómara in failing to make a correct distinction.[81] Rostworowski mentions, on the one hand, silversmiths and potters brought to Cuzco in whole groups (i.e., mitimaes) and, on the other, numerous artisans from the coast still living in a single ayllu in Cuzco whom she describes as yanas. Both potters and silversmiths were transported from the coastal region not only to Cuzco but also to many localities in the altiplano, such as Cajamarca, where potters from Collique were settled, and Huamachuco. Some of these skilled artisans from the coast formed an important part of the labor force used to produce Spanish colonial silverware.[82]

Basic Premises

As Craig Morris observes, we tend to ignore the mechanisms of Inca administration and the degree of state planning involved (though any complex scheme of imperial organization would have been hard to establish in detail in the brief century of Inca hegemony). The author stresses the importance of religion and ceremony in holding together the varied and spatially discontinuous parts of the realm; studies in Huánuco, for instance, have revealed that feasts and ceremonies were the focal point of the activities of that important Inca center. Many, if not most, of the goods sent from the hinterland and held in storehouses were manifestly destined for the city's ceremonial life and for services connected with this purpose; hence, Huánuco was a consumer center in terms of economic activities, and primary production was located elsewhere.[83]

In writing of the likely characteristics of Inca administration, one is virtually forced to resort to speculation and to *assume* that a complex state administrative service was indispensable. Any comparison with better-documented empires may surely serve to reinforce this assumption. But speculation leads inevitably to the use of the word *must,* a word suggestive of purely subjective opinions and therefore treated with caution on a professional level. But in the case of Cuzco, the expression is hard to avoid; one can only assert that there *must* have been an established and fairly elaborate machinery for making decisions and plans (even if we know so little about it) — a machinery, moreover, that could function in the ruler's absence.

Huayna Capac spent much of his reign away from Cuzco, and it is hard to see how he could control the whole empire from his second capital, Tumebamba, situated in its northern extremity. Chroniclers concur in describing Tupac's prolonged forays to remote regions long before this. Hence, notwithstanding the resources devoted to means of rapid communication, there *must* have been others able to make major decisions in the ruler's absence (quite apart from the vexed problem of succession when a ruler died). Pressing problems, some of an overall nature and others strictly military, would have arisen — for instance, what action to take against rebellious tribes in recently conquered Chile; what forces to deploy for the purpose; what steps to take if any part of the road network, say, in the Cochabamba region, needed major repair or renewal; and, in general terms, what proportion of available resources to devote to each sector of the state-controlled economy, questions demanding constant and at times instant revision in the light of changing circumstances and new challenges.

The Inca realm could hardly have functioned without a stream of orders and instructions to provincial authorities and a corresponding flow-back of data to the capital, much of which might have been recorded on quipus. The governors could hardly rule as self-sufficient potentates; moreover, they might need to be replaced instantly because of death or for other reasons. Such matters also required prompt decisions in Cuzco. Precisely who belonged to any decisionmaking body remains unclear; possibilities include a group of close relatives of the Inca, a council of four, a council of twelve, or even a single individual acting as a trusted deputy of the monarch and left in charge as governor of Cuzco. However prestigious the Inca as the sacred offspring of Inti, he could not perform the miracle of being in every place at once and was more often to be found in some distant part of his far-flung realm than in Cuzco. Hence, in the final analysis, though it may be true to regard the Inca system of government as strictly elitist, it is probably less accurate to describe it as controlled solely by a deified despot.

CHAPTER 6

The Empire and Its Infrastructure

A Diverse Pattern

Many traces of the Incas' presence throughout their empire have now been located and studied. Archaeological research denotes the existence of a complex infrastructure and suggests a pattern of orderly control. Instinctively, therefore, the temptation may arise to think of this great domain, stretching from slightly north of the Equator almost to a latitude of 35 degrees south, as a basically homogeneous realm subject to a strictly uniform system of imperial rule. But in reality each newly added province was hardly set in the precise mold of those already subdued in order to forge a more or less monolithic whole, subjected to a single set of rules.

Craig Morris, in suggesting that some kind of grand master plan might have been in place by the time of the Conquest, denies that such a plan would have aimed at reducing the Incas' domain to some easy administrative common denominator. The brilliance of their achievement perhaps lay more in their ability to accept, use, and even foster diversity.[1] Hence, factors such as the ecology of a given territory, the culture of its people, and the length of time since it was first conquered apparently led to marked differences in the way each was governed.

In the very broadest terms, the Inca Empire did indeed adhere to a single ecological pattern. Throughout most of its extent the coast was desert or semidesert (the Ecuadorian littoral was never subdued); the immediate hinterland rose steeply to the altiplano, surmounted by the Andean cordillera, and then descended gradually into tropical and subtropical plains, penetrated only at certain places by the Inca forces.

In the next chapter specific aspects of imperial rule will be considered: the established governing hierarchy, the division of the land, the imposition of taxes (levied in the form of labor or produce), and the urge for local self-sufficiency whereby certain communities would form settlements at different altitudes (the concept described by Murra as verticality). But as a prelude to any such assessment of an empire so diverse, certain other basic questions first require attention: the cultural and ecological characteristics of each principal region and the extent to which they differed; the effect of such diversity on the Inca pattern of control; and the kind of centers from which the Incas ruled their Empire. In addition, before studying the administration of this huge and heterogeneous domain, the physical means of control, in terms of both civil and military infrastructure, need to be considered.

Leaving aside for the moment the northern and southern extremities of the Empire, the basic domain might be said to consist of the core territory of the central Andes together with Collao and the Peruvian littoral — both the northern sector, previously subject to the kingdom of Chimor, and the coastal region further to the south, previously controlled by a number of separate principalities.

COLLAO

The traditional importance of Collasuyu, the region surrounding Lake Titicaca, has already been stressed. And although the splendors of the Tihuanaco civilization had long since faded, many tales bear witness to close links between Collao and the Incas' legendary past. Certain sources, moreover, imply that the Collas played a positive role in the creation of the Inca state under Pachacutec. Lumbreras, in writing of the Chanca war, refers to these Aymara-speaking principalities as major participants in the struggle to secure an Inca victory.[2] He further views the Valley of Cuzco and the Titicaca altiplano as interdependent regions.[3] Schaedel also writes of an Inca alliance with the Lupaqas some time before the confrontation with the Chancas, though he sees this alliance as excluding the Collas (whose realm also lay on the northern flank of Lake Titicaca). The Lupaqas' system of dual chieftainship might also have prevailed in the proto-Inca state.[4]

Notwithstanding any such prior links on a basis of equality between Collas and Incas, Pachacutec in the early stages of Inca long-range expansion imposed his will on the Collas by force, defeating in battle the lord of Hatunqolla and annexing his kingdom. This appears to have been an extensive domain embracing almost the entire Lake Titicaca region, excepting the Pacajes territory southeast of the lake and possibly the Lupaqa polity.[5]

The Inca administration of the region is described in some detail in the *Visita Hecha a la Provincia de Chucuito por Garci Díez de San Miguel*, written in 1557. Chucuito was the capital of the Lupaqa chiefdom and was situated a few miles south of Puno on the shore of Lake Titicaca. According to this document, as cited by Murra, the area occupied by Aymara-speaking groups was then much greater than today, and its inhabitants could be counted at least in the hundreds of thousands; the Lupaqa alone numbered more than twenty thousand households (or about one hundred thousand souls). Garci Díez writes of the dual control of the Lupaqas by two rulers, Cari and Cusi, named by Cieza and other chroniclers in describing the Inca conquest. Certain sources denounce these Lupaqa kings as mere rebels who frequently rose against their Inca masters, whereas others portray them as loyal subjects who helped to govern the whole region.[6]

Though Chucuito became the main provincial capital, Hatunqolla also developed as an important Inca center. As Catherine Julien writes, the Inca town would have been laid out on a typical grid plan, with shrines that corresponded to those of Cuzco. This pattern involved a town center with many Inca buildings, including not only a temple of the state religion but also a multitude of storehouses, as well as a convent of women chosen by the Inca government.[7]

Hyslop carried out a surface reconnaissance of Chucuito and four other Lupaqa centers of population. Evidence from surface ceramics would suggest that these communities were probably founded at about the time of the Inca occupation; the development of such urban centers would have furthered the Inca aim of pressing the Collas to abandon villages situated at or near the mountaintops and to concentrate in the plains below, a process described by Cieza. The chronicler, in writing of Collao, confirms that in pre-Inca times the inhabitants lived in fortified settlements on the high peaks, from which they would emerge to make war on each other, inflicting heavy casualties and seizing many captives for sacrifice. Few traces of Inca settlement have been found outside the cultivated zones of the plain, and any vestiges of occupation of other parts of the Lupaqa region date from pre-Inca times.[8] Copacabana retained its aura of sanctity; Amalia Castelli compares its significance as a shrine to that of Pachacamac and cites Calancha as relating that Tupac Inca introduced carefully selected *mitimaes* to guard the precincts and supervise the flow of pilgrims.[9]

The relationship between Cuzco and Collao was indeed complex. Colla contingents fought valiantly in imperial campaigns, particularly in Ecuador, but sources that report Colla rebellions in Tupac's time also mention other uprisings as late as the reign of Huayna Capac. These might in reality have occurred at an earlier date; alternatively, they could have been directed against Colla rulers loyal to the Inca, who then appealed to the latter for help in crushing such dissent.

THE SOUTH COAST

Another early objective of Inca expansionism was the series of thriving principalities on the south coast of present-day Peru, lying west and southwest of Cuzco and extending northward to the approximate southern boundary of the kingdom of Chimor. Cieza reports an early expedition by Pachacutec along the Cuntisuyu road, where he met fierce resistance.[10] Cobo also mentions this campaign, in which the ruler received a mixed reception; in the southernmost valleys of Ica and Nazca he faced little resistance, but further to the northwest Huarco fought fiercely against the invaders.[11] The Chincha polity was among the strongest and most important on the southern coast. According to Cieza, when Tupac Inca later proceeded down the coast after conquering Chimor, the Chinchas, together with the people of Nazca, initially resisted his advance, though a peaceful surrender ensued.[12]

Inca domination led to the presence of imperial officials in the Chincha Valley, the establishment of an administrative center in their capital, the building of a temple to the sun, and the cession of land for the settlement of mitimaes.[13] Much land throughout the region was evidently taken for these settlers, and many of the original inhabitants were relocated in other parts of the Empire, where they came to be well known for their skills as potters and silversmiths. The *curaca* of Chincha retained a status of great prestige in the imperial hierarchy; when Pizarro met Atahualpa in Cajamarca, he was the only other dignitary present to be borne in a litter.[14]

Though certain principalities reportedly offered little or no resistance to Tupac, a grimmer fate awaited the Huarcos, the Chinchas' northerly neighbors, who occupied the lower part of the Cañete Valley. Far from suing for peace, they fortified their territory and prepared to fight to the end. In Cieza's description of their ordeal, they struggled on for three years. Finally debilitated by this war of attrition, the Huarcos surrendered, and the chiefs and many others were massacred; the chronicler refers to great piles of bones still visible in his day.[15]

Farther to the north, the central sector of the Peruvian coast, extending as far as the border of the kingdom of Chimor, had been dominated by two principalities: Ychma, which included the Lima Valley, and Collique, north of present-day Lima, astride the valley of the Río Chillón. The surviving sites of Cajamarquilla and Pachacamac were both then situated in Ychma. Under Inca rule the latter fully retained its prestige, and when Tupac conquered the Ychma Valley he gave the shrine its present name. By contrast, Cajamarquilla, which had become a major settlement during the Middle Horizon, probably declined before the end of this period. Ruth Shady describes Cajamarquilla as having been the largest and most important town of the central coast.[16]

The religious aura of Pachacamac needs no stressing; it was famed for its influence and wealth, attracting pilgrims from regions far distant. The Spaniards were impressed by Pachacamac; Pedro Pizarro relates that Atahualpa told Francisco Pizarro of the great store of golden treasure owned by its idol.[17] Francisco de Xerez offers a dramatic description of its riches, stating that pilgrims visited the site from a distance of up to three hundred leagues bearing gold and silver gifts.[18] Pachacamac was held in such esteem that Cieza describes Tupac's occupation more as a ceremonial visit, involving a consultation with the oracle, than as a conquest. Cobo tells how, when Huayna Capac was about to die of smallpox, his servants sent two relay teams to the shrine to ask what should be done for the health of their lord. The oracle replied through the mouth of an idol that the Inca should be taken out into the sun and that he would then get well. The advice was carefully followed, but with the opposite result: When the Inca was exposed to the sun he died at once.[19]

Of the principality of Collique, north of Ychma, Rostworowski bases her description on documents that she discovered in the Archivo de Indias in Seville. Before the arrival of the Incas the ruler controlled many lesser curacas and even at one time occupied part of the Lima Valley. When Tupac conquered Collique, he met with stiff resistance, and its ruler was killed in a hard-fought battle.[20]

These maritime principalities, reportedly conquered by Tupac, collectively came to form an important part of the Inca Empire. It was valuable not only for the unique sanctity of Pachacamac but also because this was the sector of the Pacific coast most accessible to the Inca capital. From an agricultural standpoint, the two settlements offered to highland communities the possibility of vertical expansion to lands at lower altitudes ideal for the cultivation of the much-prized coca. The peoples of these ancient sites were not only noted for their skills as artisans, especially as silversmiths and potters. A document in the library of the Royal Palace in Madrid states that in the Chincha Valley there were ten thousand fishermen. Rostworowski, in agreeing that this figure might seem exaggerated, nevertheless points out that fish was not only an item of local consumption but also was used (in dried form) for the purposes of barter with the peoples of the Sierra.[21]

Chimor

At the time of its conquest by the Incas, the great kingdom of Chimor occupied the full extent of the northern coast of Peru, stretching south from Tumbez to the limits of the Río Chillón Valley. In recent times much has been written about Chimor, of which in this context a brief account may suffice. Its capital, Chanchan, sprang from ancient traditions. Kent Day cites evidence of a clear line of continuity between the Chimu and the Moche cultures. In particular this continuity is implicit in Larco-Hoyle's study of Mochica iconography, suggesting that basic features of Moche government, law, and class structure resemble closely those included by Rowe in his summary of Chimu ethnohistory.[22] The state and society of the Incas, relative newcomers, might in certain respects have been influenced both by the coastal kingdoms described earlier and, in particular, by Chimor. Long before the rise of Cuzco, Chimor ranked among the most complex urban centers of the Andean region, endowed with an elaborate system of irrigation on which it depended for much of its food supply.

Chimor, probably the largest single polity conquered by the Incas, was no moribund realm already set on the road to ruin. On the contrary, it was actively extending its bounds at the very time Inca expansion was gaining momentum. One of Chimor's later acquisitions had been Lambayeque, the realm of a powerful non-Chimu dynasty. Lambayeque lay astride the river of that name, some two hundred kilometers north of Chanchan. As Hyslop explains, many great monuments and rich artifacts usually ascribed to the Chimu are really the product of the classic Lambayeque culture that flourished from the ninth to the fourteenth century.[23]

Rowe, in his "Kingdom of Chimor," offered an informative analysis of the Chimu state. At its greatest extent, reaching from Tumbez to Carabayllo on the Chillón River, which marks the northern edge of the valley, the kingdom stretched for more than 620 miles as the crow flies. The highland valleys, before the Inca conquest, contained a number of small tribes; all were poor and weak with the exception of the people of Cajamarca, who became allies of Chimor.

As Rowe affirms, by far the most important source for the history of Chimor is the *Anonymous History of Trujillo*, written in 1604, of which the fragmentary first chapter contains a brief summary of Chimor's past. According to this source, the founder of the kingdom, Taycanamo, arrived on a big raft. It was the grandson of this legendary figure, Ñançenpinco, who really laid the foundations of the kingdom, controlling a part of the coast that stretched for a distance of about 125 miles. Seven kings succeeded Ñançenpinco prior to the time of Minchançaman, who ruled at the time of the Inca assault. This monarch, the "Chimo-Capac" of the Inca chroniclers, was among the greatest of the Chimu conquerors. The *Anonymous History* merely states that he dominated the entire coast from Tumbez to Carabayllo. However, according to Rowe, other sources suggest that Lambayeque, to the north, was probably conquered by this ruler's predecessor. The Chimu advance northward reached as far as the limits of the desert coast, but in the south it seems to have been halted by powerful resistance in the Lima Valley.[24]

More recently, researchers have sought to seek a closer correlation between the findings of archaeology and these somewhat fragmentary reports of traditional sources that Rowe tended to view as mythical. Alan Kolata identifies the earlier era of Chimu expansion with the reign of Ñançenpinco, which he suggests spanned the period between A.D. 1150 and 1200.[25] Kolata proposes that the second great phase of military expansion, the conquest of Lambayeque in the north, began between 1300 and 1370. With the annexation of this great province, additional wealth began to flow into the capital and triggered a new and vigorous program of construction.[26]

The Naylamp dynasty of Lambayeque, according to the account given by Cabello de Balboa, arrived in the Lambayeque Valley on a fleet of rafts. Nine descendants of Naylamp, according to Cabello, subsequently ruled

Lambayeque; the last of these descendants, Fempellec, reigned sometime before the kingdom was conquered by Chimor.[27] It is interesting to note that an apparently independent account of the story of Naylamp and his first successor, Cium, recorded by Father Justo Rubinos y Andrade in 1781, nearly two hundred years after Cabello, gives certain details not included in the latter's version.[28] Christopher Donnan further suggests that the Naylamp tradition could conceivably relate to much earlier times, even preceding the time of Huari influence on the north coast during the Middle Horizon.[29]

Fieldwork in recent decades has added much to our knowledge of Chanchan, a capital whose grandeur bears witness to the power of the Chimor realm. Built during the course of the Late Intermediate Period (A.D. 1000–1400), the city covers 24.5 square kilometers. Outstanding among its remains are the ten north-facing compounds, or *ciudadelas*.[30] Their original purpose is still not absolutely clear, though Conrad and others are convinced that they were the palaces of the Chimu kings.[31] Storerooms were found in large numbers in the ten ciudadelas, though specific data on kinds and amounts of stored goods are lacking. Certain structures used for storage appear to be similar to those of the Incas.[32]

As we have already seen, the sources' accounts of the Inca conquest of Chimor are cursory and contradictory; they do scant justice to one of the most dazzling, if not the most daunting, chapters in the annals of Inca military triumphs. Cabello owns that he is unable to affirm whether the army, which was commanded by Tupac's two uncles and descended upon Chimor from the north, met with stubborn resistance or whether Chimor yielded without a fight. In the case of Chimor, a state that had swallowed others by force of arms in fairly recent times, any abject surrender tends to lack credibility. Moreover, the ruler was carried off to Cajamarca and eventually to Cuzco, and it seems doubtful that such a rich and potent monarch would submit without a fight to this degrading fate. Cieza briefly describes an intense struggle between Chimor's forces and Tupac's army from the north in which the latter at one point was in danger of annihilation.[33] That one Inca force, after a grueling march, could in a single encounter destroy such a mighty kingdom, their only potential rival in the north, seems remarkable enough in itself, yet any notion that the surrender was voluntary is harder to accept. Schaedel goes so far as to suggest that Chimor's inner and outer defense works were probably the Maginot Line of their day.[34]

The Inca conduct toward Chimor was not altogether benign. The conquered domain was mercilessly looted, and some of the gold sent to Cuzco was used to make a great band of precious metal that extended around the wall of the Temple of the Sun in Coricancha. Nonetheless, in general terms the Incas' treatment of their new conquest is commended by Rowe as shrewd. The vanquished ruler was kept secluded in Cuzco, and a son mounted the Chimu throne as an Inca puppet, succeeded in turn by his son and grandson. However, any pretense of power still exercised by such phantom rulers was gradually eroded; the Incas installed each son of such rulers as hereditary lord of a town or valley, which thus seceded from the original kingdom.

The significance of the conquest lay in the excellence of Chimu organization and culture, perhaps exceeding those of any state yet taken by the Incas. We know too little about the government of Chimor to be sure just what aspects the Incas borrowed, if any. One possible feature was the system of rule through a hereditary local nobility; the political organization of the Inca Empire seems to have been established by Tupac after the defeat of Chimor. With regard to style and culture, the Incas perhaps adopted from Chimor certain techniques of metallurgy and featherwork. The paucity of Inca-style buildings or artifacts in this region bears witness to the conquerors' respect for the refinements of Chimu culture and a consequent reluctance to impose their own. By archaeological evidence alone it would be hard to establish an "Inca period" in the area, in contrast to the great constructions and copious amounts of pure Inca pottery present, say, in Pachacamac.[35]

Inca-influenced artifacts are indeed present in Chanchan, though not in great abundance. Moreover, the existing infrastructure was so impressive that the Inca state saw little need to create new centers or roads.[36] The Chimus apparently did not use the Inca *quipu*. Netherly confirms that the more recent excavations failed to reveal concentrations of Inca ceramics in the region, any demand for which was affected by the prestige of the local potters. During the period of Inca occupation, pottery in the Chimor Valley continued to display the typical Chimu stylistic elements. A hybrid Chimu-Inca style did develop but is mainly to be found outside the Valley of Chimor itself, suggesting a profound Inca appreciation of Chimu ceramics and the potters who produced them.[37]

However deep the Incas' respect for Chimu culture, they ruled the kingdom with a firm hand, notwithstanding any initial pretense of autonomy. Extensive lands were surrendered to the crown, and local nobles were obliged to house Inca officials. The kingdom was exposed to the rigors of the mitimae system, and Cieza writes that many highly skilled artisans were deported to the Valley of Cuzco.[38] Others were evidently sent to the Cajamarca area, where, Fernando de la Carrera writes, groups of people still spoke the Muchic language in the early seventeenth century.[39]

THE HOMELAND

The occupation of highland Ecuador, northwest Argentina, and north and central Chile has been reviewed in earlier chapters, and the core regions of the Empire — Collao, Chimor, and the south coast — are described above. However, certain characteristics of the central highlands of present-day Peru, the very heartland of the Inca realm, still remain to be considered.

In the Late Intermediate Period, prior to the rise of Cuzco, this extensive highland region was divided into a number of warlike principalities, of which the larger generally sought to dominate their smaller neighbors. Once conquered, a principality came under the control of one of a number of Inca administrative centers. Among the leading centers of this type was Cajamarca. It has since been the object of much archaeological research, as has Huamachuco, an important place about a hundred kilometers to the south. The Cajamarca-Huamachuco area was a highly developed part of the Central Andean region before it was absorbed into the Empire. Cajamarca itself remained important in Inca times and is described by many early sources.

Research in Cajamarca has uncovered certain pre-Inca remains but has located only one Inca structure and small quantities of Inca pottery. The Inca structure was the famous ransom room *(cuarto de rescate)*, which is said to have been filled with gold. As Hyslop points out, Inca Cajamarca did not survive the violent events of the early Spanish Conquest, and by Cieza's time the Inca buildings and storehouses were already torn apart and ruined.[40] Similarly, in other leading highland centers (such as Bonbón and Xauxa) described as thriving cities at the time of the Conquest, few vestiges of the Inca past have been recovered.

In marked contrast to Cajamarca, the important administrative center of Huánuco Pampa has in recent years yielded copious information. The site stretches over an area of two square kilometers; 3,500 structures are still visible, and 497 storehouses, with an estimated capacity of more than a million bushels, have been located.[41] The city, which is among the best-preserved Inca provincial sites, consists of four zones surrounding a large central plaza crossed by the principal road in a north-south direction. Craig Morris and Donald Thompson, in the account of their excavations of Huánuco Pampa, write both of the storage area and of residential districts in the north and south barrios, with typical Inca rectangular buildings. These bear no resemblance to the domestic architecture of local ethnic groups, and the pottery found was also Inca-inspired.[42] In another context, Morris states that one can archaeologically distinguish Inca state establishments from dwellings of local groups; not only are they more methodically planned, they are also of more recent construction. The nature of some such establishments suggests their use as accommodations for a transient population, possibly connected with military service. As an example apart from Huánuco, one may cite Pumpu, an Inca administrative center south of Huánuco.[43]

Huánuco is of special significance because, apart from reports by Cieza and other chroniclers, it was described by Ortiz de Zúñiga, whose visit took place in 1562.[44] De Zúñiga's account contains many references to the delivery to Huánuco Pampa of supplies of food and to the many storehouses; of those already identified, more than one hundred have been excavated, and it was found that of approximately 38,000 cubic meters of storage space, a large portion was used to hold food.[45] Murra and Morris also note that, notwithstanding the reports of Cieza and others on the role of Inca provincial centers, archaeological research at Huánuco Pampa revealed little evidence of any military functions.[46]

In contrast to Huánuco — which, like Cajamarca, existed in pre-Inca times — centers in other highland valleys were constructed by the Incas themselves, serving imperial personnel on a rotating basis. In such centers the greater part of the population would still be of local origin. These places in one way or another mirrored certain facets of Cuzco; many buildings were recognizably like those of the Cuzco heartland, and some used pottery in the style of the capital. The road system linked them together. Morris describes such centers as resembling miniature state enclaves scattered over a landscape originally controlled by other polities.[47]

Characteristic of such sites is Incahuasi, situated twenty-eight kilometers inland from the coast in the Cañete Valley. The layout, as described by

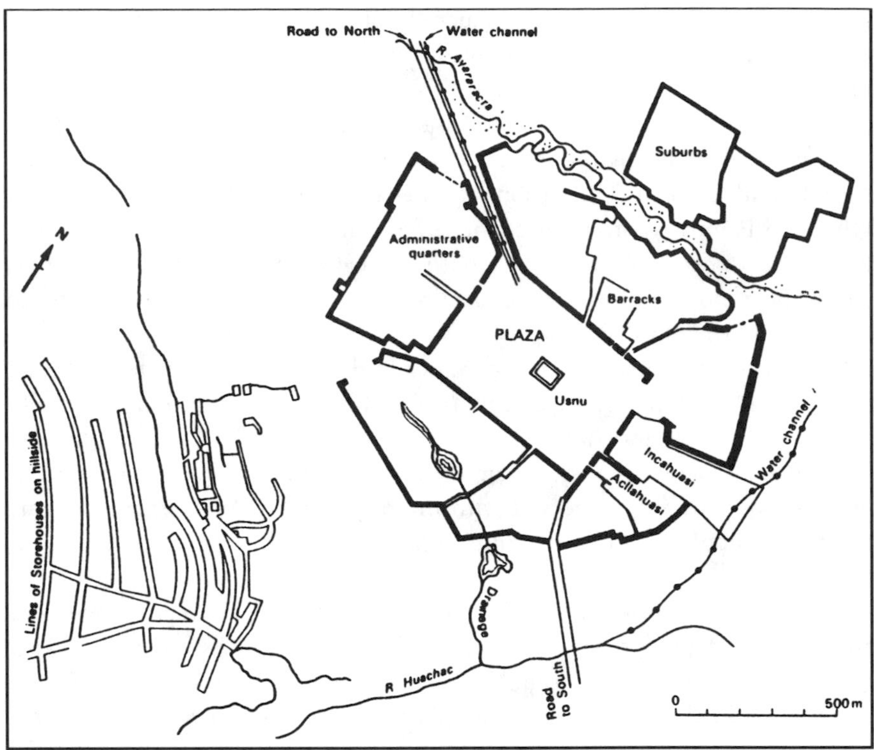

Plan of Huanuco. From Everyday Life of the Incas *by Ann Kendall. Batsford, 1973. Reprinted by permission of Ann Kendall.*

Hyslop, involved a symbolic design, based, like Cuzco itself, on the division into four *suyus*. Parts of Cuzco's formal blueprint may have been introduced; the apparent integration of important Inca astronomical sight lines into the plan of Incahuasi suggests the presence of calendrical symbolism in the layout of the town, as also proposed by Morris in the case of Huánuco. As an example of such integration, the alignment of much of the architectural remains argues that the rise azimuth of the Pleiades, of such significance in Cuzco, was important also in the design of the center of Incahuasi.[48]

Duccio Bonavía even maintains that the Incas were not basically builders of major cities, though he stops short of arguing that no urban centers were built in Tahuantinsuyu. The Incas preferred to occupy the living sites of the groups they annexed and only built new settlements when obliged to do so for the special purpose of establishing control in strategic places. These centers invariably included such typical components as a plaza, a principal palace, and a temple of the sun (almost always found in sites), though certain elements have pre-Inca antecedents. In instances where an existing town was adopted as a provincial capital, it would be partly remodeled to conform to the Inca pattern; typical of this tendency were Cajamarca and Pachacamac.[49] In Pachacamac many buildings now visible were constructed centuries before the Incas, who built the Temple of the Sun and the Pilgrims Plaza.[50]

Inca methods of control may include a natural predilection for highland as opposed to lowland settlements. This preference seems to have governed their policy toward not only Chimor but also the smaller chiefdoms of the coast. In northern Peru the Incas tended to base their major controlling centers in the neighboring highlands, to which the nearby coastal peoples were then subordinated. Huancayo Alto may be cited as an example. Discovered by Dillehay in 1976, this highland site is located on the Río Chillón, about fifty kilometers inland from the coast and from the important principality of Collique. Unlike most Inca centers found on the coast, Huancayo Alto is comparatively large, with Inca-type structures and elitist dwellings.[51]

Finally, a notable aspect of Inca rule is the apparent absence of the larger type of administrative centers in the distant marches of Empire south of Cochabamba — which, according to various sources, was itself a most important Inca center, situated in a rich valley and inhabited by numerous mitimaes. This absence of large sites in the southern part of the Empire raises the question of whether the Inca may have been capable, at least for a given period, of ruling vast areas without the necessity of massive urban development. Though Tupac Inca reportedly conquered Cochabamba, the whole province was only consolidated and reorganized in his successor's reign, leaving a rather limited time for urban development before the Empire collapsed.

Among the more notable surviving sites in the Cochabamba region are Incaracay and Incallacta. Incaracay was investigated in 1967 by Trimborn, whose description suggests that it was as much a fortress as a place of residence. Byrne de Caballero terms this an "administrative-ritual-military" site.[52] Nordenskїöld, writing of Incallacta as long ago as 1915, describes a palace with thick walls but refers to the place mainly as a fortress.[53] Farther south, major Inca centers are notably absent; though many vestiges of their occupation survive, when the Incas settled in local towns they merely adapted them to suit their residential and administrative needs. For instance, nothing in northwest Argentina can even remotely be compared with Ecuadorian Tumebamba.[54] Fine Inca stone masonry has been found as far north as Callo, about sixty-five kilometers south of Quito, but the southernmost extension of such stonework is less certain. Though apparently absent in Argentina and Chile, some remains of this type exist just south of Lake Titicaca, but none are found in the numerous Inca sites in the vicinity of Cochabamba.[55]

The Communications System

Fundamental to the control of an empire of such dimensions, embracing such varied and intractable terrain, was infrastructure. In this respect the Incas' crowning achievement was their road network, which included staging posts and ample storage facilities. Admittedly, the Incas were not the first Andean road builders; Coleen Beck's study, *Ancient Roads on the North Coast of Peru*, describes many segments of pre-Inca roads in that region, some even thought to date to Chavin times.[56] Hyslop offers much evidence of the existence of pre-Inca roads, including some built in the Huari period. The Incas are not known to have invented specific techniques, but their true innovation was the extension of formal road building into many regions where it was formerly unknown.[57]

Many Inca roads are still intact, and some have been described in fairly recent times by explorer Victor Von Hagen and others. The Inca Road Project, carried out between 1978 and 1981 under the direction of Hyslop, ranks among the more notable achievements in Andean studies. In this context one can only offer brief comments, which can hardly do justice to Hyslop's detailed account. The full extent of the system will never be known, as some roads have physically disappeared. Nonetheless, the Inca Road Project collected much new data, and it would not be surprising if future archaeological and historical surveys could properly document a network of up to forty thousand kilometers.

Some roads fall into special categories. For example, some served religious ends and led to high-altitude sanctuaries, usually well above five thousand meters; others were constructed for military purposes as a link with frontier fortresses. However, most roads were built mainly for administrative and economic purposes. The highland and coastal arteries connected the principal local and/or Inca centers in the Andes and were used by officials and technicians. The road crossing the Atacama Desert and connecting Cuzco with central Chile belongs to this category; it would have had limited military importance because water on the route was too scarce. Roads serving economic ends were used to transport basic supplies such as metals, foodstuffs, and textiles from the areas where they were produced to Inca centers and to the capital itself. The lateral routes that connected the highlands with the eastern and western valleys were also important as economic links, facilitating the exchange of products between varied environmental zones. The roads to the eastern forests also had economic significance; apart from their military use as a connection to frontier fortresses, they led to zones where wood, coca, wax, honey, feathers, and drugs were secured.[58] Of all Inca roads, however, the most important was the Cuzco-Quito highland route. Many large Inca centers lay on it, and no road in the Empire was consistently as wide; its minimum width was generally three meters and its maximum, sixteen meters. Numerous descriptions survive, as many early Spanish travelers used it.[59]

Inca road builders faced problems involving vastly different types of terrain. Coastal arteries built on a sand surface needed no formal construction; those built over rock required construction only when they confronted steep slopes. Many roads, both in mountains and lowlands, passed through agricultural land; these are characterized by sidewalls, used, according to early written sources, to protect crops from travelers and animals. The height of such walls was usually one to two meters, sufficient to serve as a real rather than symbolic barrier. On the Pacific coast the sidewalls tended to be made of *tapia*, whereas in the mountains they were generally of stone. Certain roads included stretches that were liable to flood and required stone paving over a limited distance. Others crossed long stretches of solid or nearly solid rock; these invariably lack sidewalls, as no crops were cultivated in such areas.[60]

Hyslop devotes an interesting chapter to bridges. Many of these were fairly simple log structures placed on abutments of rough or fine stone masonry. But what so impressed the early Spaniards were the suspension bridges with fiber superstructures. These were apparently new to the Europeans, and their first crossings on such swaying devices were made with intense trepidation. Suspension bridges could span considerable distances but needed continual maintenance and frequent reconstruction. In addition to the suspension bridges, the Incas at some river crossings employed the *oroya*, a device usually consisting of a basket suspended from a cable connected to both sides of the river and pulled from one side to the other by people on one bank, who hauled a rope attached to the basket.[61]

The *tampu*, the roadside lodging and storage areas sited according to various sources at a day's walk apart, formed an integral part of the road network. Though the tampu was a typical feature of the imperial system, growing evidence of the existence of pre-Inca roads and installations built on them suggests that these waysides were not an Inca invention. Comparable structures continued to be used in colonial times, and the Spaniards even expanded their use beyond the borders of Tahuantinsuyu. The main architectural element of the tampu was the *kancha*, a rectangular walled compound enclosing a number of one-room structures. A major purpose of the tampu was the storage and safekeeping of arms, clothing, fuel, and foodstuffs essential to the functioning of the Empire. Early sources tell little about activities at the tampu apart from storage and lodging, but these establishments clearly also served for craft production and played a part in local administration as well as in ceremonial and military affairs.[62]

In contrast to the more solidly built tampu, *chasqui* posts are difficult for investigators to locate. These stations were placed at short intervals along certain roads as part of the system of relay runners who passed messages and small objects over great distances in a matter of days. According to Cieza, who describes them, chasquis were houses made of wood and thatch rather than of durable materials and were occupied by two men drawn from the local population. These individuals were sworn to the strictest secrecy concerning the messages they bore.[63] As Hyslop observes, in the absence of any form of writing, verbal messages were employed (though quipus were also passed), and these perhaps ran the risk of becoming garbled when repeated many times over from one chasqui to another.[64]

MILITARY INFRASTRUCTURE

This superb communications system was invaluable, if not essential, for long-range military operations. Also of great importance were Inca fortifications. In many regions forts constituted such an integral part of the military infrastructure that their strategic importance in Inca times might almost be compared to that of castles in European warfare during the Middle Ages. Moreover, Cieza affirms that prior to the rise of the Incas, many groups lived on fortified hilltops, from which they made frequent sallies to pillage their neighbors and to take captives. In the same chapter (incidentally, quoted word for word by Garcilasco), Cieza also writes of the numerous forts built by the Incas in conquered provinces.[65] It might be added that the erection of fortifications is a most ancient practice in the annals of Andean warfare. Moseley describes Chanquillo in the Casma Valley to the north of Lima as among the most spectacular of ancient keeps, yielding radiocarbon dates as old as 342 B.C. It has three concentric walls of masonry.[66]

A distinction needs to be made between forts at key points within the Empire used to control lands already conquered and those situated in frontier zones as a protection against external aggression. Our overall knowledge of Inca frontier forts is limited, as none have been found in the eastern border regions of Peru, though some data are available from Chile in the south and Ecuador in the north. In addition, certain sites within the Empire that include fortresses, such as Incallacta and Incaracay in the Cochabamba region, have already been mentioned.

Raffino describes nine posts in southern Bolivia that were not necessarily forts but that formed a kind of protective chain to guard the eastern frontier; he lists other defensive sites in northwestern Argentina. However, without a more exact notion of where the frontier lay, it might be hard to say to what extent these were in fact frontier posts. Raffino does, however, also mention forts in Chile near the Río Maule, and these might have served to protect a frontier, as this river, as we have seen, is often described by sources as the southern limit of the Empire.[67] Alberto Rex González also gives a comprehensive list of sites in northwestern Argentina, complete with map. He cites Pucara de Andalgala (also known as Aconquija) as a good example of a frontier fortress situated at a strategic locale. This site is surrounded by walls three kilometers in length, and the structures within them are described as large and important. There is no evidence of any pre-Inca occupation.[68] Polo de Ondegardo, writing in 1571, mentions forts in central Chile, but to judge from their location these would not seem to be frontier posts.[69]

Similar doubts arise concerning Ecuador, where to the north of Quito fortified sites abound. Salomon describes both Quito and Otavalo as having undergone a transition a few years before the Conquest from defensive citadels to elite ceremonial and administrative centers. In both areas, the

Inca domain was seemingly shielded to the immediate east by fortresses of rustic construction overlooking the aboriginal communities of the valleys; at the borders of the highland basins chains of forts, apparently used during the Incaic wars, dominated the slopes of the transverse and eastern mountain ranges. However, the western slopes do not seem to have been similarly fortified. The relative openness of the western mountain boundaries might be attributable to a state of peaceful interaction with lowlanders of the forested *montaña* in this direction.[70]

Cieza relates that Huayna Capac, having established himself in Quito, took the offensive against tribes that remained hostile and that had built forts to protect themselves. In a subsequent confrontation with four other groups, including the Otavalos, Huayna Capac's forces were saved from defeat by taking refuge in a fortress, or *pucara*, they had constructed; the enemy succeeded in breaching only the outer ramparts of this stronghold, described as being situated on a hill and guarded by no less than seven or eight rings of barriers. The Incas were thus able to defend themselves and to resume the offensive after the arrival of reinforcements. Cieza also reports that in proceeding southward from Ipiales (a few kilometers north of the present-day border between Colombia and Ecuador) he came to a fortress near a place called Rumichaca, used by the Incas as a base for warfare against the Pastos.[71] This would seem to be more specifically definable as a frontier fortress.

In their accounts of these hard-fought wars, Cieza and, in somewhat greater detail, Cabello and Sarmiento mention the use of fortified hilltops with the greatest frequency. In most cases, though, these can hardly be described as frontier posts, and it remains uncertain to what extent the Incas constructed permanent defenses on their long and often only temporary borders. Plaza Schuller located no less than thirty-seven fortresses in the northern Ecuadorian Andes, and of these fifteen are situated in the Ibarra-Otavalo region. But according to Plaza Schuller, it is not very easy to determine the identity of the builders of such constructions.[72] Both Inca and pre-Inca pottery has been found in these sites, and Spanish sources insist that some were built by the Incas, though their layout is somewhat rudimentary. Plaza Schuller suggests that some of this pottery derives from provincial forces that served in the Inca campaigns in Ecuador, in particular those from Chucuito, on the shore of Lake Titicaca.[73]

The Sinews of War

The ample storage facilities, the road network, and to some extent the fortresses all formed part of the imperial infrastructure and furthered the process of military conquest and consolidation. But one further question arises: How, faced with the formidable problem of fighting at vast distances from their own base, did the Incas manage to vanquish so many peoples who bravely struggled for their independence, faced no such problems of logistics, and endured no exhausting marches before reaching the field of battle? Success surely depended in part on taking the fullest advantage of this infrastructure to deploy much larger armies than their opponents could muster. Compulsory military service, imposed on all males between the ages of twenty-five and fifty, produced an ever-increasing flow of recruits from many regions as the Empire expanded. These armies were, at least in theory, divided into units of twenty-five, one hundred, five hundred, one thousand, and ten thousand men; the sources even mention units of forty thousand men, though it seems questionable whether in practice single units of such magnitude operated as part of an even larger force.[74] The conquistadors themselves, both in Mexico and Peru, tend to offer highly implausible estimates of the numerical strength of the native armies vanquished by their own exiguous forces.

By contrast with the skill and ingenuity the Incas devoted to their means of communication and methods of military deployment, the actual weapons used by their armies did not constitute any advance over those of other Andean peoples and certainly did not impress the Spaniards, who marveled at their roads and buildings. Though the bow and arrow was known throughout the Andes, the Incas seldom availed themselves of this weapon; it was mainly used by tribes living near the Amazonic forests, against whom Inca triumphs were reportedly hollow. Among their principal weapons was the sling, a belt of wood or fiber that one twirled above the head before releasing with some force and accuracy a fairly large stone. Another favorite arm was the club, originally fashioned from stone and made in Inca times of hard jungle palm with a head of bronze, often fitted with sharp spikes, as can still be seen today in many museums and collections. They also employed wooden lances, but these were much shorter than those the Spaniards used to such effect against the native armies.[75] The Inca armament hardly seems to represent a very major advance over that of the Mochicas, whose warriors, as depicted on their pottery, carried large clubs and used slings and spear-throwers. Elizabeth Benson concludes that they also fought wars of conquest against their neighbors; she observes that they were apparently intent on taking prisoners, perhaps for sacrifice.[76]

Francisco de Xerez offers an eyewitness account of an Inca force. The forward troops carried slings, whereas those behind bore clubs and axes (bows are not mentioned). The slings could cast stones about the size of an egg, and their users were protected by jackets of padded cotton. The clubs were about three feet long, tipped with five or six metal prongs about the size of a man's thumb. Behind those with clubs and slings followed others with lances. Xerez describes the Inca armies as very well trained and commanded, to a point that a mere thousand men could overcome rebel or enemy forces numbering twenty thousand. But Xerez's generous praise of Inca prowess hardly accords with his account of how the tiny band of Spaniards to which he belonged took a mere half-hour to decimate the countless thousands of warriors in Atahualpa's escort when the ruler went to Cajarnarca.[77]

Cieza does mention archers, but they seemingly had only a ceremonial role as part of the rulers' personal guard, accompanied by a much larger force of troops equipped with slings and clubs. He further describes a typical large expedition heading into battle armed with slings, lances, and clubs but does not mention bows. He relates how such a force numbering three hundred thousand soldiers (a palpable exaggeration), accompanied by a sizable retinue of camp followers and women to serve their needs, would proceed from Cuzco and march in orderly fashion along the road from tampu to tampu (normally a day's journey apart). The inhabitants of the places through which they passed were obliged to serve the troops; the latter were forbidden on pain of death to rob a single ear of corn or to molest the local women. As a consequence, good relations were maintained between the army and the local population.[78]

Although Francisco de Xerez asserts that the Incas defeated their enemies in part because they were better trained, such training or discipline alone could hardly ensure automatic victory in battles against enemies armed with similar weapons. Shirley Gorenstein seeks to account for Inca military achievement more in terms of superior tactics; their units cooperated as a single force to attain a common objective and to achieve surprise. They were also fully aware of the principle of concentration, the necessity of massing forces at a decisive point during an opportune phase of the campaign. Moreover, their elaborate storage system enabled the Incas to keep a large force in the field for a long period.[79]

The Incas were perhaps favored by the fact that they were nearly always on the offensive against opponents who adopted a static defense, often based on fortified strongholds. Ever since the Chanca war, originally a *defensive* action, the Incas almost invariably pursued aggressive tactics. As an example one may cite the defenders of the kingdom of Chimor, who, far from attacking the rather vulnerable lines of communication between Cuzco and Inca territory to the north of Chimor, seemingly adopted a static defense based upon a resolve to protect their capital, Chanchan.

It may be conceded that the Incas, as the attacking force, were thus often (but not always) at an advantage over their enemies, who were on the defensive. However, the chroniclers' reports, particularly Cabello de Balboa's account of the Ecuadorian wars, suggest that the Incas and their adversaries employed almost identical tactics, with both sides in many instances adopting a strategy based on fortified points and aggressive sorties. The Incas' success, then, may in part be attributed to another factor: the skill and determination of their high command. The initiation of the process of empire building might be ascribed to the inspired leadership of Pachacutec. His son, Tupac, was also a superlative commander, the range of whose conquests was staggering. Moreover, he and his successor were served by generals of undoubted ability. As we have seen, the high command was basically the preserve of the elite of Cuzco, including *orejones* who were close relatives of the ruler.

But neither sound tactics nor competent leaders can altogether account for the Incas' dazzling record of victory against so many opponents. Their success in wars of conquest, extended into regions remote from the center, is perhaps more readily explained by their evident ability to deploy superior numbers by drawing on the manpower of an already extensive domain, many of whose peoples the Incas had managed to convert into dependable subjects. If the Inca forces faced a setback in Ecuador, they could use their road and message network to summon ample reserves of, say, Collas, or of many other loyal peoples from the rest of the Empire; their adversaries, hopelessly outnumbered and worn down by a stream of fresh levies, themselves had no means of replenishing their depleted strength. Hence, the Incas' military success might be said to have been due, at least in part, to their political skill in winning over conquered peoples, who, though formerly inveterate foes, would later prove willing to march huge distances to fight for the imperial cause. Moreover, though some accounts may exaggerate the extent to which peoples would refrain from resisting the invaders, there seems little doubt that in some instances the Incas were able to achieve conquest more by skillful negotiation than by force.

Certain doubts arise as to how far these large Inca forces formed part of a full-time standing army in the modern sense. Both historical sources and modern authors make fairly frequent use of the word *garrison*. However, Trimborn, in writing of Incaracay and Samaipata, denies the existence of a standing army charged with the defense of such strongholds, stating that any "garrison" was in reality more a resident peasant colony.[80] Cieza implies that, at least in the Cuzco region itself, warriors were mobilized for specific campaigns rather than kept permanently under arms. Whenever the need arose, the ruler would summon the provincial curacas and command them to levy specified numbers of recruits for the coming expedition. Such a procedure presumably applied more to the earlier stages of imperial conquest; when the Empire extended to remoter regions, forces could have been raised in other places as well as in Cuzco.[81] Rowe, in reviewing data on the Inca military machine, also affirms that there was no standing army except for the imperial bodyguard.[82] It should perhaps be added that Murra cites Espinosa Soriano as implying that the Aymara-speaking Charcas were full-time warriors, though the wording of this report is somewhat ambiguous.[83]

The orejones constituted a more regular force of officers and commanders, even if many also had nonmilitary duties. However, it would seem that the ordinary soldiers were basically farmers who were liable for military service, admittedly for longish periods, rather than warriors with no other occupation, as in a modern standing army.

The Inca Empire, unlike many Old World empires, could maintain forts without the presence of a contingent of full-time soldiers because of the special features of the mitimae system. As we have seen, Huayna Capac settled many mitimaes in the Cochabamba Valley, and if, as Trimborn states, Incaracay was both a fort and a residence for farmers, then such loyal mitimaes would have offered not only sustenance but also security, able both to cultivate their new lands and to guard them in times of emergency. Cieza states that mitimaes not only ensured the civil obedience of a new province in a general sense but also restored order in times of crisis. For example, the eastern frontier regions, the home of recalcitrant tribes such as the Chunchos, Mojos, and Chiriguanos, were so far from Cuzco that any emergency expedition would tend to arrive too late upon the scene; locally resident mitimaes could be used to man the fortresses and to suppress sudden insurgencies.[84]

At the same time, in view of the distances involved and the duration of campaigns, Inca levies might at times have served for such long periods at a stretch as to become almost full-time soldiers, even if that was not their official vocation. For such forces military lodging, as well as storage of supplies, became part of the indispensable infrastructure.

CHAPTER 7

The Imperial System

THE RELEVANT EVIDENCE

Having studied certain aspects of the imperial infrastructure, I now turn to the systems employed by the Incas to govern their Empire. As in the case of accounts of Inca conquest, the problem once more arises of interlinked records, at times partly copied one from another with mere variations in spelling. A number of chroniclers deal with major aspects of imperial rule, such as the powers of provincial governors and other officials generally described as "visitors," the status of the *curacas*, the system of justice, the ownership of wealth, the redistribution of merchandise, as well as the somewhat theoretical application of the decimal system as a means of controlling Indian communities and their labor service.

The problem of such sources has been studied by Åke Wedin. He explains that much of the basic information derives from two early local chronicles, that of Damián de la Bandera on the region of Huamanga, written in 1557, and that of Cristóbal de Castro and Diego Ortega Morejón on Chincha, written in 1558. A third account is that of Hernando de Santillán, probably dating from 1563. Wedin adds a fourth, anonymous source, *La Relación del Origen e Gobierno Que Los Incas Tuvieron, Por Señores Que Sirvieron al Inca Yupangui y a Topa Yupanqui*, which he calls simply "Los Señores."

Wedin first proceeds to demonstrate that at least part of Santillán's text is copied from de la Bandera's. He cites three passages from the two chroniclers — on the distribution of herds of llamas, the system of marriage, and the punishment of crime — that not only give the same information but also contain certain phrases copied word for word from de la Bandera by Santillán.[1] One might add to Wedin's observations the fact that another passage, in whichde la Bandera sums up in some five hundred words the overall system of provincial government imposed by Tupac and Huayna Capac, is reproduced by Santillán with only minor adjustments.[2] Wedin also sets out a synoptic table of the material presented by Castro and Ortega, "Señores," and Santillán. He is able to demonstrate that the three accounts offer their basic data in almost exactly the same order and bear an uncanny resemblance to each other. Wedin's table shows that Santillán also gives fairly copious additional information not contained in the other two sources.[3]

A further problem arises because "Los Señores" turns out to be a mere copy of de la Bandera's work with the exception of the last six pages, which are preceded by a statement that the previous text was indeed written by Damián de la Bandera in the city of Huamanga.[4] Differences between the two texts amount to nothing more than variations in spelling and the use of accents. In one instance, a single line in de la Bandera on the division of contingents of a thousand Indians into ten groups of a hundred is (apparently mistakenly) omitted from "Los Señores."[5] It may be fair to add that the available text of "Los Señores," published in 1921, was re-edited in about 1572 based on an earlier version that no longer exists.

Other sources provide important information on the Inca system of government. For instance, Cieza and Sarmiento write about Inca provincial governors. Polo de Ondegardo is another valuable source much used by Murra in writing of land distribution. But once more the question of copying and repetition arises: Murra points out that some of Polo's original comments — for instance, on the landholdings of the Inca state and church — are reproduced almost exactly by Acosta and by Cobo (who may also have had some information from sources no longer available); in another instance Polo's information is copied by Acosta, Montesinos, and Cabello.[6] Hence it must be borne in mind that studies of Inca provincial rule cite many sources but that the relevance of these sources depends on the degree to which their material is original as opposed to mere repetition of another work.

Governors and Visitors

Many sources report that each province of the Inca Empire was ruled by a governor chosen from the ranks of the Inca elite. These officials resided in the main provincial centers, which invariably contained a temple of the Inca sun god. Cieza mentions some of these provincial capitals *(cabezeras)*, including early conquests such as Bonbón and Xauxa, as well as distant centers in Ecuador and Chile. He writes of the presence of silversmiths and other artisans in these places, as well as strong garrisons, implicitly manned by loyal *mitimae* groups on whom the governor could depend to combat external attack or internal uprisings. The chronicler observes that in cases where the Incas failed to settle such mitimae groups, they often were faced with serious revolts. The governors were *orejones* of high status *(de gran confianza)*; the majority of them possessed property in the vicinity of Cuzco. If any governor spent too much time in his Cuzco domain, he was removed from office. Periodically the reigning monarch would visit a province, where he was received by his representative with elaborate pomp and ceremony. Cieza adds that he came to know a few governors who continued to exercise a certain authority in their province even after the Spanish Conquest.[7]

Damián de la Bandera, writing of the province of Huamanga, states that the governor had his capital in Vilcas and that his domain stretched for fifty leagues from Uramarca (six leagues distant from Vilcas), as far as Acos, on the edge of the Xauxa Valley. The *Relaciones Geográficas* in their report on Huamanga confirm that the governor resided in Vilcas and merely differ in describing the extent of his province as forty leagues.[8] Murúa describes the governors, who were always orejones, as viceroys. They had the privilege of traveling in a litter; they were responsible for the construction of temples and fortresses, as well as roads and bridges.[9]

Mention of the high status of provincial governors is also to be found in other sources. Polo de Ondegardo refers briefly to governors, stating that they were obeyed by all.[10] Sarmiento mentions governors quite frequently in his description of the reigns of Pachacutec, Tupac, and Huayna Capac.[11]

Sally Moore observes that the question remains open as to how far the office of governor might have been hereditary, as some sources state and as Cieza perhaps implies when he mentions a continuance of their influence in certain cases after the fall of the Empire. It is also hard to determine whether the governors possessed lands in the provinces they ruled in addition to their estates in the Cuzco region. It appears that they could obtain funds from the lands owned by the state in each province, but it is not clear whether they derived most of their income from such lands. Moore cites sources, including Cobo, who write of the governors' personal holdings in provinces but concludes that no certainty exists that the Inca governors had such private lands, nor that their families had an enduring interest in local state and church property.[12] Murra, though stressing the power exercised by these governors (the Quechua word *tocricoc* means "he who sees all"), admits that it is hard to be specific about their precise functions. The data from each province, recorded in *quipu* form, were all sent to Cuzco, but we know little of the specialists who handled this information, and it appears that such records disappeared very soon after the Spanish Conquest.[13]

In addition to governors (tocricoc), reportedly resident in their respective provinces, the sources also write of a different class of officials usually described as "visitors" *(tocoyricoc)* who appeared from time to time to report on the proper functioning of specific aspects of imperial rule. Castro and Ortega wrote of envoys called *runaquipo* who were sent by the Inca to verify statistics on population provided by quipus; another category of visitor, *ochacamayo*, was responsible for the administration of justice and the collection of tribute.[14] Castro and Ortega do not describe resident provincial governors; by contrast, de la Bandera mentions the presence of a governor in each province. The latter also writes of *visitadores*. The first category of visitors to be named is that of the *hochaycacamayoc*, a title also referred to by Castro and Ortega. Both sources attribute a similar function to this official: the punishment of crime. Two other types of visitors are also named by de la Bandera, one responsible for checking quipu records and the other for overseeing the care of the *mamaconas*, the women devoted to the cult of the sun. In a subsequent passage the same source again refers both to resident governors and to visitors sent to each province every three years.[15] Santillán mentions visitors in a passage that is partly copied from de la Bandera.[16]

Sarmiento also writes of visitadores as distinct from the governors whom they visited periodically. They returned to Cuzco after two years and were concerned with such matters as land cultivation and payment of tribute. Other high officials, described as *orejones proveedores*, were sent to supervise the construction and maintenance of roads. In another passage the same chronicler writes of visitors sent to collect tribute.[17] Cieza in a brief passage also mentions orejones acting as "judges"; these were sent each year to oversee the levying of tribute and the administration of justice.[18]

Because of the apparent overlapping of the functions of governors and visitors, it has at times been questioned whether any true distinction should be made between the two. This is surely a question of major importance. But in such a tightly controlled empire, if the different provinces were ruled by a resident governor, it might be logical to suppose that he would in turn be subject to periodic inspection by officials specialized in accounting and related matters, including deliveries of goods to Cuzco, or in the construction of roads, as mentioned by certain sources.

But it is surely also reasonable to suppose that such an empire, in which only limited power was delegated to the curacas, could hardly be governed by mere visiting officials. Resident governors closely linked to the reigning Inca, of a kind so often mentioned in the sources, would almost certainly be crucial. On the basis of this assumption, the respective roles of governors and visitors appear to be distinct.

The Local Lords

Many of these curacas could boast of a long dynastic history. In the first stages of their expansion the Incas confronted the important kingdoms of the Collao region. Early conquests also included the traditional principalities of the south coast of Peru; a few were still in the process of extending their own bounds at the time when they succumbed to the Incas. Their institutions may have influenced their new masters and thus become a factor in the development of Inca statecraft.

Curaca was a generalized term for rulers of domains of very different size and standing. Certain curacas reigned over substantial territories; others were relatively small fry. Murra points out that, according to both Garcilasco and Cobo, those in charge of fifty or fewer households worked in the fields like taxpaying commoners. Such a settlement would amount to two hundred to three hundred souls, whose leader would be a local man, linked by endless ties of kinship to his community. Those responsible for a hundred or more households were allegedly free of the imperial corvée labor service, though some chroniclers say that only curacas in charge of five hundred or a thousand households were exempt.[19]

As Murra also observes, information on these ethnic lords derived from traditional sources is incomplete. The terms *cacique* and *principal*, used to describe them, are imprecise, as they are applied equally to the headman of a small valley with three or four villages and to the king of Chimor (sometimes described as an emperor). Only with the publication of the Lupaqa and Huánuco *visitas* has it become possible to assess the role of the curacas within the Empire and to appreciate the great disparities in their status. Such disparities arose not only from the size of their domains but also from the profound cultural differences between the sierra and the coast, between groups of herdsmen in the altiplano and communities that controlled irrigated lands at lower altitudes.[20]

The Inca ruler (in effect, the Inca state) became the theoretical owner not only of all land in conquered provinces but also of all mines and herds. Murra, however, stresses the key role of the curacas in imperial administration; Inca control was somewhat indirect, and the curacas were left in charge of local affairs. From the Inca point of view, the most important function of these traditional lords was to provide manpower, both for military and civilian purposes. According to the available evidence, curacas were seldom removed from office.[21] Moreover, the curaca retained the right to labor service from the people of his community; reports from Spanish administrators who had daily contact with local lords after the Conquest confirm that they were entitled to labor sufficient for the cultivation of their lands in Inca times, though they did not receive tribute. Such service formed part of their established rights, and their houses were also built by communal labor.[22] Garcilasco writes of curaca landownership and confirms that in each community the people had an obligation to cultivate the holdings of the curaca. Always anxious to stress the benign nature of Inca rule, he further states that the poorer people only had the duty to serve the curaca *after* they had worked on their own fields and claims that during the reign of Huayna Capac an official was put to death because he arranged for the cultivation of the lord's property before that of a poor widow. Garcilasco adds that cultivation of the lands of those on military service or of widows and orphans was also a communal responsibility.[23]

Wachtel writes of the numerous texts that bear witness to the curacas' possession of land cultivated by the city. The extent of these curaca properties, however, varied greatly from one region to the next. Wachtel cites reports of fairly large holdings, such as those in the Chincha Valley and others in the Lupaqa territory.[24] Because the lands belonging to the Inca and the curaca would have served no useful purpose for their owners if they had no labor force under their control, local and imperial rulers in effect received tribute in the form of labor. According to Cobo, the curacas even exercised a certain authority over groups of mitimaes whom the Incas had settled in their territory; he writes that whereas they were freed from obedience to their former caciques, they were ordered to submit to those controlling the lands to which they were sent. The settlers retained their traditional dress and emblems but in other respects were expected to follow the customs and way of life of the place in which they were settled and to obey its rulers.[25]

Apart from their administrative functions and their rights to the service of labor to till their fields, the curacas played a key role in the exchange of gifts, basic to the complex Inca system of reciprocity. Polo is adamant that the peasants' only obligation was to till the soil. He insists that if the curaca had large quantities of clothing, this had been woven not by the community but by his numerous wives. However, Castro and Ortega include the fabrication of textiles among the services to which curacas were entitled. As a possible explanation for this discrepancy, the curacas might have pretended after the Conquest that they had indeed received such benefits during Inca times, even if their subjects denied this.[26]

Though the curacas retained certain powers and privileges, Inca control was fairly strict. The sons of provincial lords — presumably only those of the more important members of this elite — were obliged to reside at the Inca's court from the age of fourteen or fifteen, enabling their Inca masters better to judge which son would be the most suitable successor.[27]

Cobo describes the pragmatic approach of the Inca authorities toward the curacas, who on the whole seem to have managed to preserve the loyalty of their people. The Incas took advantage of the prestige of local rulers in order to bolster their own standing and did not hesitate to change the boundaries of the curacas' domains, adding to some at the expense of others. The governors kept a careful watch over the local lords and prevented them from treating their subjects badly. If a curaca was judged guilty of any grave misdemeanor, he could be removed.[28] Cieza, however, implies that in practice they were loathe to depose curacas because such a course would arouse the people's resentments.[29]

The state seemingly had the last word in the choice of a curaca's successor, who was not necessarily his eldest son. Castro and Ortega affirm that both on the coast and in the sierra a curaca would select the successor, whether son, brother, or nephew, who would best conform to Inca notions and present him to the Inca authorities. If the successor was not a close relative, he inherited only the office of ruler but not the possessions of his predecessor.[30] Damián de la Bandera suggests that normally the curaca preferred to nominate as heir the most apt of his own sons. In cases where a curaca died without having put forward a successor, the Inca governor would choose a suitable candidate with the aid of quipu records.[31]

Other limitations were placed on the powers wielded by the curacas over their subjects. They were forbidden to put individuals to death, for example, but could flog them in certain instances.[32] The curacas, moreover, were held to certain rules of protocol whereby the most important took precedence over those of lesser standing. Garcilasco relates that only a high-ranking curaca had the privilege of making a ceremonial toast to the ruler (to whom he would present his cup after drinking). For his part, the Inca could drink with all the orejones, or *capitanes*. The Inca was nonetheless careful to treat with great affability even the lesser provincial lords and instructed certain Incas by privilege to take his place in drinking toasts with them.[33]

In general terms, it was not in the Incas' interest to suppress the ancient institutions of the conquered peoples. Out of respect for local tradition, they granted curacas a certain authority but kept them on a tight reign and compelled them to serve imperial ends. Curacas' resources were considerably curtailed by comparison with pre-Inca times, when surplus wealth drained off from the population would have been at their entire disposal. Moore, aptly summing up the situation, says that although local rulers were not removed nor stripped of their property, they ceased to enjoy their previous powers; they could not exploit the local population for their own ends beyond a fixed point. This was not entirely an indication of Inca benevolence toward the people; there also probably was concern that the curacas might rebel or that they might compete too successfully with the central power for local resources.Even the Inca governors, who formed a trusted inner circle, were spied upon and forced by law to depend upon the king for certain sumptuary goods.[34]

A further unresolved matter is the degree to which these local potentates were single rulers or whether, in at least some instances, they operated in pairs, presiding over the upper and lower portions of their domain. Polo, for instance, implies that this division into upper (Hanan) and lower (Hurin) existed throughout the Empire.[35] The degree to which such division was a uniform pattern of social organization has been much debated in recent times. Its presence in the Inca Empire was perhaps regional rather than universal; such divisions are rarely mentioned, for instance, in the case of Huánuco. Many Spanish chroniclers erroneously wrote of a single dynasty among the Lupaqa, whereas Chucuito was subject to two kings having equal access to its resources. Subordinate centers within this realm were also controlled by pairs of lords, subject to the chief rulers.[36]

Certainly dual rule was present in the Inca provinces of the south coast; for example, Rostworowski discusses the possible division of the principality of Maranga, "as also occurs in the other coastal *curacazgos*."[37] The use of the name Hatun Xauxa in Inca times suggests also the presence in that center of the Hanan-Hurin system, and Rostworowski even suggests that the kingdom of Chimor might have possessed two rulers.[38]

The Imperial Cult

The imperial cult, as an instrument that served to unify the Empire, is attributed to its founder, Pachacutec. As Laura Laurencich-Minelli writes, this ideology, centered on Cuzco, served as a model not only of the Empire but of the entire universe, as Tahuantinsuyu was conceived as corresponding with the universe itself.[39] Before further discussion of other aspects of administration, this spiritual, or religious, factor should first be mentioned, both as a possible motive for conquest and as a means of securing the Incaization of those conquered. The religious factor, moreover, is inseparable from secular concerns, as the church was granted large holdings of property throughout the Empire.

The sources stress the widespread imposition of the solar deity, Inti, who serves as dynastic ancestor to the Inca ruler himself, the son of the sun. Demarest refers to the Incas' manipulation of the Andean high god based on their emphasis of the solar aspects of this celestial godhead, as compared with the sky-creator deities of other highland groups. For instance, the sun was not extensively worshipped by the Colla and was certainly not their dominant sky god, as it was among the Incas.[40] To quote another example, Castro and Ortega state that the Yungas of the Peruvian south coast worshipped a variety of *huacas* and that it was Tupac Inca who had ordered them to adopt the cult of the sun as part of their religion.[41]

The Incas reportedly would take hostage the main idol of a newly conquered province and place it in Cuzco, where it was honored with the same ceremonies as in its place of origin. People from that province were sent to Cuzco to ensure the correct observance of the rites of their local deity, whose effigy was now lodged in the capital. Whereas provincial deities were thus honored in Cuzco, Cobo suggests that the Incas tended to limit the local observance of the previous rites of these conquered peoples. Cieza, by contrast, confirms the general imposition of the cult of the sun but denies that this implied the suppression of older religious customs.[42] The latter view seems more acceptable, as the Incas would have surely been loathe to circumscribe, for instance in Collao, the worship of deities that in some form or another were fundamental to the genesis of their own pantheon.

In Cuzco, solar worship came to be the dominant religious force, and the sun cult was preeminent in coronation and funeral ceremonies and in most of the principal rites. This emphasis served to deepen the veneration for the ruler as a prince of solar descent. In the main centers the principal temple was dedicated to the cult of the sun, imposed as the symbol of imperial rule. Cieza writes of the magnificence of the sun temple in Tumebamba, Huayna Capac's northern capital. Some of its inhabitants reported that much of the finely cut stone of which the shrine was built had been brought from Cuzco; Cieza further describes its vast store of valuable objects and relates that two hundred of the most beautiful Cañari virgins were dedicated to its service.[43]

Language and Culture

Imperial cohesion was also furthered by the use of the Quechua language throughout the Inca domain. At least the provincial elite were expected to know the language of Cuzco.[44] Moreover, Quechua would have been useful as a lingua franca among the babel of tongues created by the relocation of so many groups of mitimaes from one corner of the Empire to another. Levillier writes of the confusing medley of languages among such migrants, obliged at times to use Quechua and conserve their native idiom in places where another native tongue prevailed. Faced with this situation, the viceroy, Francisco de Toledo, convinced that Quechua would be the best instrument for spreading the Gospel, established chairs in Lima University for teaching that language, in which the catechism was also printed.[45] In spite of the rather short period of Inca rule in Ecuador, there is little doubt that the lingua franca use of Quechua was well established in Otavalo, and from Quito southward in the sierra its prevalence is unquestioned. Nearly all communities affirmed its presence, and even those who did not do so introduced Quechua words beyond the common Hispano-Quechua jargon of administration.[46] Equally, Spaniards reported that in northwestern Argentina some seventy years after the Inca conquest, Quechua was spoken in addition to local tongues such as Kakan. However, it seems that by a process of diffusion, elements of Aymara had also spread to this region.[47] In Collao itself Quechua was used in areas where foreign colonists were settled; for example, it was spoken in Paucarcolla, ten kilometers distant from Hatunquolla.[48]

Apart from their imposition of the solar cult and the diffusion of the Quechua tongue, it is open to question how far the Incas sought, in their brief spell of rule, to establish a uniform cultural pattern in general. Among the surest signs of their occupation of a given area is the presence of Inca or Inca-inspired pottery, nowadays perhaps a more reliable guide to the extent of their conquests than the written texts.

Quite apart from its use as an indication of imperial frontiers, archaeological evidence gives clues as to the intensity of Inca cultural penetration. In particular, elements of Inca culture tend to be more apparent in the sierra than in the coastal provinces, which were more able to preserve their own traditions. According to Dorothy Menzel, most Late Horizon sites on the Peruvian south coast show comparatively little sign of Inca influence. Evidence from the Late Intermediate and Late Horizon suggests that the Chinchas had established a highly centralized pattern of control before the coming of the Incas, who merely took over the existing machinery of government. Their administrative center in the Chillón Valley had probably been built before the Incas conquered the territory.[49] Dillehay even suggests that in regions already as highly developed as the Chillón Valley, the Incas could exercise control without heavy permanent occupation.[50] Farther north, in the Moche Valley, the heart of the kingdom of Chimor, no concentration of Inca-type pottery has been located.[51] In marked contrast, in the Lupaqa territory Inca cultural artifacts are much more visible, to the point that it is almost impossible to distinguish between Chucuito- and Inca-type ceramics, whether utilitarian or ceremonial. Indeed, not only the elite but also the ordinary people commonly used Inca-style pottery among the Lupaqa.[52]

The time factor is naturally a crucial element affecting the intensity of Inca penetration. For instance, Meyers points to the presence of Cuzco-type pottery in Tumebamba, whereas Quito, a more recent conquest, can scarcely even be regarded as an imperial center.[53] Similarly, in Chile evidence of Inca settlements suffers a notable decrease to the south of the Río Maipo, though Stehberg does describe one site, the fort of Chena, near present-day Santiago. Pottery found at Chena with Inca-type designs suggests the existence of some significant administrative center in the vicinity.[54]

Intermediate cases can also be cited in which Inca-style ceramics are less in evidence than pottery that represents a local form blended with certain Inca influences. Raffino describes the Diaguita ware, found in the present-day Chilean provinces of Atacama and Coquimbo, parts of which were conquered somewhat earlier than the Santiago region. In the phase known as Diaguita III, a hybrid pottery was produced that combined local and Inca forms. Another mixed style, Inca-Paya, appears both in northern Chile and in northwest Argentina, as well as in southern Bolivia.[55]

Vestiges of Inca-style construction also shed light on Inca occupation. In general terms, their architecture was characterized by the use of finely cut stone as opposed to adobe or wood; it thus derives from a long tradition already present in the Huari-Tihuanaco era. Another distinguishing feature is the use of trapezoidal doors and windows. As identifiable in the important center of Huánuco, for instance, an Inca city normally consisted of four principal sectors situated around a large central plaza.[56] Close scrutiny of the fine buildings of Huánuco indicates that most were constructed by local personnel rather than by people imported from Cuzco.[57]

Outside the area of central Peru, the nature of Inca constructions depended not only on the time depth of Inca occupation but also on the importance of the site. Cieza's account of the magnificence of the remains of Tumebamba has already been cited.[58] But this city was important enough to rank as a second capital under Huayna Capac, with architecture that displayed Cuzco's best stonecutting techniques. A few finely constructed Inca buildings in sites around Lake Titicaca, such as Sillustani and Coati, bear witness to the significance of Collasuyu to the Empire as a whole; the impressive temples were the product of a policy of close integration of this region. By contrast, no large Inca temples have been located farther to the south, and in northwestern Argentina architectural remains tend more to represent an attempt to blend Inca and local styles.[59] Only in the Cochabamba region of Bolivia, southeast of Lake Titicaca, are certain more positive Inca traits to be found in such sites as Incallacta and Incaracay, but the latter was as much a fortress as a place of residence.

LAND AND PROPERTY

As in other preindustrial societies, possession of land symbolized both wealth and status among the Incas. However, accounts of the system of landholding throughout the Empire expose apparent discrepancies between theory and practice. Cobo's résumé of earlier data gives a useful outline of this rather complex problem. He asserts that when the Incas conquered a town or province, they would divide the cultivated land into three parts: the first for the state religion, the second for the ruler himself, and the remaining third for the community as a whole. Church lands were used to cultivate maize, whose ritual significance was important, and possibly other products required for ceremonial purposes, as well as to provide food for the priests of various deities. In many places the division between church and state was not equal; in some cases the ruler's share was the largest, but in others the greater part of the land belonged to the cult of the sun and other religious entities.

Cobo writes that care was taken to leave the people enough land to produce their food, but holdings assigned to the community in theory also belonged to the ruler, and the population was only granted the usufruct. The curacas were responsible for the division of these community holdings among the common people in accordance with the size of each family; if any members were absent, presumably on military or corvée service, others would till their fields. In addition, certain individual holdings of land represented a gift from the ruler as a reward for the performance of some outstanding service, whether in war or in civil administration.[60] Murra cites Polo and Huaman Poma as suggesting that community holdings were reallocated annually, though he questions the accuracy of this statement.[61]

Though countless reports, such as those of Polo de Ondegardo and Cobo, insist that the Inca state disposed of all conquered lands, Murra interprets this assertion as a legal fiction propagated by Inca authorities and designed to afford the sovereign the power to assign and manipulate land.[62] This situation also prevailed elsewhere; for example, in parts of Africa the kings "owned" land that in fact was under the control of their warriors. However, in practice the authority of the monarch, whether Inca or African, was always limited by the prevailing economic system, bound by traditional rights and needs. In such systems, royal or state rights and those of the community were basic factors. Inca conquest had put an end to warfare between various ethnic groups, but disputes surely continued over boundaries, particularly those of communal lands; copious evidence survives of litigation in Inca times as a substitute for violence in the settlement of such differences.

Murra, in seeking to analyze reports of what was in effect more a ritual than an actual pattern of distribution of conquered land, outlines features that were probably basic to the Inca system as it existed in practice. First was the continued cultivation by peasants of typical Andean crops, involving a plan of ethnic holdings that survived the act of Inca domination. Such holdings of necessity continued to survive because it would be dangerous for the Incas to place limits on the self-sufficiency of the peasants. The second feature was the assignment, after Inca conquest, of productive holdings to the state or to the solar cult. Part of these holdings might have been obtained from previously uncultivated land made productive through the introduction of improved forms of farming, such as irrigation or terracing, by the conquerors. When this was not sufficient, particularly on the coast, lands cultivated by the peasants would have been expropriated by the state.

In addition, certain other categories of holdings surely existed: lands that provided for the traditional lords, whether important princes such as the Chimu rulers or local curacas of lesser status; lands presented by the Inca to individuals as a reward for special services; domains assigned to the ruling dynasty, whether to the present monarch or to his dead predecessors; and new assignments to mitimae settlers brought in by the state. With regard to royal holdings, European chroniclers consistently confuse these with state-held lands. The ruler and his predecessors had considerable estates in the vicinity of Cuzco, but their personal property in the provinces, though mentioned by the sources, was not necessarily as extensive as that of the state.[63]

The curacas' rights over land, according to Murra, are hard to define because of confusion in the sources between traditional entitlements and those subsequently conferred by Inca rulers. It is very possible that gifts of land by the ruler to a curaca were nothing more than a confirmation by the state of existing rights or a reformulation of the pretense that all conquered lands belonged to the state and that it was only through the magnanimity of this state that such rights were preserved.

Certainly much evidence points to the existence of curaca holdings, though reports from Castro and Ortega on the Chincha Valley and others on the kingdom of Chimor suggest that curaca landownership could take various forms. Basically, such lands were not really gifts from a bounteous Inca but properties retained by their original owners after their domain had been conquered. Moore, as we have seen, suggests yet another possible category of landholding, that of the Inca provincial governors.[64]

As Schaedel also observes, the Inca system of land control can only be partly reconstructed from the available data. The lands of the sun present no real problem, as they were administered by the state religion in corporate fashion.[65] The situation of the state lands is less clear. In the Cuzco region, part was divided into holdings of the *panacas*; at the provincial level, at least two types of state lands existed, as the mitimae enclaves formed a specialized version of state tenure. Polo de Ondegardo, who is almost alone among the chroniclers in assessing the relative shares of land assigned to church and state, affirms that in general terms the latter's portion was larger.[66]

Whereas outright state ownership of all land may thus have been in many respects a legal fiction, the Inca claim to ownership, or at least control, of mining rights is perhaps more clearly defined. Among the Andean civilizations metallurgy was an ancient craft, but only in the second half of the fifteenth century did the Inca thirst for gold lead to intensive exploitation over a large area. Inca control of gold mining is widely reported. De la Bandera affirms that all mines and herds belonged to the Inca.[67] A major incentive for the conquest of part of distant Chile was the presence of precious metals, the mining of which was controlled by the Inca rulers. Historical evidence exists of Inca mining activity in northwestern Argentina, and perhaps the lure of gold was also the main motive for the Incas' conquest of this region, though data pertaining to this point are hardly conclusive.[68] Archaeological evidence, moreover, demonstrates that the quest for other metals also motivated the Inca advance into Chile. Hans Niemayer writes of the Copiapo region as rich not only in gold but also in silver and copper. He describes furnaces and other equipment brought by the Inca conquerors to that region for the purpose of refining these metals.[69]

Mining activity was widespread throughout the Empire. Jean Berthelot, in writing of the mines of Collao, also points to the chroniclers' insistence that the precious metals were destined for the Inca ruler — which may be taken to mean the ruling caste in general — and the state cults. But the same author observes that both provincial governors and caciques made presents of gold and silver to the ruler, which suggests that the curacas also participated in the exploitation of the mines, if only to the degree that would have enabled them to bestow gifts on their sovereign. Writing more specifically of the Carabaya and Larecaja mines, situated to the northeast of Lake Titicaca, Berthelot cites colonial documents to the effect that certain mines in this region could be freely exploited by the local population, thus making a clear distinction between the "Inca's mines" and the "community's mines."[70] Though the chroniclers stress the use of gold and silver, copper, which since Moche times had been used for making implements, was probably also important.[71]

The same point applies to another major source of wealth: the great herds of cameloids consisting of llamas, *vicuñas,* and alpacas. They originally abounded above all in Collasuyu, where the local rulers possessed large herds. They were prized for their wool, which provided the luxury textiles used in religious rites, and also for their value in the complex procedure of offering gifts to the ruler and to the elite. Cumpi, the finest cloth of all, was made of alpaca wool. The Inca himself consumed an abundance of cloth; he seldom wore a garment more than once and would change clothing several times a day, and his litter was completely covered with the finest material. The llama was also important as a beast of burden, though it carried a relatively light load. The animal itself, as well as the textiles made of its wool, played a part in Inca religion as an important sacrificial offering, white llamas being the preferred victims of the sun. Llamas were offered in southern Bolivia not only to the sun but also to Illapa, the thunder god.[72] In important funerary rites, at times involving human sacrifice, the principal offering would consist of the finest textiles, including woolen robes threaded with gold.[73]

A large proportion of the herds seem to have belonged to the imperial authorities, though any statistical comparison between those of the state and those of the church is hard to make. The Inca, moreover, established herds in many regions where none had existed before. Hence, the state herds were very numerous, serving military as well as ceremonial ends.[74] It is probable that in places where herds had existed before the Inca conquest, the curacas and their subjects were not altogether deprived of cameloids. In view of the Incas' tendency to maintain good relations, local potentates, particularly in Collao, would surely not have been completely stripped of their possessions in this respect.[75]

It seems, therefore, that throughout the Empire the claim to full and outright state ownership, whether of land, mines, or herds, was more a concept than a fact. It simply served to assert the imperial power's right to general control over wealth. Such rights, however, did not in practice allow the Inca to confiscate all property of either the local lords or their subjects, without whose compliance such an unwieldy domain would have been ungovernable.[76]

Mass Resettlement

I have already stressed the supreme importance of the mass settlement of mitimae groups from the Valley of Cuzco in pacifying and controlling newly conquered provinces and ensuring their adoption of elements of Inca culture. The Incas were usually able, after a certain time had passed, to instill such a total subservience to the will of the divine ruler that their subjects meekly obeyed his command to forsake their cherished homeland and migrate to a remote and newly conquered region. Here they would preserve their own rites and customs, at the same time fostering the process of absorption whereby the local inhabitants were converted into loyal subjects.

Murra sums up the wide use of the system in Ecuador: "Where serious opposition was met, as in the case of Cañari, Puruha and Cara, native organization was smashed by removing a large part of the population and replacing it with mitimaes, settlers from other parts of the Empire who were by then regarded as thoroughly acculturated and reliable. Thus thousands of Palta were taken to Collao and replaced with Bolivians." According to Oviedo, as cited by Murra, all the inhabitants of the Quito region were in his time either Quechua- or Aymara-speaking Indians from Bolivia, the natives having been deported south. Murra describes this as an overstatement, as the Puruha language, native to the region, was spoken as late as 1692, even though very many inhabitants had been deported long ago by the Incas. Murra names various peoples in northern Ecuador whose land had been settled by southern colonists. Such enclaves within the aboriginal population served as focal centers of Inca influence, and today some of these settlements can still be distinguished by the dress and customs of their inhabitants.[77]

Not all the mitimaes settled in Ecuador came from afar. Waldemar Espinosa relates how Tupac conquered the Huayacuntus (situated to the east of Piura in southern Ecuador). Their chief, Apo Guacal, became a fervent Inca supporter; he brought a contingent of his warriors to help Huayna Capac in the fierce struggle against the Caranquis and other tribes to the north of Quito. When the war ended, the ruler settled a large number of Huayacuntus in Quito itself, where they were active in repressing opposition to Inca rule.[78]

Cieza divides the mitimaes into three categories. The first, having both social and military functions, consisted of those sent when a new territory was organized into provinces. They were relocated not only for security reasons but also to aid the process of educating the local inhabitants and converting them into loyal subjects. The second category, serving purely military ends, comprised those dispatched to establish garrisons for protection against savage frontier peoples, such as the Chunchos and Mojos. Mitimae enclaves of this type were also stationed farther north along the critical frontier region of the ever-rebellious Bracamoros and Chachapoyas, as well as among the Caranquis, who fought for so long against Huayna Capac. The third type of mitimaes, economic rather than military, were those sent to populate mountain valleys that were fertile but lacked people to till the soil.[79] Cobo also describes this system:

> The Inca induced this change of residence in order to keep his domain quiet and safe. The city of Cuzco was far away from the most remote provinces in which there were many nations of warlike and barbaric people; thereafter the Inca felt that he could not maintain peace and obedience in any other way, and since this was a reason why this measure was taken, the Inca ordered that the majority of the *mitimaes* who are made to go to recently subjugated towns settle in the provincial capitals so that they could serve as a garrison and *presidio* — not for a salary or for a limited time; rather the *mitimaes* and their descendants would remain perpetually. And, as would be the case with warriors, they were given some privileges so they would appear to be more noble, and the Inca commanded that they always be very obedient and do whatever their captains and governors might order.

Cobo further states that when the ruler subjected a province, he would remove as many as six or seven thousand families to a more settled region and replace them with groups of mitimaes that sometimes even included orejones from Cuzco. Though these mitimaes were instructed to follow the customs of the places to which they had been relocated, they retained the dress and outer symbols of their own nation. Even at the time when Cobo wrote in mid-seventeenth century, such people could be still distinguished from the original natives.[80]

The mitimae system was doubtless expanded in the time of the later rulers; Cabello suggests that it was initiated by Tupac. However, resettlement had also occurred in Collasuyu, which was among the very earliest conquests. For example, according to Díez de San Miguel, a group from Chinchasuyu was located in the Colla province of Umasuyu.[81] Waldemar Espinosa, who has contributed much to the study of the mitimae system, describes it as vital to the very existence of the Empire. In stressing its military aspect, Espinosa quotes Garci Díez as relating that Huayna Capac employed six thousand men brought from the Lupaqa region against the Cayambis; of these, five thousand perished. The same author adds the interesting detail that in the Lupaqa kingdom 80 percent of the mitimaes who had been settled there (probably at a relatively early date) came from the Valley of Cuzco; of the remaining 20 percent, some were Chancas.[82]

Examples of the use of mitimaes survive throughout the Empire. For example, they played a key part, as mentioned earlier, in the absorption of the important center of Cochabamba, first conquered by Tupac, who sent contingents of its inhabitants eastward to Pocona. Wachtel cites documentary evidence of the dispatch to Cochabamba of contingents of Charcas, as well as Quillacas and Carangas (situated in the region between Cochabamba and the coast of Chile). Wachtel states that further large contingents of mitimaes were brought to Cochabamba by Huayna Capac and that in his reign their function had become more economic than military. Some of these settlers had come from places as far distant as Quito. Huayna Capac also introduced a group of silversmiths from Chinchasuyu, who were compelled to cross over the Andes on their arduous trek. Artisans from the Pacific coast are also known to have been settled in Cuzco.[83]

Labor Service and Tribute

Many chroniclers write of the imperial system of taxation and tribute. Santillán's information (in this instance not borrowed from earlier sources) suggests that the Inca, in fixing the quota of a given province, would only demand goods produced locally or available in nearby lands. The curacas were obliged to give orders to their subjects to work for the Inca; once their task was done, the same people would then help to produce crops and clothing for the curacas, who thus also received a form of payment. The latter were themselves exempt of any contribution. Santillán cites as examples of tribute not only food but also fine clothing and featherwork, together with objects of gold and silver; in case of war, arms were supplied to the Inca forces. Luxury items such as gold and feathers were sent to Cuzco, along with some food, the remainder being consigned to local storehouses.[84]

Cobo confirms that not only orejones but also curacas were exempt from payment; they did give valuable presents to the ruler, but these were "voluntary" and hence did not rank as tribute. As part of the elaborate system of reciprocity, the Inca would give jewels and fine garments to captains who had showed valor in war, but the most prized gift of all was that of a maiden from among those gathered as tribute, along with livestock and farmlands. Cobo affirms that payment by the common people was made in the form of personal service:

> In place of paying tribute, the craftsmen worked in the service of the Inca, the religion, or their *caciques*; each one performed the craft that he knew, such as making garments, working gold or silver, extracting these metals from the mines and processing them, making clay and wooden cups, and the other crafts. As long as they were employed in fulfilling their quotas and tributes with the crafts and jobs, both the craftsmen and the artisans, as well as the communities of the towns and *mitayos*, were supported at the expense of the owner of the estate where they worked or the person they served, even though it might be the estate of the Inca or religion; and from this same estate they were also given the tools along with the rest of their instruments and necessary equipment; they did not invest anything of their own except manual labor.[85]

Cobo goes on to explain that officials and curacas were not paid in the form of gold or silver but received as payment the personal service of the subjects residing in their districts and placed under their command. They were assigned a certain number of laborers, the number that would suffice for their own needs; the ordinary rate was one laborer for every hundred subjects. Quite apart from performing services within the curacas' houses, local inhabitants cultivated their fields and looked after their livestock; such service took the place of a salary.

These and other reports lead Murra to stress that "tribute" consisted basically not of goods or cash but of labor that the peasant community gave to the state and the curaca. For instance, certain groups, such as the Uru, a rather primitive people living on the shores of Lake Titicaca, provided only fish and had no obligation to serve in the army or participate in major public works.[86]

Mit'a was the term generally used for the part-time labor service imposed upon the peasant population. Such labor was far from limited to cultivation of fields and production of goods for the ruling class. In addition, mit'a labor met the demand for construction of temples and palaces in both Cuzco and the provinces, as well as for road building, work on fortresses, irrigation, mining projects, and transportation of goods and materials from one place to another. The labor needed for transportation alone must have been colossal. For instance, Huayna Capac ordered that plentiful supplies of timber for making rafts should be carried from the coast of Ecuador all the way to the shore of Lake Titicaca, a distance of 1,500 kilometers! It is hard to determine whether some of these tasks, particularly those involving infrastructure, were performed by rotative mit'a laborers or by *yanas*. Nor do we know how such tasks were reconciled with the agricultural cycle.[87]

Any full-time labor force basically of yanas, who were, in effect, state (or, at times, individual) servants. Information as to their origins, their numbers, and their precise status is far from complete. Murra states that he simply does not know if they were slaves; present studies of dependency and slavery hardly provide any ready classification.[88] Huaman Poma treats the term *yana* as synonymous with "slave" but states, nonetheless, that the authorities managed to extract from some of them payments of gold and silver.[89]

In view of doubts over the availability of sufficient numbers of yanas or of part-time mit'a workers to fulfill the massive demands for state labor, the question arises as to how far mitimae colonists, at least in certain regions, might have taken the role of yanas, working as full-time serfs. Waldemar Espinosa, on the basis of colonial documents stating that large groups from the north coast of Peru were moved to the sierra regions of Cajamarca, questions whether these coastal mitimaes might have served in this capacity. Some of these mitimaes were relocated in Shultin on the edge of the Valley of Cajamarca; they were expert potters, and their only task was to produce ceramics for the state.[90] In certain instances the term *mitimae* was perhaps becoming a euphemism, used as a protective label for people who in pre-Hispanic times had been captives or yanas. Whereas the yanas were recruited individually, the mitimae system would have provided a method of obtaining servile laborers not singly but in groups.[91]

Another aspect of the division of labor is the reported use of the decimal system, not only for the army but also as a means of apportioning the tasks of the inhabitants of a given area. The sources concur in saying that the peasants were divided into bodies of ten thousand to be placed under the control of a leading curaca. These would then be subdivided into ten contingents of one thousand and thereafter into smaller groups of one hundred, each administered by a lesser curaca; the group of one hundred might be further split into yet smaller fractions of fifty, ten, and even five workers. Numerous chroniclers report — with certain variations — this systematic division of Inca subjects into numerical groups. The partly interlinked accounts of Santillán, Castro and Ortega, and de la Bandera follow this report with an account of the subdividing of Indians into twelve "ages," ranging from the first, consisting of people over sixty years old, to the twelfth, formed of infants between birth and two years.[92] Though earlier investigators, such as Means, tended to take such statements at their face value, clearly such a bureaucratic round-numbers scheme could not correspond to demographic reality, as village populations cannot be made to conform to a precise decimal system. Nonetheless, a preference for such a neat arrangement might account for a tendency to adjust the boundaries of communities in order to attain a certain uniformity.

An approximate decimal system could more easily be applied to military service, which formed such a major component of the mit'a system. The numbers recruited through the mit'a are hard to quantify, but there is little doubt that, given the ever greater distances involved in the waging of imperial wars, the obligation became increasingly burdensome. The very nature of the system, requiring both the cultivation of land and many other nonmilitary tasks, makes it improbable that such recruitment involved full-time service in the army. Even if military service was the principal obligation of males, just as the weaving of cloth was the main task of females, the soldiers surely had to return to their villages for part of the time, as old men and women could hardly be expected to cultivate not only their communal holdings but also the state lands.[93]

The universal obligation to serve the state, whether in a military or civilian capacity, was fundamental. Murra cautions against underestimating the redistributive function of the crown but refutes any general notion of the Inca domain as a benign welfare state; at the same time, he draws attention to the insistence of many sources that tribute was paid not basically in goods but in labor. However, as Moore points out in the case of food production on lands assigned to the Inca or to the sun, what Polo, Cobo, and other Spanish writers saw was the *labor* rather than the produce subsequently paid as tax. The chroniclers accepted without question the notion that the Inca and the sun held title to this land; they obviously reasoned that the Inca could hardly tax land that he already owned and that therefore the only tax levied took the form of labor. But if what the laborer contributed was service, what the Inca, as well as the governors and curacas, actually received was produce. A distinction surely needs to be made, therefore, between the many instances where a service was indeed personally rendered and received and those in which service was rendered in the form of productive labor but in which the state actually received *goods.*[94]

Moreover, certain chroniclers quite plainly describe tribute payable in goods rather than labor. Cieza, for instance, writes of specific quantities of gold, silver, clothing, and arms, the correct delivery of which was monitored by quipus.[95] The cornucopia of sumptuary articles produced by craft specialists amazed the Spaniards, who found them both in Cuzco and in the provinces. This hoard presumably consisted both of items produced directly for the Inca by the local peasantry and of others made for the curacas and then presented to the Inca as presents. The tributary system was not confined to goods produced solely for immediate use; it therefore necessitated an imposing storage network, both for sumptuary items and for regular supplies of food, arms, and clothing.

In his archaeological study of Inca warehousing, Craig Morris describes facilities of enormous size and sophistication. Though the administrative records of storage for the most part perished with the last interpreter of the quipu knots, the storehouses themselves still dot the hills above the ruins of many Inca towns and cities, inviting archaeological research. A large portion of fine cloth and other goods that conferred status naturally was sent to the capital, where much of the elite resided. But the quantities mentioned in the reports and actually seen by Spaniards appear to have far exceeded any conceivable needs of the upper social strata among the residents of Cuzco. Many, if not most, of these goods went to the army and to others in service of the state; one reason they went to Cuzco was so they could then come *from* Cuzco. The prestige of gifts and issues was greatly enhanced by association with the ruler himself and with the imperial city. The huge amounts of cloth the Spanish saw in Cajamarca when they first set eyes on the Inca stores were probably a temporary result of the sovereign's presence rather than a sample of Cajamarca's usual supplies.[96]

Morris further stresses that the ordinary subsistence goods were mainly carried not to the capital but to the big provincial centers, such as Huánuco Pampa, and for the most part were consumed or stored there in order to support state activities. In centers built by the Incas along the principal roads, massive quantities of foodstuffs were stored, drawn from the surrounding hinterland. In villages, as opposed to towns, storage was usually limited to households, and no large quantities were accumulated either for the state or for the local authorities. Evidence from the Lupaqa territory suggests that fairly large amounts of goods were taken out of state storehouses and given to the local rulers, who might in turn use them to regale Inca capitanes and other leaders who passed through the province; it seems unlikely that any major portion trickled down to the common villagers. Hence, it becomes rather harder to pursue the welfare theory originally elaborated by Baudin and rather solidly refuted by Murra.[97] In every storehouse, including the *tambos* situated at regular intervals along the roads, goods were meticulously counted by a *quipocamayo.* Huaman Poma provides an illustration of such a functionary, seen conversing with the reigning Inca, to whom he displays a quipu.[98]

The tributary and storage regime operated even in distant Ecuador in a limited zone, perhaps reflecting an early phase of imperial consolidation rather than the later stage of full-blown dominion. In the case of Hurin and Hanan Chillo, situated in the Quito basin to the south of the city, local lords who actually managed the tribute testified that after a large maize field was harvested, half the crop was sent to Quito; the other half was stored by the curaca, to whom mit'a workers were also sent to serve his house and make him some woolen clothing.[99]

In the final analysis, it may be right to describe the whole system as a form of redistribution but one that ministered to the well-being of the ruling classes more than to that of their humbler subjects. The latter at least derived some benefit from the additional employment thereby created, even in the case of sumptuary goods. What the elite received was not simply direct peasant labor but the fruits of that labor in the form of goods. In the case of gold, the mines seem to have mainly served the Inca, even if the curacas were to a limited extent involved; in this instance, therefore, what the subject cities contributed was indeed basically labor. It must constantly be borne in mind that in the tributary, or redistributive, system, the common people provided not only for the Inca conquerors but also for their own curacas. As such, the system surely had ancient roots. Local lords of some kind had held sway since time immemorial, and agriculture and even mining had existed for countless centuries. Archaeology demonstrates the presence from Huari times of storage facilities with capacities far surpassing mere local needs. What cannot be stated in exact terms is the extent to which the Incas, who improved the productivity of agriculture, herding, and mining, might have increased the total burden on the common man over what had already been imposed by traditional local lords.

Vertical Archipelagoes

In general terms, the Inca Empire differed from that of the Aztecs in that it lacked the latter's established merchant class, honored by the ruler and second only to the nobles in power and prestige. The Incas, by contrast, displayed an aversion to the creation of an open market, in which goods native to different provinces might be traded freely throughout their empire. They tended instead to favor a system aimed at securing for each region the maximum degree of internal self-sufficiency, even though some interchange of goods between provinces seemingly continued.

Fundamental to the attainment of such self-sufficiency was what Murra identified as the principle of verticality, whereby certain polities of the sierra established a series of productive settlements at lower and warmer levels on or near the coast and occasionally also at altitudes higher than their main centers. These settlements formed a kind of vertical "archipelago," through which the main center was able to obtain a variety of produce, native to a wide range of ecologies, without recourse to formal trade with other regions. Jorge Flores Ochoa writes that such settlements might consist of both farmers and llama herders, who provided transport. Many of the latter were native to the Lake Titicaca region.[100]

Data provided by Ortiz de Zúñiga's account of his 1562 visits to Huánuco, supported by fieldwork at Huánuco, convinced Murra of the probable existence since comparatively ancient times of a system that he described as "the vertical control of a maximum number of ecological levels"; the establishment by the Incas of mitimae colonists in the Huánuco region was merely a later and altered manifestation of this system.[101] Murra cites other examples to prove this hypothesis, of which perhaps the most striking is that of the Lupaqa kingdom, documented by the visits of Garci Díez de San Miguel in 1567. This domain, much larger than Huánuco, possessed its own oases on the coast, stretching from Arica, on the Chilean border with Peru, as far as Moquegua, about 150 kilometers to the northwest. Here the Lupaqa cultivated cotton and maize and obtained a whole variety of marine produce. They also had settlements in Larecaxa in

Bolivia. The Lupaqa were only one of various kingdoms of the Lake Titicaca region, and there is a strong possibility that others also possessed land and forests at lower elevations, thus giving rise to a veritable maze of multiethnic population distribution.[102]

Murra and Wachtel stress the great expansion of the system in the final decades of Inca rule: "One particularly Andean feature is that these complementary outliers were frequently multi-ethnic. Representatives of polities quite distinct from each other in the mountains found themselves in close, if tense, proximity at the periphery. These settlements were five, ten and sometimes even more days' walk distant from their respective power centers. . . . the vertical archipelago thus implied a rather closed economic circuit, linking several tiers through ties of kingship and political subordination."[103] The greatly expanded scale of operations under the last rulers led to the settlement of mitimaes up to sixty days' walk from their homelands, suggesting that the vertical archipelago was undergoing fundamental change in the decades immediately before 1532. Some such colonies were assigned to mining or garrison duties rather than to agriculture; colonists sent so far away from their ethnic homelands could no longer return there easily to exercise residual rights in farming.

Mid-sixteenth-century documents from highland Ecuador consisting of reports of Spanish visitas suggest that in certain areas some form of verticality was established even in the more recently incorporated northern marches. In particular, the five ethnic lords of the Puruha communities were interviewed in 1556; the Puruhas occupied the Río Bamba territory, situated to the south of Quito. In this region, recognizably central or southern Andean techniques were adopted, and the previous dependency of these highland peoples on interchange with *montaña* groups of the tropical forest was eliminated. Instead, the Puruhas were endowed in the montaña with their own outposts, which bloomed into a full-blown archipelago system; of these forest settlements, many were cotton plantations. Maize tribute for the Incas was also produced in special enclaves at a different altitude. The Puruha visita is one of a small number of sources that write in some detail of the internal management of archipelago systems. Nonetheless, Salomon, who describes the archipelago system as a radical measure, does not suggest that it was applied with the same intensity in Ecuador as in certain provinces farther to the south.[104] Oberem also writes that in Ecuador a form of microverticality was practiced rather than Murra's macroverticality.[105]

Murra's hypothesis ranks as a major contribution to Andean social studies. But Murra himself has been the first to concede that the system of vertical archipelagoes had its limitations.[106] Possibly conditions in certain parts of the Andes favored its development, whereas other parts were not as well disposed. The kingdoms around the shores of Lake Titicaca established "islands" toward the Pacific coast, but those of the Mantaro Valley had none on the ocean, though they did make settlements on the edge of the forest.[107] It might be added, moreover, that there is less historical evidence that coastal principalities practiced what might be termed "verticality in reverse." Conquest and consolidation by the Moche and later by Chimor limited penetration into the highlands above about two thousand meters.[108] Pease also refers to Oberem's "microverticality" in the north; although the system of verticality is generally accepted in the southern Andes, strong evidence of its presence in other areas has not been fully established. This is especially the case for the coast of present-day Peru, perhaps because this region lacks the sort of documentation available for Chucuito and Huánuco. The possible existence of markets (as an alternative to archipelagoes as a means of obtaining specific types of produce) requires further research.[109]

Moreover, any Inca predilection for a maximum degree of regional self-sufficiency could only be partially realized through the archipelago system. Self-sufficiency would also have required a major increase in the production of the core region, both to provide for a growing population (including settlements at different levels) and to satisfy the tributary demands of the Inca state. Cieza, for instance, records that the mitimae system populated barren areas to such an extent that in Inca times very little fertile land remained uncultivated. (The chronicler sadly remarks that whereas the idolatrous Incas cared for their extensive lands, the methods of the Christian Spaniards were basically destructive.)[110] Considerable evidence, moreover, bears witness to the Incas' skill in extending irrigation works. One may recall Huayna Capac's development of the Cochabamba Valley with the introduction of large numbers of mitimaes. Ever greater quantities of food were needed to maintain the large provincial centers that supported Inca conquest and expansion.

The drive to increase production was, if anything, gaining momentum at the time of the Conquest, to a point that leads Craig Morris to write that projects aimed at improving output appear hardly to have begun when the Spaniards arrived. If the Incas introduced few new skills, their intensified use of established techniques achieved impressive results.[111]

TRADE AND BARTER

Though the Incas may have preferred such practices as the use of vertical archipelagoes, the question nonetheless arises as to how far this rather closed economic system was or was not supplemented by more traditional types of interchange in the form of trade and barter. Some interchange of goods unquestionably occurred, but its volume and significance are less clear. Rostworowski, in her work on the pre-Hispanic Peruvian coastal peoples, devotes a whole chapter to the merchants of Chincha. Much of her information stems from an unpublished colonial document, according to which no less than six thousand merchants traveled from Chincha to Cuzco and Collao; they also went to Ecuador, from whence they obtained gold and emeralds for the curacas of Ica. According to the same document, the Chincha merchants were the only ones in the whole Empire who used a kind of currency, in the form of pieces of copper; they also had established a fixed ratio of exchange between gold and silver. Rostworowski expresses surprise at the high number of traveling merchants, as the use of traders was for the Incas a somewhat alien concept. Though questioning the numbers involved, she nonetheless accepts that in Inca times there was some continued presence of merchants in the Chincha coastal region and cites examples of Chincha merchandise, such as shells and dried fish, that reached the sierra. As she remarks, the Inca Empire was not as static as some historians would pretend, and because of its short span of existence, its laws and customs had not been fully imposed throughout its vast expanse.[112] Cieza writes of an impressive market in Potosí. However, he mentions the presence of Spaniards, and because Potosí is basically colonial this must surely have been a post-Inca development.[113]

Murra, notwithstanding the stress he lays upon the Inca preference for vertical settlements as a substitute for trade, acknowledges the existence of merchants and markets in the north. However, he suggests that it is not yet possible to draw firm conclusions on Inca "commerce" because of the incomplete data offered by the sources.[114] Susan Ramírez cites various chroniclers who tend to imply that, relatively late in pre-Conquest history, the Incas encountered organized exchange in certain areas and, recognizing its significance, took measures to accommodate it within their system.[115] Murra accepts as historical the description Sámano-Xerez heard from Pizarro's pilot, who sighted a great raft off the coast of Ecuador; it included a cabin, had cotton sails, and carried an impressive cargo. The merchandise, as described by Sámano-Xerez, was of a strictly ceremonial nature, consisting not only of shells but also of luxury textiles and gold and silver adornments.[116] The only chronicler recorded as having personally seen native crafts was Zárate, who tells of a veritable fleet of sailing rafts in the vicinity of the island of Puná. Some were big enough to have carried fifty men and three horses. Murra poses the all-important but uncertain question as to whether such craft were employed by the state or by private merchants.[117]

In her work on the Chincha merchants, Rostworowski also offers concrete examples of trading activity in Ecuador. She quotes the *Relaciones Geográficas* as reporting that in Otavalo, a comparatively recent Inca conquest in the north of Ecuador, the local ruler treated his people like slaves — except for the merchants, who merely paid tribute. Such traders even had dealings with people who lived beyond the imperial frontiers.[118] Salomon, in describing certain changing patterns of trade, also mentions the presence of merchants and a market in the Quito region. Even peoples of the Amazon montaña, such as the Quijos, probably sent exchange specialists of their own to Quito.[119]

Any tolerance on the part of the Incas for traditional trade and barter in Ecuador might partly be due to the ritual importance attached to the *mullu* shells *(spondylus pictorum)* available in the warmer Ecuadorian waters but not in the colder sea farther south. These shells, already greatly prized by the elite of Chimor, were in demand in the heartland of the Empire and have even been found as far afield as northwestern Argentina and in Chile. Netherly, in writing of the Inca conquest of the southern coast of Peru, suggests that the Incas might have used the Chincha merchants as intermediaries to obtain supplies of spondylus from farther north.[120]

The conclusion might therefore be drawn that in specific instances, such as that of Ecuador, the Incas were slow to impose their general policy of state-controlled redistribution to the exclusion of private trade. Because the Incas did not control coastal Ecuador, it is hard to see how any state mechanism that excluded trade could have satisfied their insatiable demand for the spondylus shells for ritual use.

However, Murra is probably correct in asserting that commerce in the Inca Empire was somewhat marginal. Further archaeological studies may shed more light on the question, but it might be hard to distinguish between genuine commercial links and "administered trade," described by Polyani as a form of state-sponsored exchange of goods. The basic Inca policy seems to have been to eliminate pure commerce where practical and at all events to limit its scale.[121]

Theory and Practice

Inca imperial administration, as we have seen, embodied certain fundamental principles. Basic to their system of provincial rule, as indeed to that of most great empires, was the control exercised by leading members of the central hierarchy — in this instance, orejones of the highest standing, who acted as viceroys of the Inca ruler. The spiritual symbol of the imperial presence was an imposing temple to the sun. Still important as part of the machinery of government were the curacas, the former rulers of conquered lands. These local dignitaries were permitted to retain part of their wealth, together with certain powers and privileges, but were subject to strict Inca control and obliged to send their sons to be educated in Cuzco. The common people were compelled to devote part of their time to the state, whether to till the fields, fabricate goods, or serve in the army. Their output met the requirements of the state redistribution network, backed by massive storage facilities. To ensure a degree of self-sufficiency, each region became in effect a kind of state within a state, supplying its own needs to the greatest possible extent. This aim was reinforced by the establishment of vertical archipelagoes and the settling of large mitimae groups from other regions, both to supplement the local labor force and, where necessary, to provide more skilled craftsmen.

But in an empire that was a mosaic of different ecologies, languages, and traditions, any theoretical model had to be applied with flexibility. It was almost impossible to impose identical conditions, for example, on petty highland chiefdoms, the great kingdom of Chimor, and the traditional Aymara principalities of Collao. If in theory the state was supreme and the Inca ruler and his gods owned almost everything except the peasants' holdings, in practice many concessions were made to established interests in terms of both power and property. Local traditions were respected; where these were ancient and deep rooted — as, for instance, on the southern coast of Peru — Inca cultural penetration was more limited than in less developed regions.

Equally, although the principle of verticality was significant as a means of achieving a degree of local self-sufficiency, it was far from all-embracing. It was one means to a given end, the reinforcement of a state-controlled redistributive system. This system served, among other things, as a substitute for a market economy by providing for the interchange of the products of different ecological zones — for instance, maize and cotton from temperate regions for wool from the altiplano.[122] But in this respect also, notwithstanding the predilection for state-controlled interchange, there was a certain flexibility in practice, if one is to believe the reports of the existence of thousands of Chincha merchants. The presence of traders in Ecuador is also demonstrable and probably would have continued unless the Incas were ready to commit themselves to the conquest of the coast in quest of the greatly prized spondylus shells.

It may be true, as certain authors maintain, that merchants were alien to the Inca spirit even if in practice their usefulness was acknowledged. Yet one may wonder why private trading, usually present in ancient empires as the most practical way of exchanging goods, was so little favored. Admittedly, the Incas practiced a strict system of control and were reluctant to delegate authority. In addition, their elites were small in number; possibly they feared the rise of a large, enterprising, and prosperous class of merchants, hard to confine by force to one locality and free to move from place to place.

CHAPTER 8

The Decline and Fall

The Rival Contenders

With the death of Huayna Capac, the period of Inca achievement moved toward its close. The events of both the civil war and the Conquest need to be briefly considered in any attempt to assess this achievement and in particular to understand how the mighty structure of Tahuantinsuyu could suffer such a dramatic collapse.

The first portentous event was the civil war, which arose on the death of Huayna Capac. Such discord was not wholly without precedent, given the absence of precise rules governing the succession to the throne. In this instance, the Inca hierarchy was reluctant to accept without question the deceased ruler's choice of successor. According to Sarmiento, Huayna Capac declared on his deathbed to the leading *orejones*, including close relatives, that his first choice as heir was his son, Ninan Cuyochi; however, if the omens were not favorable to him, he would accept another son, Huascar, as successor. The entrails of two llamas were examined by the high priest of the sun; the omens for Cuyochi were most unpropitious, and Huascar was thus proclaimed the twelfth Inca. Ninan Cuyochi died of smallpox soon after this.[1]

Huascar was duly enthroned in Cuzco, escorted, according to Cieza, by no less than forty brothers. He appointed as his captain general, or "second person," a prince named Atoco.[2] A deep rivalry, however, prevailed between Huascar and another brother, Atahualpa, usually described as an illegitimate offspring (though his mother, Palloca, was reportedly descended from Pachacutec).[3] Atahualpa remained in Tumebamba, but numerous orejones who accompanied Huayna Capac's body to Cuzco were accused of supporting Atahualpa as a rival Inca and, on Huascar's orders, killed. These orejones were all from Hanan Cuzco, as was Atahualpa himself, whereas Huascar was from Hurin.[4] Atahualpa had apparently not yet made a formal claim to the throne of his father; accordingly, he sent further supporters with conciliatory messages to Huascar, but these individuals were also killed. According to Santacruz Pachacuti, at this stage Atahualpa merely asked to be confirmed as governor of Quito; the chronicler relates that Huascar had the skins of most of his brother's envoys made into drums but sent a few back to Tumebamba with insulting messages to their master, together with bundles of female attire.[5]

Cabello's detailed account of the civil war diverges in certain respects from that of Sarmiento. He mentions Huayna Capac's great affection for Ninan Cuyochi, whose premature death left Huascar as the natural heir. Cabello confirms the murder of the orejones who accompanied Huayna Capac's body to Cuzco but states that Atahualpa's subsequent emissaries, after conferring with Huascar and with his wife and mother, were allowed to return to Tumebamba bearing conciliatory messages. Nonetheless, after their departure, a Cañari leader convinced Huascar that Atahualpa planned to usurp the throne.[6]

Following this episode, Huascar, persuaded that Atahualpa would eventually rebel if allowed to remain in Ecuador, sent three successive envoys to his rival. Atahualpa was commanded to present himself in Cuzco and warned that if he failed to obey the summons an army would be sent to fetch him. The first to take up arms was Huascar. Cabello, Sarmiento, and Cobo describe a rather involved conflict in which Huascar initially triumphed. Atoco, Huascar's general, advanced northward and apparently succeeded in occupying Tumebamba. With the aid of his Cañari supporters, Atoco captured Atahualpa, but the latter miraculously escaped from his prison, according to one account by drilling a hole in a wall with a silver bar given to him by an important lady who had been allowed to visit him.[7] The Spaniards, alas, were to prove themselves more efficient as captors.

Following his liberation, Atahualpa assembled a large force, which eventually defeated Atoco at Ambato (south of Quito); Atoco and many of his men were killed. Atahualpa's army then marched southward under the command of two loyal captains, Chalco Chima and Quizqiz, and fought a series of engagements with forces commanded by Huascar's brother, Huanca Auqui, including the battles of Xauxa and Bonbón.[8] As Atahualpa's army approached Cuzco, Huascar entered the field in person; he mobilized a huge force, drawing on his supporters from the principal provinces of the Empire, including Collas, Charcas, and even Chile. After an initial triumph near Cotapampa, in which Atahualpa suffered huge losses, the fortunes of war were reversed, and Huascar himself was captured by Chalco Chima and Quizqiz.[9]

These accounts are confirmed in broad outline by that of Betanzos, who offers an abundance of seemingly factual material, to which he adds details that are more allegorical. He is an implacably harsh critic of Huascar; in the very first chapters of his story of the civil war, he writes of the drunken and licentious behavior of the newly crowned ruler, together with his profanity in despoiling the former rulers' *panacas* of their lands. Betanzos also describes his cruelty in torturing Atahualpa's emissaries.[10] More addicted to the bottle than to the din of battle, Huascar fell from power on a tragic note. Awakened from his drunken slumbers at midday by his captain, Aguapante, and warned that Atahualpa's generals, Quizqiz and Chalco Chima, were approaching Cuzco, Huascar precipitously set forth with a large army to stem their advance. But he then devised a stratagem so inept that it failed to deceive those seasoned commanders and instead led to his capture.[11]

Betanzos is scarcely more flattering when writing of Atahualpa, his own father-in-law, whose atrocities he also describes in detail. As an example, perhaps apocryphal, of such barbarity, he relates that on Atahualpa's orders, the hearts were cut out from the living bodies of three Cañari chiefs, chopped into very small pieces, and eaten raw.[12] To an account of Atahualpa's deeds, in some respects more factual, he adds other bizarre incidents, such as the upstart Inca's consultation of a famous stone oracle, or *huaca*, in the vicinity of Huamachuco. He was tersely told by the huaca that the god Viracocha disapproved of his wanton killings; not content with beheading the huaca with an axe (as a result of which the old man inside the huaca also lost his head), in his rage he determined to level the hill on which the idol had stood.[13]

Surviving accounts stress the gruesome ferocity of the civil war and the huge toll of casualties inflicted in a whole series of battles. Not surprisingly, the victor's vengeance was pitiless, leading at times to extremes of both cruelty and vandalism. According to Huaman Poma, Huascar, when held in captivity, was fed a diet consisting of the excrement of humans and dogs; in place of *chicha*, he was forced to drink the urine of llamas.[14] Because of Huascar's association with his grandfather, Tupac Inca, the men and women of Tupac's panaca were slaughtered, and this ruler's own mummy was burned to cinders, an act of sacrilege so horrendous as to be unthinkable in more settled times. Huascar himself was forced to witness such abominations in person, including the killing of eighty of his own children. Adherents to his cause throughout the Empire, such as the Cañaris, were also butchered. The forces of Atahualpa, the descendant of Pachacutec, even pillaged the shrines of the holy city of Cuzco.[15]

Relating the fluctuating fortunes of the rival contenders in more detail can add very little to our understanding of the inner workings of the Inca Empire. Nonetheless, certain aspects of the conflict are perhaps revealing and relevant. Among the more curious of these, belying the traditional image of the Inca ruler as the resplendent supreme warrior, is the apparent reluctance of the two claimants to the throne to take the field at the head of their armies. Huascar only fought in the last and most disastrous battle of all; Atahualpa merely dallied in the north, entrusting to his leading generals the forces that won the war, occupied Cuzco, and exacted a merciless revenge. The apparent absence of both Huascar and Atahualpa from the main battles that were to decide their fate might seem surprising, though the tendency was perhaps increasing for the ruler to delegate military command to others. Such a tendency was to a certain degree unavoidable because of the vast extent of the Empire, in which several major campaigns might be in progress at the same time. Such operations were not always reported by the chroniclers, who nonetheless do at times refer to forces sent by the emperor to specific regions to make new conquests or to suppress uprisings.

The accounts of the civil war also draw attention to the process whereby a new Inca ruler acceded to the throne, a sequence of almost Byzantine complexity. Huascar is more often described as the "legitimate" successor and thereby as enjoying a certain consensual support; however, he also is generally portrayed as fecklessly cruel and debauched, an image somewhat at variance with the principle of choosing the "fittest" son as heir to the throne.

Huascar's rival, Atahualpa, was the confirmed favorite of the armies of the north, who had fought so hard for Huayna Capac and who thereafter proved themselves to be the strongest force in the Empire. But Atahualpa hardly seems to have owed this loyalty to any reputation as a genial commander. On the contrary, according to Sarmiento he was out of favor with his father at the time of his death because of his dismal failure as leader of a force sent against the Pastos.[16] Betanzos, though differing in certain details, tells a similar tale of this event, recounting how Atahualpa fled from the field of battle, followed by his large force; his enraged father tore his clothes, expostulating that an army of women would have given a better account of themselves.[17]

Such reports not only stress the complexity of the process of succession but also draw attention to the latent rivalry that seems to have persisted between Hurin and Hanan Cuzco. The sources tend to identify Huascar's lineage with Hurin Cuzco; Sarmiento even writes of the extreme animosity *(aborrecimiento)* of those of Hanan Cuzco towards Huascar.[18] Betanzos explains the problem in somewhat different terms, citing a statement by Huascar that his lineage also derived from Hanan but that such was his hatred of Atahualpa, heir to the strictly Hanan identity of Pachacutec, that he henceforth would owe allegiance to a re-created lineage of Hurin.[19] The sources generally give the impression that, at least since the time of Pachacutec, Hanan Cuzco, identified to a marked degree with the army, came to enjoy a certain primacy over Hurin Cuzco, mainly associated with the established priestly hierarchy of Coricancha. Hence, the elevation of Huascar to the throne might conceivably be viewed as a kind of counter-revolution on the part of this conservative religious hierarchy, based in Hurin, against the Hanan military establishment, in particular against Huayna Capac's great northern army. Huascar, the protagonist of Hurin, unquestionably enjoyed very wide support not only in Cuzco but throughout much of the Empire, from many parts of which he freely recruited ample forces for his army. Even the north was divided in its allegiance, as the formidable Cañaris were among Huascar's staunchest allies.[20]

Such loyalties and associations need to be borne in mind in weighing the true balance of forces in the Inca realm at the time of its destruction. Certain aspects of the civil war suggest that the more traditional and conservative forces of Hurin had perhaps not wholly succumbed to Pachacutec's reforms. It might also be added that Spanish sources, obsessed with notions of primogeniture, perhaps exaggerated the strength of the provincial support for the "legitimate" successor, although these writers freely admit that Huascar's treatment of his own supporters finally served to alienate them.

Rostworowski, citing various chroniclers, concludes that the accounts of the respective lineages of the two claimants are ambiguous enough to suggest that it was more a war of opposing cliques than a struggle between rival houses. As she points out, Cieza maintained that Atahualpa, as well as Huascar, was connected on his mother's side with Hurin Cuzco.[21] However, Betanzos, as we have seen, refers to Huascar as speaking of his Hanan lineage. Pease describes the struggle as fomented by the Cuzco ruling establishment's inherent resentment of the political ascendancy of the Tumebamba military coterie, established during the reign of Huayna Capac. This ascendancy, endowing Tumebamba with the status of a rival "center of the world," created a grave situation for the Cuzco religious hierarchy; hence, the outbreak of war might be attributed to the quest for vengeance by this group, motivated by mystico-religious necessity to restore its supremacy.[22]

A Short-Lived Triumph

If Atahualpa's victory was total, it was short-lived. In the spring of 1532, at the very moment he was celebrating the news of the battle of Cotapampa and the capture of Huascar, he received in Huamachuco the portentous tidings of the landing of Pizarro's small force of Spaniards. Having savagely crushed the resistance of the islanders of Puná, they had crossed the Gulf of Guayaquil and stormed the city of Tumbez in a night attack. The civil war, which had spread to almost every corner of the Inca realm, also left its mark upon this region, never fully incorporated into the Empire. When Hernando de Soto rode inland from Tumbez to Cajas, he found the town in ruins, and from the trees hung many bodies of Indians loyal to Huascar who had refused to surrender to the victorious Atahualpa.[23]

Francisco Pizarro was by now no stranger to the Ecuadorian littoral. His first voyage in 1524 had achieved little; a second expedition to Ecuador in 1527 or 1528 made a few discoveries but sustained heavy casualties. In 1530 he set sail once more from Seville with a flotilla manned by would-be conquistadors. After a wearisome march along the coast of Ecuador, ending in the occupation of Puná, he eventually reached Tumbez. At the head of an exiguous force of 62 horsemen and 106 foot soldiers, Pizarro then set forth on his march into the interior on September 24, 1532. Atahualpa's first envoy, sent from Cajamarca, soon located the Spaniards and after a two-day stay in their midst invited Pizarro to proceed to Cajamarca to meet Atahualpa. Pizarro readily accepted and sent the Inca the gift of a fine Holland shirt and two goblets of Venetian glass.[24]

The eyewitness account by Miguel de Estete, a European, of the first face-to-face meeting confirms all that the chroniclers' informants related of the pomp and ceremony surrounding an Inca ruler:

> In a very fine litter with the ends of its timbers covered in silver, came the figure of Atahualpa. Eighty lords carried him on their shoulders, all wearing a very rich blue livery. His own person was very richly dressed, with his crown on his head and a collar of large emeralds round his neck. He was seated on the litter, on a small stool with a rich saddle cushion. He stopped when he reached the middle of the square [of Cajamarca] with his body half exposed. The litter was lined with parrot feathers of many colors and embellished with plates of gold and silver. Behind it came two other litters and two hammocks in which other leading persons traveled. Then came many men in squadrons with headdresses of gold and silver.[25]

This formal entry into Cajamarca followed Atahualpa's decision to convert his visit to the exotic strangers, now themselves ensconced in the town, into a kind of ceremonial pageant. He was accompanied by a large escort, unarmed according to major sources except for small battle-axes and slings concealed beneath their tunics. The anonymous French account of the Conquest does state that many of Atahualpa's men bore heavy clubs hanging from their belts and that others were armed with bows and arrows.[26]

What then occurred is familiar to every student of the Spanish Conquest. Though the chroniclers may vary in certain details, they concur as to the principal events: the capture of the Inca; the carnage that followed (mainly outside the walls of Cajamarca), leaving six or seven thousand Indians dead on the plain; the offer of a room full of gold as the Inca's ransom (an unexpected proposal that astounded the Spanish captors); the killing of Huascar on Atahualpa's orders; the melting down of countless masterpieces of the Inca goldsmiths, yielding a total of 13,420 pounds of 22.5 carat gold; the judicial murder of Atahualpa, strangled after he had solemnly embraced the gentle faith of his conquerors; and, finally, the Spanish march on Cuzco. By killing Atahualpa, the Spaniards had cast themselves in Indian eyes in the role of champions of the cause of Huascar; as such, they had to face the implacable resistance of Atahualpa's northern armies, commanded by his general, Quizqiz, at that moment in occupation of much of central Peru. Against these forces the Spanish fought no less than four battles; after the final, conclusive encounter in the mountains above Cuzco, the Quitans lost heart, and Quizqiz's army simply vanished. The triumphant conquistadors, when they first beheld Cuzco, described the buildings of the Inca capital, as their counterparts had done in Mexico, as superior to anything they had ever seen in Spain.

THE FINEST HOUR

A few episodes from the early years of Spanish occupation may be relevant to our study and shed some light on the sociopolitical structure of Tahuantinsuyu itself. After the deaths of Atahualpa and Huascar, the Spaniards already controlled the central part of the Inca Empire, roughly corresponding to modern Peru, and were in the process of occupying Bolivia and Chile. But the northern armies still held out against the invaders in Ecuador. These forces were now ruled with a very firm hand by Rumiñavi, Atahualpa's third-ranking general, acting more as an independent condottiere than as the trusted lieutenant of the dead ruler and his heirs. During his master's captivity, Rumiñavi held the ruler's sons and many of his women in custody. Atahualpa managed to send his brother in an attempt to rescue his children, but the prince was murdered by Rumiñavi, skinned, and made into a drum.

The Spaniards' attention was naturally drawn to this northern stronghold and its ruthless tyrant. Accordingly, Sebastián de Benalcázar set out from the port of San Miguel de Piura (about 120 miles south of Tumbez). John Hemming, in his account of the Conquest, describes the opposition Benalcázar encountered as the finest hour of the Inca army. Though the Quitan forces had no prince of the blood to lead them, their resistance was staunch. Benalcázar occupied Tumebamba, where three thousand Cañaris, still loyal to the cause of Huascar, joined his forces. The Spanish general continued his northward march and at Teocajas, situated near a mountain pass at an altitude of 14,000 feet, met ferocious resistance. This was the greatest pitched battle of the Conquest; though the Inca force failed to stem the Spanish horsemen, the latter achieved no decisive victory. The Spaniards had to continue to fight bands of natives until they eventually reached Quito; finding that all the men of this principality had left to join the Inca forces, Benalcázar sought to make an example by slaughtering their women and children.

Meanwhile, other contenders had unexpectedly entered the field. The well-known conquistador of Mexico, Pedro de Alvarado, proceeding from Guatemala, had landed a powerful force on the coast of Ecuador in February 1534. However, unfamiliar with the harsh conditions of the Andes, he and his expedition initially achieved little, and thereafter many of his men and horses froze to death as he tried to penetrate the cordillera and took the wrong route. The Inca forces faced their own struggles. Quizqiz,

Atahualpa's trusted general, having fought inconclusive battles against the Spaniards in the region of Xauxa, returned to Ecuador; he failed to join forces with Rumiñavi. After both generals had been defeated and killed, the Ecuadorian resistance gradually subsided.[27]

The occupation of the southernmost marches of the Empire presented fewer problems. In July 1535 Diego de Almagro left Cuzco for Chile at the head of a well-equipped army, supported by great trains of native porters and accompanied by a force of twelve thousand men under the command of Paullu, another surviving son of Huayna Capac. The march through Collao and Charcas met with scant resistance; both provinces tended to accept the authority of Paullu and demonstrated their loyalty to the latter as heir to Huayna Capac. In Chile there was some resistance, and isolated groups of Spaniards were ambushed and killed. In the province of Copiapo, most of the Indians simply fled from the invaders.[28]

PUPPETS AND REBELS

Meanwhile, however, an entirely new situation had arisen in the capital. The story of the Spaniards' dealings with a series of phantom Inca kings constitutes a bizarre page in history, though its details hardly fall within the scope of this work. The first attempt to maintain the fiction of a subservient "empire" was short-lived. Immediately after the Christian burial of Atahualpa, elaborate preparations began in Cajamarca for the coronation of Huascar's younger brother, Tupac Huallpa. Every detail of the traditional ceremonies was punctiliously observed, commencing with a three-day fast of the "emperor" in a specially constructed edifice and ending with the placing of the royal fringe on his head, as his followers turned their faces toward the sun. The reign of this compliant puppet came to a most untimely end when the Inca died a few months later, in October 1533, while staying in Xauxa in the company of Francisco Pizarro; the Spaniards, chagrined by their loss, convinced themselves that Tupac had been poisoned.[29]

Undaunted by this setback and determined to maintain the fiction of Inca rule, the conquistadors were not slow to seek a new champion for their cause. On entering Cuzco in November 1533 they were greeted by the young Manco, yet another son of Huayna Capac, who impressed them by his obsequious devotion to Spanish rule. Manco was duly crowned and regaled with the same ceremonies previously observed for the coronation of his half-brother, Tupac Huallpa.[30] Miguel de Estete offers a vivid description of Manco's coronation, at which the Spanish witnessed all the panoply of Inca ritual, including the presence of mummies of the former kings seated on thrones. The new Inca led the procession, flanked by the mortal remains of his father, Huayna Capac. The mummies were attended by numerous members of their panacas, both male and female, holding fans and showing reverence for the former monarchs as if they were still living; de Estete adds the curious detail that a little vessel at the side of each mummy contained the remains of nails and hair that had been cut from their bodies.[31] Such was the Spaniards' fear of suppressing heathen ceremonies, alien and even repugnant to the tenets of their own faith, that Manco was allowed to practice certain traditional rites. Cristóbal de Molina in 1535 witnessed the great feast known as Inti Raymi to celebrate the harvesting of the maize crop; on this occasion also the mortuary bundles were paraded and placed under feather awnings. They were attended by many orejones, splendidly attired and wearing medallions of fine gold on their heads. Once again, the rulers' effigies were accompanied by many female attendants, who kept away flies with fans made of swans' feathers.[32]

Manco, however, had some unpleasant surprises in store for his Spanish sponsors. He managed to flee from Cuzco, was recaptured, but escaped again on the eve of Easter 1536. His departure heralded the beginning of the great rebellion. Manco first led a massive force against the Spanish capital, Lima; this attack was finally repulsed by cavalry. However, following a dramatic siege of Cuzco, during which a small group of conquistadors were reduced to the most dire straits, Inca fortunes were gradually reversed with the help of a never-ending flow of reinforcements sent from many parts of Spanish America. Manco eventually took refuge in the far-off province of Vilcabamba, which he ruled as a kind of rump empire until he was murdered in 1545. This realm survived in its remote fastness, ruled successively by the sons of Manco, until it finally succumbed to an expedition sent by the Viceroy Toledo in 1572. The last ruler, Tupac Amaru, was condemned to death. Huge crowds of grieving Indians lined the streets of Cuzco as Tupac Amaru was led to his execution by decapitation; his body was buried in the high chapel of the cathedral.

The Inevitable Triumph

In weighing any possible conclusions that might be drawn from the civil war, reference has already been made to the reportedly limited attainments of the two claimants to the throne, resulting perhaps from the inadequacies of the process of selection. The civil war was also seen as arising from a built-in imbalance, occasioned by Huayna Capac's resolve to establish Tumebamba as a second Cuzco and the consequent antagonism between north and south, exposing the ruler to the perils of a counterrevolution on the part of the traditionalist hierarchy of Hurin Cuzco.

From the first stages of the Spanish Conquest, as outlined above, certain conclusions may also be drawn concerning the fallen Empire. In spite of debilitating internal divisions, the Incas staged a tenacious resistance based on native pride and valor, demonstrating the strengths as much as the weaknesses of their realm. Such resolve on their part is exemplified by the opposition met by the conquistadors in Ecuador. Moreover, Spanish tolerance of Inca rites arose from their reluctance to provoke a population whose reactions they still feared. But in fighting the Spanish, the Incas' greatest limitation may have been the fact that in Indian warfare, ritual considerations were never wholly absent. As Hyslop points out, the sources describe rituals and divinations that accompanied almost every step taken before, during, and after military campaigns, including rites performed and offerings made to strengthen Inca efforts and weaken those of the enemy. Favorable auguries were an indispensable prelude to the taking of important initiatives.[33] Ritual considerations were ever present in the savage civil war, though any tendency to cite that war as the main cause of the Empire's destruction is probably exaggerated. Pease expresses doubts as to the degree to which the conflict affected the struggle against the Spanish; in drawing attention to certain aspects of the civil war, he stresses the fact that Cuzco at no point really lost its status as a holy city, the center and the place of origin of the Inca world.[34] But as the adversary of this resurgence of Cuzco (the original founders of Inca rule had come from outside the capital), Atahualpa could pose as the new emissary of the sun and even recreate the special role of "founder." His miraculous escape from captivity marked the initiation of the conception of Atahualpa as the semidivine hero receiving the direct aid of his father, the sun.[35]

Betanzos, who incidentally rejects the story of Atahualpa's imprisonment in Tumebamba and his miraculous deliverance, offers other examples of his assumed role in Inca ritual as leader of a spiritual renewal. For instance, Atahualpa adopted the curious procedure of causing a "bundle" to be made of portions of his hair and nails, in conformity with similar bundles that accompanied the mummies of former rulers on ceremonial occasions. Moreover, when proclaimed ruler, he adopted the appellation "Caccha Pachacuti Ynga Yupanqui"; because Caccha was the name of the war god associated with his great-grandfather, Pachacutec, Atahualpa thus in effect assumed the mantle of that monarch as the new "founder."[36] According to Betanzos, it was not Atahualpa but Aguapante, Huascar's general, who was imprisoned by the Cañaris.[37]

Atahualpa is at times portrayed as the embodiment of Inca valor, a man who would have reunited and revitalized the Empire. However, it remains hard to explain why, following his ruthless treatment of other adversaries, Atahualpa insisted on making an essentially ceremonial occasion of his visit to Pizarro, ensconced in Cajamarca. He led an elaborately caparisoned but lightly armed host of retainers into an obviously dangerous situation, a decision that cost him his kingdom and his life. Surrounded as he was by factious tribes openly disloyal to his cause, such as the Cañaris, he surely had no reason to trust the Spaniards, already known to have ravaged Tumbez and other coastal polities, or to believe they would simply regale him as the guest of honor in a ceremonial reception. Betanzos, the ruler's own son-in-law, relates in detail how Atahualpa's assembled captains had stressed the base intentions of the invaders and besought him to treat them not as benevolent guests but as inveterate foes, to arm his forces and seek the first chance to cut the Spanish to pieces in the open field. The same chronicler also relates at length a previous conversation between the ruler and Ciquinchara, identified as the messenger who first contacted the Spaniards on their march from the coast. He was obviously a keen observer of Spanish habits and offered perhaps the best proposal as to how to deal with them: Because they tended to sleep in one place, huddled together, they should be induced to occupy a structure with gates that could be barred at night, after which the building could be burned and its inhabitants incinerated. Unfortunately, Atahualpa was not a good listener when offered such practical suggestions.[38]

Hence, in asking the inevitable question of how it was conceivable that this tiny band of Spaniards could overthrow an empire whose forces outnumbered them by perhaps a thousand to one, it must be stressed first and foremost that the invaders fought a total war, bent on maintaining the offensive until victory was achieved. Their adversaries, by contrast, fought a different kind of war and were imbued with different concepts, and their conduct of military operations involved ritual and ceremonial considerations wholly irrelevant to victory in the field.

At the same time, superior arms and tactics obviously were a very significant factor. In pitched battles, however vast the native armies and however gallant their resistance, the ultimate victory of the Spaniards was assured. One may cite the four battles fought on the Spaniards' road to Cuzco, as well as the subsequent encounters during their conquest of Ecuador. At best the Inca forces withdrew and lived to fight another day; usually they were more successful in ambushing smaller groups of Spaniards than in facing them in the open.

The shock caused by strange and fearful arms was no doubt stunning, at least at the outset, and even in subsequent encounters the horses and firearms were often used to good effect. My previous conclusions as to the Spaniards' ability to defeat the Aztecs broadly concur with Hemming's observations on the triumphs of Spanish conquistadors against the Incas.[39] Our views coincide as to the importance of Spanish armor and the effectiveness of their steel swords. For both Aztecs and Incas, a principal weapon was the club, with a head fitted with sharp spikes. As I pointed out in describing Aztec arms, such clubs had to be lifted on high to inflict a mortal blow, thus exposing the whole body; the Spaniards could dispatch Indian after Indian with lightning sword-thrusts before the latter could strike back with their more unwieldy arms.[40] We also reach the same conclusions as to the comparative inefficacy of the arquebus as a decisive arm (at that time it was still a rather clumsy weapon, particularly in wet weather) and also as to the limited usefulness of the crossbow, which had already proved inferior to the Welsh longbow at the Battle of Crécy, 173 years before the Conquest of Mexico. Hemming inclines to the view that Spaniards owed everything to their horses, which gave them mobility and instilled terror into their Inca foes. However, it needs to be borne in mind that Cortés was still able to crush his enemies at the Battle of Otumba after his calamitous retreat from Tenochtitlan, at a time when the Spaniards not only had lost all their artillery but were left with only twenty-three extremely debilitated horses.

Contrary opinions are expressed by many authors as to the demoralizing effect of the initial belief, reported to have been held both in Mexico and Peru, that the Spaniards were identified with important native deities. However, such convictions were probably a less than decisive factor. Hemming suggests that there is little evidence that the eventual outcome was affected by any native identification of the invaders with the returning creator god, Viracocha.[41] This was in effect a replay of the notion that reportedly arose in Mexico — i.e., that the Spaniards personified the creator, Quetzalcoatl, a belief that was fairly quickly dispelled.[42] The American Indian empires in both Mexico and Peru were pitted against the greatest soldiers of the age; for a century and a half no Spanish army was ever defeated in a pitched battle. Perhaps the most vital factor of all, decisive but hard to assess, was their superiority in tactics and morale. The Inca armies fought bravely but would more easily lose heart if the tide of battle turned against them, whereas the Spaniards positively thrived on adversity and always displayed an absolute resolve to retain the initiative.

Saga and Substance

Ample data survive from the rather confused four decades during which an Inca chief grimly clung to a remote corner of the fallen Empire. Such events might prompt a cynic to proclaim that Inca history in the strictest sense, far from ending when the Spaniards arrived, *began* at that very point. The foregoing brief résumé only offers glimpses of a scenario in which some Incas resisted colonial rule but others backed it to the hilt; moreover, during this period not only did Inca fight Inca but Spaniard fought Spaniard. The record, however convoluted, is nonetheless replete with dates, giving the day and the month of many incidents, together with countless names of leaders who are without question historical figures and on whose deeds we have fairly precise Spanish records.

In contrast, attempts to describe the deeds of the pre-Conquest kings in historical terms face greater problems. A major limitation is the sheer brevity of the imperial period as a whole; Rowe assigns a time span of a mere eighty-seven years from the date of Pachacutec's accession to that of Huayna Capac's death. Even those who question this chronology might nonetheless agree that the length of the period of dynamic expansion, assuming that it embraced only three reigns, is not very likely to have exceeded a single century.

Huayna Capac's end was premature, and Tupac was reportedly still engaged in active warfare in the year of his death. In contrast to these three conquerors, of whose deeds many details survive, the sources write of no less than eight rulers (with the possible exception of Viracocha) whose claim to qualify as historical figures is at best slender. Hence, as we have already seen, the temptation arises to dismiss most of Inca history as mere myth, a tendency backed by the notion that oral accounts are too subjective to be trusted and that without chronology there can be no history.

My own conclusion is that at least from the time of Pachacutec onward the record of the Inca past may in broad terms be treated as history. Because it derives from oral rather than written accounts, the more remote events become progressively blurred, and a perhaps disproportionate attention is focused upon Huayna Capac's reign, to a point where even some accounts of Tupac's deeds may reflect acts more strictly attributable to his successor. But in this respect it may be worth stressing that much of what we know of the Aztecs and their empire, notwithstanding their capacity to record the past, also derives from informants rather than from codices; in particular, the monumental work of Fray Bernardino de Sahagún was recorded in Nahuatl from a carefully chosen band of high-ranking informants. It may be more pertinent to add that even for the history of ancient Greece, a comparable situation arises. Thucydides, perhaps the greatest Greek historian, relied much more on verbal reports than on documents and did not believe that the past was really discoverable beyond the span covered by oral testimony from living sources.[43]

Leopold von Ranke is still probably regarded as the leading historian of the nineteenth century. He spent his life studying and discovering written sources; in one of the most famous of all pronouncements about the nature of history, he declared that his aim was not to judge but only to tell "how it really was" *(wie es eigentlich gewesen war)*. But, as M. I. Finney points out, even history based on precise written records is of necessity selective, and Ranke's omissions, as the Italian philosopher Benedetto Croce insisted, are apparent from his work, together with a certain narrowness of focus.[44] To cite the English historian, Lord Acton: "All that he [Ranke] says is often true, and yet the whole is untrue. . . . Ranke deceives not by additions but by selection."[45]

Yet any tendency to deny historical validity to Inca sources surely derives from this very need for selectivity. In dealing with the Inca Empire, the historian is faced with the absolute necessity of evaluating sources containing conflicting information and deciding which are the more credible. But in questioning the validity of the Inca record, we have to admit that such problems confronted even the very greatest of both ancient and modern historians, Thucydides and Ranke.

Inca history is open to challenge on the grounds that it is based on verbal accounts of past traditions; but such accounts should not automatically be branded as unacceptable. One of the most practical ways to check the potential reliability of oral traditions and recollections is to examine those with which one is oneself familiar. I may perhaps, therefore, be forgiven for striking a rather personal note. Because of an unusually long age gap between generations in my own family, I descend from a father born in 1881, whose own father was born in 1840. Apart from many other stories of my grandfather that were more anecdotal (but probably also fairly accurate), I remember being told that his eldest brother, born in 1835, had been severely wounded before the Battle of Sebastopol in the Crimean War at the age of nineteen and had died in the harbor onboard ship in 1854. Of this event I had seen absolutely no written record and only quite recently chanced upon documentary proof that the information was correct. Yet the time span involved is much greater than that which elapsed between the traditional dates for Pachacutec's accession and Huayna Capac's death.

In assessing the relevance of Inca historical material, archaeology today assumes an ever increasing role. The findings of scientific research tend to confirm rather than to deny documentary reports as to the extent of Inca conquests in Chile and even in Ecuador; in addition, in recent decades new evidence has helped us better to define imperial boundaries in Peru, Bolivia, and northwest Argentina. From archaeology we also learn that the chroniclers' euphoric accounts of elements of the Inca infrastructure, such as the road system, are far from exaggerated.

Obvious Limitations

The proper role of archaeology as a means of interpreting and understanding history has admittedly been the subject of much discussion during recent decades. Bruce Trigger even refers to the positively antihistorical bias of the "New Archaeology"; such research may tend to be viewed as confined more to generalizations about human behavior, with the ultimate goal of defining social systems.[46] Archaeology has been able to contribute substantially to the making of such social definitions in the Andes, but in certain respects it has surely gone further. In studying the process of not only social but also political change from one horizon to another it has contributed as well to the history of the Late Horizon through its affirmation of what preceded it, particularly in the Middle Horizon. This period began almost a millennium before the Inca era, and its remains, now investigated, bear witness not only to the existence of urban sites but also to the possible construction of roads.

But assuming that meaningful studies of Inca history can indeed be undertaken, it has to be accepted that they have obvious limitations. The dividing line between almost undiluted myth and stories founded on at least an element of fact is at best ill-defined. Our own standards distinguishing between myth and reality are perhaps hard to apply to the Inca world; as Robert Berkhofer points out, in order to determine what is myth as opposed to what is knowledge, the historian must produce evidence that the actors of the past themselves believed a certain proposition to be real or false.[47]

It must be further admitted that it is easier to describe the Inca past in terms of traditional history than in terms of certain contemporary trends in historical research. As described by Gertrude Himelfarb, "Where the old (history) features kings, presidents, politicians . . . the new takes as its subject the anonymous masses. The old is history from above, 'elitist history,' as it is now said; the new is 'history from below,' or 'populist history.'"[48] Admittedly, "history from below" is not altogether lacking; one may cite, for instance, the outstanding work of Murra in unraveling whatever it may be possible to learn from the written records and even from present-day ethnological data on the "anonymous masses," including *mitimaes* and *yanas*. Nonetheless, surviving Inca history, like that of so many pristine realms, is basically "history from above"; the chroniclers learned from their informants much more about rulers and the ruling class than about the common people. In societies of a certain type, stories of kings and their conquests are what survive for the most part. One may assume that the task of the historian indeed embraces not only the deeds of great men but also the life of the community; in heroic polities such as that of the Incas, though, the king is the colossus around which the life of the community revolves. The history of ancient peoples further differs from our own in being designed to edify rather than merely to instruct. Precise details, such as which ruler conquered which place and when, were often of lesser consequence. More remote events in particular become blurred. But here again the Incas are not unique in such failings. Notwithstanding the use of hieroglyphic writing, the enumeration of the conquests in Asia of the Pharaoh Ramses III consists simply of a list of the triumphs of his predecessor.[49]

One has only to peruse Spanish eyewitness descriptions of the ceremonial that surrounded the person of Atahualpa or study the many chroniclers' accounts of land distribution throughout the Empire to appreciate that the Inca *was* the state. As a form of heroic history, the chroniclers' records tend to focus upon the deeds of the ruler, mainly concentrated in the northernmost marches of the Empire, during the latter years before the Conquest. The record is therefore very incomplete, as we learn little of events occurring in other parts of that huge domain, where the ruler was less often present in person.

Information on the upper echelons of the civil administration tends to be fragmentary. Any search for institutional forms and systems of government does not lead us very far; the data on so many aspects of this problem are almost nonexistent. Obviously the monarch had to delegate power to a complex array of officials. Imprecise references occur to a kind of alter ego, or second person to the ruler, but we have little idea as to his functions, though the king's closest relative is sometimes named as governor of Cuzco in his absence. The chroniclers write much of the orejones, but little is said of precise functions apart from their command of armies in the field. Surely, though, they must have been responsible for a variety of other aspects of government.

Economic data on ancient societies are notoriously hard to unravel, and statistics are usually nonexistent. Chronology is itself a form of statistics and is often the most difficult form to clarify. For instance, some Mesoamerican codices and written sources recorded the passing of the years, but there exists no consensus as to the correlation of the various regional calendrical systems with dates in our calendar.

The Unique and the Recurrent

However imprecise our knowledge of the Incas gleaned from chroniclers' reports, the surviving archaeological remains, whether in the form of infrastructure or of monuments, are more than sufficient to demonstrate the magnitude of their achievement. In terms of imperial architecture one need only cite the best-preserved, if not the largest, of such remains: the site of Machu Picchu. This clearly was an important Inca town with impressive buildings and fine masonry. It did not stand alone as an isolated outpost and today it is no longer regarded as a fortress. Bingham's 1915 expedition located and cleared a number of other settlements within a few miles of Machu Picchu. In 1940 and 1941 another major expedition discovered a whole string of towns on the slopes between Ollantaytambo and Machu Picchu, including the sites of Winay Wayna and Inti Pata, each of which possessed spectacular systems of terracing, greater even than those of Machu Picchu itself. But this whole cluster of sites was situated in a relatively remote corner of their realm; the mind boggles at the potential richness of Inca construction throughout the length and breadth of the Empire, in so many places where little has survived. Machu Picchu was merely the last of a string of towns in that remote region, whose flights of superb agricultural terraces were possibly designed to provide special crops and luxuries for the court in Cuzco.[50]

Notwithstanding its remoteness, Machu Picchu's very survival serves to stress the most unique aspects of the Inca achievement (assuming that many comparable sites indeed existed). It might easily be supposed that the Incas, far from being themselves innovators, merely repeated on a greatly expanded scale the innovations of pre-Inca times. But today leading scholars tend to insist that it is at best half true to treat the Inca Empire as merely having repeated the achievements of the past on a vaster scale. This dramatic process of expansion must have involved radical changes from anything previously accomplished, for instance, in the production of food and in the immensely expanded storage system.

One wonders what the Incas might have accomplished if their Empire had endured, like that of Chimor, for centuries. As Theresa Topic stresses, moreover, the vast difference in scale between Inca and Chimu storage facilities in itself illustrates fundamental differences between their overall achievements, in particular between Inca and Chimu state finances.[51] One may further stress that by its very size, apart from other considerations, the Inca domain was an intricate structure that achieved a delicate balance but that inevitably collapsed in the hands of new masters who had no experience of such a structure or of Andean conditions in general.

In recent decades a tendency has prevailed to seek a nomothetic approach to human culture as governed by definable laws and to establish models that might serve as a norm for predicting a given pattern of change.

Such notions tend to be questioned by some authors; one may again cite Bruce Trigger as insisting that there is no quick and easy way by which archaeologists can create a body of evolutionary theory that will allow them simultaneously to predict or retrodict (predict backwards) the course of history.[52]

Notwithstanding such reservations, probably few scholars today would reject out of hand the potential use of models, especially where there are ample examples of a comparable set of circumstances. Nomothetic concepts may, for instance, help to clarify differences and similarities between the progress of certain nations following the inception of the industrial revolution in the nineteenth century. Generalizations of another kind may be applicable to smaller chieftainships in earlier times throughout the globe.

But history is the study of both the unique and the recurrent. The formation of major empires involving the subjection by one conquest state of a whole series of peoples over an extensive area is a rare phenomenon. The number of instances is perhaps rather small to allow for the establishment of any standard that might serve as a norm for the development of others. At best one may propose tentative generalizations. If we divide these conquest states into maritime empires, such as the Spanish and British, and contiguous land-based empires, in which conquering armies simply subjected many neighboring peoples to their rule, the number of comparable instances becomes even smaller. Though certain aspects of the history of other empires may be relevant to the Inca case, there surely exists no model that bears strict comparison, given the territory's daunting ecological circumstances. The only Asian mountain range comparable to the Andes, the Himalayas, served more as a dividing line between cultures.

The Reasons Why

In the absence of obvious physical parallels and of any detailed knowledge of the Incas' pre-imperial past, it remains hard to explain why they, rather than some other group, became the dominant power of their era. As Conrad and Demarest observe, had there been a bookmaker in 1430 taking bets as to who would control the southern Sierra in the near future, he would probably have established two peoples as odds-on favorites: The top contender would have been the Lupaqa, who had become the strongest kingdom in the rich Titicaca basin through their victory over the Collas; the other choice would have been the Chancas, who in a startling turn of events had completely upset the balance of power north and west of Cuzco after defeating their traditional enemies, the Quechuas.[53]

In the absence of a more concise explanation, one might only observe that the Incas, apart from their martial skills (indispensable for any would-be conqueror), also displayed notable political talents not shared by all their neighbors. The turning point in their history, the defeat of the Chancas, was accomplished largely through their ability to form a kind of coalition, enabling them to achieve victory against considerable odds. They also consistently demonstrated a certain political acumen in their ability to conciliate many conquered peoples; for instance, Collas or Charcas were willing to march vast distances and to fight and die to further the process of Inca conquest. Explanations as to why a given group may succeed in establishing control over its late neighbors, whether in the Old World or the New, are seldom easy to formulate. The factors that motivated a few such groups to go much farther and to make long-range conquests are even harder to determine.

In studying the forces that motivated both the Inca and the Aztec Empires, Conrad and Demarest propose first and foremost religious, or ideological, factors for a process that eventually led to overexpansion. They suggest that for the Mexicas the sacrificial cult became a driving force in generating expansionist policies; for the Incas, the elaboration of the royal ancestor cult, with its crucial extension of a king's property rights beyond his demise, created an institutional imbalance in the dynastic system, virtually imposing expansionistic policies on each heir to the throne. Split inheritance thus ensured the militarism of the Inca state's rulers, and the dogma of Inti gave those rulers the justification and propaganda they needed to carry out imperialist policies. Conrad and Demarest conclude, "We are convinced that ideological elements were the cutting edge of Mexica and Inca imperialism."[54]

It may, however, be fair to add that the two authors insist that the processes involved in both imperial expansions are extremely complex and that care must be taken to refrain from proposing a purely monocausal explanation. It may indeed be generally accepted that the Incas "solarized" the Andean creator god, thereby forging an instrument of imperial conquest that took formal shape in the sun temples built throughout their realm. However, in the Inca creation myth, the creator is inseparable from the sun from the very beginning. The myth offers an interpretation of Viracocha as an agent of the sun.[55] The creator deity, however, was already basic to the pantheon of many of the conquered peoples; hence, this form of religious manipulation may have served admirably as an instrument of domination, but it hardly amounted to any new ideology (as compared, say, to the fanatical determination of Islamic conquerors to impose on others an absolutely distinct faith).

The case of the Mexicas is perhaps comparable to that of the Incas. Ostensibly, Huitzilopochtli was their tutelary deity, yet so profound was their veneration for Tezcatlipoca (the Smoking Mirror) that it becomes hard to determine which of the two ranked as the senior god. Tezcatlipoca, who had evolved from the original feline god of Mesoamerica, was in one form or another universally revered, whereas Huitzilopochtli was virtually an alter ego of the god Camaxtli, closely linked with Mixcoatl, another deity whose cult was very widespread. It is hard to insist that the Mexicas made war simply to convert people to gods whom they already worshipped in one form or another.[56]

Split inheritance may indeed have provided a motive for Inca expansion, though it is far from clear, as we have seen, how far the Inca rulers established personal holdings (as opposed to state lands in theory belonging to the Incas) in distant provinces. The truly royal and panaca constructions and estates near Cuzco far exceeded in their magnificence and elegance any state settlements beyond the Cuzco region.[57]

As an alternative, or supplement, to ideology, the most obvious incentive for wars of conquest is surely the quest for material gain, whether in the form of land, trade, or mere booty. Though the Incas were ostensibly reluctant traders, state control not only of land in conquered provinces but also of the local labor force yielded a massive surplus of agricultural produce and other goods. Much of this was stored locally, partly for military use, though a large proportion of the sumptuary items, particularly gold, was dispatched to Cuzco. The ruling elite of Cuzco seemingly developed a veritable passion for amassing immense quantities, far beyond any rational requirements, of such tribute, much of which was then simply hoarded. In discussing motivation, it may therefore be relevant to stress once again the phenomenon of accumulated spoils.

Nothing had prepared the Spaniards for the gigantic stores found in Cuzco. According to Pedro Sancho, the quantities are so vast that it was hard to imagine how the natives can ever have paid such enormous tribute consisting of so many items. The stores included whole buildings full of utilitarian things such as cloaks, wool, metal, and cloth. But what most struck the conquistadors was the accumulation of smaller items of exquisite quality simply stored in leather chests; they included deposits of iridescent hummingbird feathers, each little larger than a fingernail. These were threaded together and made into garments that contained staggering amounts of such iridescents. Many other hoards of feathers were found, of a kind used for robes worn at the great festivals.[58] Needless to say, such finery was of scant interest to the Spaniards, who were consumed with the urge to acquire pure gold and melted down countless treasures for this purpose.

In previous chapters, the temptation to draw conclusions between the Inca and Aztec Empires has been generally avoided. However, given that both empires met the same ultimate fate, dramatically collapsing when confronted with small contingents of Spanish conquistadors, the parallels are surely close enough to merit attention, notwithstanding certain marked differences.

Once they had defeated their enemies, the Aztecs virtually left local rulers in full charge of their former domains, subject only to the obligation (enforced in case of default by punitive expeditions) to make fairly onerous tribute payments every eighty days, payments strictly supervised by imperial officials. Detailed documentary evidence survives of the exact quantity of each item extracted from a given province. The Aztecs, like the Incas, did have an effective system of military recruitment, and both states were remarkably successful in mobilizing levies from conquered peoples to fight their battles. However, the Aztecs' more loose-knit domain offers a striking contrast to the Inca Empire, over whose curacas provincial governors exercised tight control. The imposing infrastructure, including the road network and the storage facilities, has no true counterpart in Mesoamerica.

Ironically, perhaps, in view of their patent dissimilarities, in the two New World empires conquered by the Spaniards a comparable phenomenon seems to have arisen. For both, a powerful factor in the process of continuous expansion was the urge to acquire ever-increasing supplies of sumptuary objects; many were sent from provinces so far distant that it was hardly feasible to haul the more bulky goods to the capital for general consumption (notwithstanding, in the case of the Incas, the fine road network). Such sumptuary goods, including much of those used to reward the elite of Cuzco and of Tenochtitlan, served basically ritual purposes. These rituals, celebrated on an ever more stupendous scale, are amply described by Sahagún and other Aztec chroniclers. Spaniards witnessed Inca rites of comparable splendor in the early post-Conquest years. Hence, for both Aztecs and Incas, spiritual and material motives for conquest were inextricably linked as part of the need to satisfy an appetite for luxury products. If these also helped to enrich the privileged few, such redistribution served basically ceremonial ends.

Immense efforts were, of course, also made to reinforce the economy of the core regions of the Valley of Mexico and the Valley of Cuzco by massive public works; in both instances, spectacular results were brought about. However, it becomes hard to see the process of long-range expansion as contributing in a very direct manner to such achievements, for which conquest on a much less ambitious scale might have provided an adequate surplus of materials and manpower. Nonetheless, the Incas placed much emphasis on the quest for more gold.

In addition, vast quantities of trophies, fashioned from such exotic components as feathers from the breasts of hummingbirds, were found by the conquistadors in Cuzco. The Codex Mendoza lists the tribute supplied to the Aztecs by the province of Soconusco, on the border of present-day Guatemala; bunches of feathers predominate, including those taken from the tails of the quetzal bird, native to that region. In both empires such items became as much a necessity as a luxury; they were required for the ever more elaborate rituals, which were viewed as indispensable for the honoring of the gods, for the ordering of the cosmos, and for the well-being of the rulers of the two empires and of their elite hierarchies.

Conrad, who tends to reject pure cultural materialism as an adequate explanation for the expansion of both the Chimu and Inca empires, draws attention, in writing of split inheritance, to the massive ceremonial attached to the mummies of past rulers, maintained in state, consulted in times of stress, and brought out to attend important rites.[59] The existence of this whole series of establishments of defunct Inca rulers surely magnified the demand for ceremonial paraphernalia from remote provinces, even if these territories did not serve to provide the panacas with additional estates.

It may indeed be fair to suggest that the process of endless expansion had slackened some years before the Spaniards arrived. Moctezuma II made little attempt to expand his realm beyond the limits reached by his all-conquering predecessor, Ahuitzotl; he concentrated his efforts on consolidation and on the attempt to supress enclaves within his empire that retained a measure of independence. Equally, following Tupac's dazzling career of conquest, Huayna Capac seemingly made less spectacular advances, even refraining from attempts to gain control of the Ecuadorian littoral. It should be added that for the Aztecs (for example, in the case of the Oaxaca Valley), and to a much greater extent for the Incas, distant provinces were not treated solely as suppliers of sumptuary goods. Much of the labor and its produce throughout the Inca realm was dedicated to the maintenance of the local infrastructure; of this, the Valley of Cochabamba may serve as an example. As we have already seen, the sources report the massive introduction of mitimaes by Huayna Capac, a measure that served to greatly augment the output of nonluxury produce and to make of this valley a veritable breadbasket that served to support the Inca power structure in the southern part of the Empire.

Other causes may also be cited that impel certain peoples to embark on a career of conquest, apart from the ideological and material motives discussed above. Of these, perhaps the most significant factor is that once a given polity begins to conquer others, there is no obvious place to stop; it becomes very hard to set any limit to the process, even when faced with diminishing returns. Though precise models for empire building may be elusive, many of the world's greatest empires seem to have displayed this compulsive tendency toward overexpansion, leading the conquerors to press ever forward, almost blindly, regardless of the cost in blood and resources, before initiating a process of consolidation. This was often hard to achieve after expansion had been carried so far.

The British Empire might be cited as an example. Though it may be an oversimplification to say that the empire was won "in a fit of absent-mindedness," it would be hard to describe the process as motivated by a set ideology. To India, in particular, the British originally went not to impose dogma but to earn profits; for a century and a half they clung to their status as humble petitioners of the Mogul Emperor and his viceroys. They were servants not of the English monarch but of the East India Company of London, governed by a board of directors; they, in turn, were chosen by shareholders who sought dividends rather than domains and who were opposed to military involvement. But in the long term, the British had little alternative but to impose direct rule on province after province in order to protect that trade. This initially protective approach became an imperative. Clive's decisive victory at Plassey in 1757 over forces backed by the

French marked the outset of an inexorable process of conquest; dominion, once acquired, as a final resort can often only be defended by gaining yet more dominion. By the second half of the nineteenth century, British expansionism had gained a momentum of its own, resulting in a vast but somewhat purposeless acquisition of countless other territories, large and small, throughout the globe.

Conrad and Demarest may be accurate in insisting that both the Inca and the Aztec Empires became overextended. As the authors imply, such expansion may surely be seen as having developed a momentum of its own, offering little in terms of any corresponding material or spiritual rewards. The Ecuadorian campaigns, reportedly involving crippling losses, convulsed the whole fabric of empire and upset its equilibrium. As we have already seen, incentives for northern conquest were few. Salomon points to the favorable conditions prevailing in highland Ecuador for the cultivation of maize and to the possible mystico-religious significance for the Incas of its situation on the equatorial line, but he agrees that such incentives hardly compensated for the price in terms of blood and resources.[60]

Inca southward expansion, though less fully documented, might be viewed in almost similar terms; the resistance of the natives to any form of alien rule eventually may have almost borne comparison to the ferocity of those of Ecuador. The Incas encountered implacable opposition before some kind of border was established in central Chile; the Spaniards were to face comparable resistance. The Araucanians were among the first American Indians to adopt the horse, and in 1598 three hundred mounted warriors annihilated a Spanish force of comparable strength. In the extreme south they held out for centuries against the Spanish and subsequently against the forces of the Chilean republic, to whom they only finally surrendered their freedom in the 1890s.

The distances involved in advancing into central Chile were so immense that, were it not for archaeological proof of an Inca presence, some scholars might be tempted to dismiss reports of such feats as mere fables. As we have already seen, the ostensible attraction of Chile was its mining resources, but the Incas could have extracted similar or larger quantities of metal from mines much nearer home. The first Spaniards to arrive in the Potosí region of Bolivia were surprised to note that the Incas extracted metal only during the warmer months of the year; it was left to the conquerors to greatly intensify work in existing mines, apart from the vastly more productive silver mines that they were quick to discover. According to Jean Berthelot, scouts sent by Pizarro in 1533 were told that at the Chuquiago mines in Bolivia a mere fifty men and women were employed, at times even fewer. At another center, Carabaya, the mines were merely worked in summer when their fields did not require the Indians' presence.[61]

Hence, in seeking motives for imperial expansion, sheer greed, in terms of the search for ever greater material wealth, surely played its part but can hardly be viewed as a sole determinative goal. Perhaps a compulsive tendency to indulge in overexpansion applied as much to the Incas as to other empires. Salomon, in writing of Ecuador, describes the forward momentum of the Inca frontier as a precondition to the pacification of areas farther to the rear. Such expansion, often involving immense costs (as in the Imbabura area, in which the epic battle of Yahuarcocha was fought, and in Chile), was the price of consolidating military efforts already expended. The alternative, the hermetic sealing off of a static boundary, does not seem to have been attempted.[62]

An Untimely End

Of the tale of doom and disaster that befell the Inca Empire when confronted with invaders from another world, poignant details survive. In some respects, the Inca collapse followed the Aztec pattern a decade earlier; in others, the course of events differed. In particular, the pitiful and parallel fates of their respective rulers have been recounted and reenacted in every detail; improbable versions of their small talk have been confected to enrich the dialogue of dramas, novels, motion pictures, and even operas inspired by their misfortunes.

One may concur that these empires, having enjoyed a similar life span, were facing comparable problems at the time they were overthrown. However, the premise that even if no Spanish invasion had occurred their days were numbered is surely more open to question. The Incas' capability for long-term survival if no such invasion had taken place may be a strictly hypothetical subject; it is nonetheless relevant, as it poses the fundamental question as to whether their achievement, in terms of human history, represented an advance over what had gone before in the central Andes or whether it was nothing but a passing phenomenon, a bubble that was soon to be burst in any event.

Every empire inevitably must have an end as well as a beginning. In Arnold Toynbee's terminology, familiar to all historians, civilizations ultimately engender universal states, subject to a somewhat predictable but fairly long, drawn-out process of rise and fall. It may be worth adding that most Old World empires did enjoy a fairly prolonged life span. To cite one example, Josef Vogt writes of the existence of a state of crisis in the ancient world, ruled by Rome, in about A.D. 200. By the time Diocletian became emperor in A.D. 284, Vogt claims, the situation was " desperate."[63] But that empire endured for yet another two centuries before the last emperor was deposed by the Goths in A.D. 476. Meanwhile the empire of the new, or second, Rome, Constantinople, survived for almost another thousand years, until it was overthrown in A.D. 1453 by the Turks; their empire, in its turn, was to live on into our own century!

As I have proposed in another context, it is hard to say whether the Aztecs could have overcome the problems of overexpansion if no Spaniards had arrived. But estimates of the potential life span of such empires often fail to take into account another factor: Their trajectory does not always follow a consistent curve. Established empires may have their ups and downs, enjoying more than one peak period of power before the ultimate collapse. Of this, I propose Assyria as an example. After the thirteenth century B.C., Assyria had conquered the Babylonian Empire. After succumbing once more to Babylon two centuries later, Assyria acquired in the eighth and ninth centuries B.C. an empire more extensive than the first.[64]

Though predicting the possible future of an Inca Empire that was spared the Spanish onslaught is obviously a speculative exercise, it is surely worth suggesting that any survival of Inca power need not automatically presuppose the maintenance of the notably elongated domain of 1532. After the conclusion of the civil war, the situation in Ecuador might have become stabilized, at a time when the Chilean frontier region was apparently also more settled. But given the unwieldy proportions of an empire stretching from northern Ecuador to central Chile, it is surely not inconceivable that at one end or the other of this extended line of provinces some territory could eventually have been yielded without any calamitous effect on the economic or political stability of the whole fabric.

Though the tendency toward a disputed succession may have been the Achilles' heel of the Inca Empire, in other respects, such as the massive infrastructure and the well-established systems of control, it was held together by certain bonds, not altogether shared by the Aztec realm, that endowed it with innate strength. Many of these subject peoples, though they had lost their independence, were perhaps not wholly unmindful of benefits derived from the infrastructure created by the Empire, which served to increase the production of food and raw materials, part of which were used locally.

Given the Incas' fairly stubborn resistance to the Spaniards, which lasted for decades before it was finally extinguished, they could surely have faced up to any sporadic uprisings among their own conquered peoples almost indefinitely if the Europeans had not arrived. Aside from any such speculation as to its inherent solidity, the Inca realm was without question a stupendous achievement, deserving to rank high in the annals of empire building throughout the world. Its memory survives not as an overromanticized enigma but as a supreme triumph of human genius over the challenge of some of the harshest conditions to be found on our planet.

Appendix A

A Résumé of the Campaigns of Tupac Inca and Huayna Capac as Related by Sarmiento de Gamboa and Cabello de Balboa

Tupac Inca

	Sarmiento de Gamboa		Cabello de Balboa
p. 118	Tupac named successor to Pachacutec. Sets out for Chinchasuyu. Names two generals: Anqui Yupanqui and Tilca Yupanqui.	p. 318	Tupac, named successor to Pachacutec, takes road to Chinchasuyu. Names as captains Topa Capac (his brother), Auqui Yupanqui, and Tillca Yupanqui.
p. 119	In "Province of the Quechuas" takes forts Tohara, Cayara, and Curamba. In the "Province of Angaraes" takes forts Urcocolla and Guayllatucara and captures chieftain Chuquis Guaman. After expedition from Cajamarca against kingdom of Chimor in Pacsamayo Valley, Tupac goes to province of the Cañaris.	p. 319	In "Province of the Quechuas" takes forts Toara, Cayara, and Curamba; in "Province of Angaraes" takes forts Orcolla and Guaila Tucara. Chieftain Chuquisguaman captured. Proceeds to Cajamarca and launches expedition against Chimo Capac, a kingdom irrigated by the Río Pacaz Mayo.
p. 121	Tupac then proceeds to Tumebamba and captures Pisar Capac.	p. 320	Tupac fights the Paltas (in Ecuador) and proceeds to Tumebamba, where he captures Pisar

			Capac. Builds forts in Azuay, Pomallacta, and Quichi Caxa (not mentioned by Sarmiento).
pp. 122–123	Defeats Quitos and Cañaris and builds fort at Guachalla on his march toward the ocean, where he defeats the Huancavilcas and conquers Manta, Tumbez, and the island of Puná.	p. 322	After subduing the Cañaris and Quitos, builds fort at Guachalla on his advance toward the seacoast, where he occupies Manta, Charapoto, and Piquaza.
pp. 124–125	Builds many rafts *(balsas)* and makes expedition lasting nine months to islands of Auachumbi and Ninachumbi. On return, sends expedition against Chimor (Trujillo) and returns to Cuzco.	p. 323	Using many rafts *(balsas)*, makes expedition lasting one year to islands of Haguachumbi and Nina Chumbi. Sends expedition against Chimo Capac.
		pp. 325–333	Digressions on Lambayeque and on dynastic feuds (not in Sarmiento).
pp. 128–130	Makes expedition to Antisuyu, enters Andes via Aguatona, and names two captains (Otorongo Achachi and Chalco Yupanqui).	p. 334	Expedition to Antisuyu accompanied by Topa Yupanqui (brother), Otorongo Achachi, and Apoc Chalco Yupanqui.
p. 130	After suffering great casualties Tupac conquers four "great nations" — Opataries, Manosuyo, Yanaximes, and Chunchos — and then attacks the Chiponauas.	p. 335	Suffered great hardships but conquered four provinces: Opitarisuyo, Mamansuyo, Chunchos, and Chipomaguas.
p. 131	Expedition to Collao; names as captains Achachi, Conde Yupangui, Larico, and Quigual	p. 336	Expedition to Collao. Names captains Gualpac, Alarico, Cuyuchi, and Achachi. Takes four

	Topa. Takes four forts — Llallaua, Asilli, Arapa, and Pucara — and captures their commanders (Chuchachucay, Pachacuti, and Coaquiri).		forts: Pucara, Asillo, Arapa, Lana. Captures *caciques* Chuca Chuca and Chasuti Coaquiri.
	Proceeds to Chile, fights chieftain Michimalongo, reaches Coquimbo and Río Maule. Discovers gold and silver mines (unnamed).	p. 337	Proceeds to Chile and reaches Coquimbo. Discovers rich mines of Porco and Tarapaca.
p. 132	Suppresses rising in Chachapoyas.	p. 338	Goes to Xauxa, then down to Pachacamac and Chincha, thence via Cajamarca to pacify Chachapoyas.
		pp. 341–347	Digression on events in Europe and Africa.
p. 133	Goes to Yanacayo.	p. 347	Goes to Yanacayo. After long digression, Tupac's death mentioned on page 356.
pp. 136–137	Builds Cuzco fortress and dies.		

Huayna Capac

	Sarmiento de Gamboa		Cabello de Balboa
p. 141	Huayna Capac attacks and defeats the Chachapoyas.	p. 361	*Some* reports say Huayna Capac campaigned against the Chachapoyas.
p. 142	Sends his uncle, Guaman Achachi, to Quito and himself proceeds to Charcas via Collao and then on to Chile. Goes via Coquimbo and Copiapo to Arequipa. Goes to Antisuyu, settles *mitimaes* in Cochabamba, and goes to Pocona, a fort built by his father. Thence to Tihuanaco, where he instructs the Urus to fish in the lake.	p. 362	Reports also exist that he went to Collao. Attacks Chiriguanos, thence to Cochabamba, where he settles *mitimaes.* Thence to Pocona, where he terminates the fort built by his father. From there to Lake Titicaca where he instructs the Urus on fishing.
p. 143	Huayna Capac prepares to leave for Quito. Appoints Guaman Achachi (uncle) governor of Cuzco and names Michi and Auqui Topa generals for the campaign. Reaches Tumebamba and constructs great buildings. Sends expedition against Pastos, commanded by Auqui Topa and Colla Topa, of the lineage of Viracocha Inca, assisted by two captains from Collao and two from Condesuyu, Apo Cautar and Conde Mollo. The Pastos surprise the Incas and inflict great casualties before they are defeated.	pp. 363–367	Returns to Cuzco, leaves (uncle) Apoc Larquita as governor, and names as generals Mihi and Auqui Topa. Proceeds to Tumebamba, where he erects great buildings. (Cabello gives description of buildings not included in Sarmiento text.) Sends expedition to Pastos commanded by two captains from Collao, by two from Condesuyu (Apoc Cauzar and Cuntimollo), and by two Incas, Auqui Topa and Colla Topa, descendants of Inca Viracocha. Pastos eventually defeated after Incas have suffered great losses due to their own negligence. Cuntimollo killed.

p. 144	Huayna Capac returns to Tumebamba, mounts expedition, and conquers Macas, Quisna, the people of Ancamarca, and provinces of Puruuay and Nolitria. After short excursion to Tumbez, turns against Caranquis and Cochisquis. Cayambis sally from fort and defeat Incas. Huayna Capac falls to the ground. Huayna Capac returns to Tumebamba.	pp. 368–370	Huayna Capac goes to Tumebamba, campaigns first against Puruaes, Angamarcas, Tomaveles, Sicchos, Lactaccumgas, and others. Reaches Cochisqi fort. After initial defeat, conquers Cochisquis. War against Caranquis. Huayna Capac falls to the ground. Caranquis defeated in counterattack. After building forts, ruler returns to Tumebamba.
p. 145	Some *orejones* dissent and threaten to return to Cuzco (*short* description). Cayambis defeat Inca force. Auqui Topa attacks Cayambi fort. He is killed after forcing entry to four successive walls.	pp. 371–377	Long description of discord among *orejones* who say they will go back to Cuzco. Huayna Capac eventually appeases them with gifts. Auqui Topa attacks Caranqui fort. After he has scaled four out of five ramparts of a fort, he is killed.
		pp. 379–380	Digression on Columbus.
p. 146	Cayambis retire to fortress. They eventually make a sortie and are defeated. Many perish in a lagoon called Yahuarcocha.	pp. 381–382	Incas besiege Caranqui fort. Caranquis make sortie and are routed. Many drown in lagoon called Yahuarcocha.
p. 147	Cayambi chief, Pinto, escapes but is captured, flayed, and made into a drum.	pp. 382–383	Caranqui captain, Pinto, escapes but is caught, flayed, and made into a drum.
p. 148	War against the wild Chiriguanos, who have invaded province of Charcas. Yasca sent from Cuzco; defeats Chiriguanos, rebuilds forts, leaves garrison, and sends prisoners to Huayna Capac in Quito.	pp. 384–385	The savage Chiriguanos revolt. Yasca goes via Cochabamba and defeats them. Leaves garrison in fortress and sends prisoners to Huayna Capac in Quito.

p. 149	Huayna Capac leaves Tumebamba for campaign to Río Angasmayo. Army suffers great hardship and thirst before achieving victory.	p. 385	Huayna Capac marches northward to Pessillo Pucara and to Rumichacha. Reaches Río Angasamayo. Surrounded by savage Indians in mountains. Troops nearly die of thirst but finally defeat enemy.
p. 149	Huayna Capac proceeds to seacoast; visits island of Puná and Guancabilica.	p. 393	Huayna Capac visits Puná, sends force to Guanor Villca, crosses Guayaquil River, returns to Quito. His uncle, Apoc Yllaquita, and his brother, Auqui Topa, have died of pestilence. Huayna Capac falls ill and dies.
p. 150	Huayna Capac returns to Quito, where his two governors, his uncle, Hilaquita, and his brother, Auqui Topa, have died of pestilence. Huayna Capac dies, possibly of smallpox.		

Notes

Chapter 1: In Search of the Past

1. Pease, "Notas Sobre Historia," 95–6.
2. Wedin, "El Concepto," 39.
3. Cieza, *Señorío*, 47.
4. Ibid., 45–6.
5. Ascher, *Code of the Quipu*, 62–7.
6. *Declaración*, 21, 23.
7. Cieza, *Señorío*, 44.
8. Baudin, *A Socialist Empire.*
9. Xerez, *Verdadera Relación*, 228, 233, 248.
10. Pizarro, *Relación*, 501.
11. Wedin, "El Concepto," 54–73.
12. Pease, "Las Fuentes," 51–9.
13. Zuidema, "The Origin," 733.
14. Salomon, *Native Lords*, 7.
15. Baudin, *A Socialist Empire*, 207.
16. Means, *Ancient Civilizations.*
17. Valcárcel, *Historia*, 182.
18. Rowe, "An Introduction."
19. Uhle, *Pachacamac.*
20. Bingham, *Machu Picchu.*
21. Rowe, Collier, and Willey, "Reconnaissance."
22. Bennett, "Excavations."
23. Bushnell, *Peru*, passim.
24. Isbell, "City and State," 172–3.
25. Isbell, "El Origen," 67.
26. Isbell, "City and State," 184–5.
27. Isbell, "Huari Urban Prehistory," 107.
28. Lumbreras, *The Peoples and Cultures*, 177.
29. Isbell, "City and State," 172–3.
30. Cook, "Aspects," 164.
31. Rowe, "Inca Culture," 295.
32. Cabello, *Miscelánea*, chapters 20–2.
33. Plaza Schuller, *La Incursión*, 38–9.
34. Zuidema, *The Ceque System.*
35. Murra, *Formaciones*, 279–80.

36. Lévi-Strauss, *La Pensée*, 25–7.
37. Oakeshott, *Experience*, 204.
38. Sahlins, *Islands*, 154.

Chapter 2: The First of the Incas

1. Eliade, *Myth and Reality*, 13, 19.
2. Betanzos, *Suma y Narración*, 13.
3. Cieza, *Señorío*, 18–9.
4. Sarmiento, *Historia*, 35–40.
5. Garcilasco, *Primera Parte de los Comentarios*, Book I, chapter 15.
6. Kubler, "Written Sources," 200.
7. Gómara, *Historia*, 200.
8. Rostworowski, *Etnía y Sociedad*, 141–54.
9. Kubler, "Written Sources," 199–203.
10. Wedin, "El Concepto," 87.
11. Ixtlilxóchitl, *Obras*, II, 23–5.
12. Demarest, "Viracocha," 52–3.
13. Rowe, "The Origins," 414–5.
14. Eliade, *Myth and Reality*, 8.
15. Garcilasco, *Comentarios*, Book IV, chapter 3.
16. Puhvel, *Comparative Mythology*, 2.
17. Pease, "Las Fuentes," 67.
18. Dumézil, *The Destiny*, 3.
19. Dumézil, *L' Héritage*, 106.
20. Rowe, "Absolute Chronology," 267.
21. Garcilasco, *Primera Parte de los Comentarios*, Book II, chapter 20; Book III, chapter 2.
22. Rowe, "Absolute Chronology," 270.
23. Cieza, *Señorío*, 67–8; Sarmiento, *Historia*, chapter 3; Cabello, *Miscelánea*, chapter 9.
24. Sarmiento, *Historia*, 59–60.
25. Cieza, *Señorío*, 122; Cobo, *History*, 116.
26. Cieza, *Señorío*, 132; Sarmiento, *Historia*, 75–7.
27. Sarmiento, *Historia*, 64; Cobo, *History*, 115.
28. Cieza, *Señorío*, 119; Cobo, *History*, 113.
29. Cieza, *Señorío*, 130.
30. Sarmiento, *Historia*, 65–7; Cabello, *Miscelánea*, 284–6; Cobo, *History*, 119–20.
31. Sarmiento, *Historia*, 69–70; Cabello, *Miscelánea*, 293–4.
32. Urton, *Pacariqtambo*, 3, 31.
33. Rowe, "Inca Culture," 198–9.
34. Gonzáles Corrales, "La Arquitectura," 197–8.
35. Bauer, *Development*, 24, 41, 141.
36. Moseley, *The Incas*, 244.
37. Davies, *The Aztec Empire*, chapter 1; Van Zantwijk, *The Aztec Arrangement*, chapter 3.
38. Métraux, *The History*, 42.

39. Zuidema, *Inca Dynasty,* 197–8.
40. Zuidema, "Myth and History," 173.
41. Rostworowski, *Pachacutec,* 24.
42. Moseley, "Structure," 24.
43. Rostworowski, "Ethnohistorical Considerations," 449.
44. Sarmiento, *Historia*, 83.
45. Rostworowski, *Estructuras*, 131–2.
46. Murra, "Una Apreciación," 26.
47. *Relaciones Geográficas*, I, 166–9.
48. Rostworowski, *Estructuras*, 131–2.
49. Zuidema, *Inca Dynasty,* 180.
50. Zuidema, "El Ushnu."
51. Duviols, La Dinastía, 68–76.
52. Wedin, *El Concepto,* 77.
53. Cieza, *Señorío,* 121.
54. Duviols, "La Dinastía," 79.
55. Bandera, *Relación*, 496.
56. Sarmiento, *Historia*, 43, 140; Cabello, *Miscelánea*, 306.
57. Huaman Poma, *Nueva Corónica*, I, 119, 130.
58. Ellefsen, "La División," 24–5.
59. Rostworowski, *Estructuras*, 139.
60. Sarmiento, *Historia*, 94.
61. Betanzos, *Suma y Narración*, 85.
62. Rostworowski, *Estructuras*, 141–5.
63. Rowe, "Inca Culture," 253–5.
64. Zuidema, "El Ayllu," 408–11.
65. Rostworowski, *Estructuras*, 146.
66. Zuidema, *The Ceque System*, chapter 4.
67. Zuidema, *Inca Dynasty,* 191–4.
68. Cabello, *Miscelánea*, 269.
69. Sarmiento, *Historia*, 58–9.
70. Brundage, *Empire,* 13–5.
71. Toledo, *Informaciones*, 132–3.
72. Cieza, *Señorío,* 122; Sarmiento, *Historia*, 66; Cabello, *Miscelánea*, 284.
73. Toledo, *Informaciones*, 137.
74. Rostworowski, *Los Ayarmacas*, 2.
75. Ibid., 22–3.
76. Ibid., 14.
77. Sarmiento, *Historia*, 81, 99.
78. Rowe, "What Kind," 59–63.
79. Rowe, "Inca Culture," 203.
80. Rostworowski, "Reflexiones," 351.
81. Pease, "Las Fuentes," 87.

Chapter 3: The Era of Pachacutec

1. Rostworowski, *Pachacutec*, 61.
2. Sarmiento, *Historia*, 109.
3. Cabello, *Miscelánea*, 317–8.
4. Cobo, *History*, 133.
5. Rostworowski, *Pachacutec*, 35.
6. Cieza, *Señorío*, 136.
7. Ibid., 139.
8. Rostworowski, *Tawantinsuyu*, 52.
9. Sarmiento, *Historia*, 52.
10. Cobo, *History*, 132.
11. Ibid., 128.
12. Cieza, *Señorío*, 152–7.
13. Sarmiento, *Historia*, 91; Cabello, *Miscelánea*, 301.
14. Murúa, *Historia General*, 68, 110.
15. Cobo, *History*, 137.
16. Cieza, *Señorío*, 162–3.
17. Rostworowski, *Pachacutec*, 84.
18. Cieza, *Señorío*, 166.
19. Ibid., 165.
20. Ibid., 159.
21. Schaedel, "Formation," 113–4.
22. Rostworowski, *Pachacutec*, 26, 41.
23. *Relaciones Geográficas*, I, 171.
24. Cieza, *Señorío*, 136.
25. Lumbreras, "Sobre los Chancas," 216.
26. Ibid., 236–7.
27. Rowe, "Inca Culture," 204.
28. Cieza, *Señorío*, 161–6.
29. Sarmiento, *Historia*, 86; Betanzos, *Suma y Narración*, 32; Santacruz Pachacuti, "Relación," 238.
30. Betanzos, *Suma y Narración*, 27–47.
31. Sarmiento, *Historia*, 91.
32. Sarmiento, *Historia*, 84–5; Cabello, *Miscelánea*, 299; Cieza, *Señorío*, 160; Betanzos, *Suma y Narración*, 43.
33. Sarmiento, *Historia*, 90; Cabello, *Miscelánea*, 300.
34. Garcilasco, *Comentarios*, Book IV, chapter 21.
35. Ibid., Book V, chapters 19–23.
36. Ibid., Book IV, chapter 22.
37. Cobo, *History*, 26–7.
38. Ibid., 132.
39. *Declaración*, 16.
40. Rowe, "Inca Culture," 203.
41. Rostworowski, *Pachacutec*, 114.

42. Rostworowski, "Reflexiones," 350–1.
43. Betanzos, *Suma y Narración*, 49–53.
44. Loredo, *Los Repartos*, 42–3.
45. Garcilasco, *Comentarios*, Book III, chapter 21.
46. Betanzos, *Suma y Narración*, 59–60.
47. Cieza, *Señorío*, 181.
48. Hyslop, *Inca Road System*, 67.
49. Schaedel, "Formation," 116–8.
50. Rostworowski, "Nuevos Datos," 130–4.
51. Rowe, "Inca Culture," 261.
52. Rostworowski, *Los Ayamarcas*, 15–6.
53. Rostworowski, *Pachacutec*, 131–2.
54. Rowe, "Origins," 414.
55. Demarest, "Viracocha," 6.
56. Ibid., 17.
57. Ibid., 18–41.
58. Ibid., 45–50.
59. Pease, "Las Fuentes," 66.
60. Sarmiento, *Historia*, 100–110.
61. Sarmiento, *Historia*, 104–5; Cabello, *Miscelánea*, 305–6.
62. Cieza, *Señorío*, 186.
63. Cobo, *History*, 141.
64. Hyslop, "El Area," 56–7.
65. Sarmiento, *Historia*, 107.
66. Cieza, *Señorío*, 177.
67. Sarmiento, *Historia*, 106–8; Cabello, *Miscelánea*, 317–9.
68. Cobo, *History*, 142.
69. Cabello, *Miscelánea*, 318–37.
70. Sarmiento, *Historia*, 120–5.
71. Katz, *Ancient*, 297.
72. Murra, "Inca Political Structure," 31–2.
73. Conklin, "Information," passim.
74. Cobo, *History*, 128.
75. Cieza, *Señorío*, 150–1.
76. Garcilasco, *Comentarios*, Book VI, chapter 34.
77. Rostworowski, *Pachacutec*, 204.
78. Murra, "Inca Political Structure," 31.
79. Zuidema, "El Puente," 322.
80. Zuidema, "Myth and History," 173.
81. Zuidema, "Inca Dynasty," 194.
82. Pease, "Las Fuentes," 42–3.
83. Murúa, *Historia General*, 105.
84. Eliade, *Myth and Reality*, chapter 1.
85. Pease, "Las Fuentes," 66.
86. Ibid., 68–70.
87. Wedin, *La Cronología*, 15.

88. Ibid., 58, 61.
89. Ibid., 48–9.
90. Sahlins, *Islands*, 35–6.

Chapter 4: The Last Conquerors

1. Garcilasco, *Primera Parte de los Comentarios*, Book VIII, chapters 1–6.
2. Betanzos, *Suma y Narración*, 157.
3. Huaman Poma, *Nueva Corónica*, I, 114.
4. Garcilasco, *Primera Parte de los Comentarios*, Book IX, chapters 1–14; Betanzos, *Suma y Narración*, Part I, chapter 48.
5. Betanzos, *Suma y Narración*, 192, 199.
6. Cieza, *Crónica*, 121–4.
7. Salomon, *Native Lords*, 146–7.
8. Larrea, "La Cultura," 29.
9. Plaza Schuller, *La Incursión*, 21; Pizarro, *Relación*, 474.
10. Cobo, *History*, 186.
11. Romoli de Avery, "Las Tribus," 26–7.
12. Murra, "Historic Tribes," 786.
13. Cabello, *Miscelánea*, 384.
14. Uribe, "Asentamientos," 60–83.
15. Cabello, *Miscelánea*, 380–2.
16. Murra, "Historic Tribes," 809; Hyslop, *Inca Road System*, 35.
17. Cieza, *Señorío*, 229.
18. Cieza, *Crónica*, 130–2.
19. Cabello, *Miscelánea*, 393.
20. Cobo, *History*, 159.
21. Rostworowski, "Ethnohistorical," 450–1, 457.
22. Casevitz, "Las Fronteras," 118–21.
23. Saignes, "El Piedemonte," 154–6.
24. Cabello, *Miscelánea*, 336; Sarmiento, *Historia*, 142.
25. Cieza, *Crónica*, 222.
26. Raffino, *Los Inkas*, 280.
27. León, "Expansión," 97–100.
28. Idrovo, "Tomebamba," 94–5.
29. Dillehay and Netherly, *La Frontera*.
30. Hyslop, "Las Fronteras Extremas," 35–58.
31. Ibid., 49.
32. lbid., 41.
33. Saignes, "El Piedemonte," 154–67.
34. Strube, "Vialidad," 24–6, 33–8, 51–4.
35. Raffino, *El Imperio*, 77–82.
36. Ibid., 102.
37. Hyslop, "Las Fronteras Extremas," 43.

38. Ibid., 44.
39. Bibar, *Crónica y Relación*, 91, 137.
40. Silva Galdames, "Donde Estuvo," 45–8.
41. Dillehay, "La Actividad," 228–38.
42. Means, *Ancient Civilizations*, 228–38.
43. Means, "Biblioteca Andina," 436–7.
44. Rowe, "Absolute Chronology," 269–73.
45. Ibid., 267–8.
46. Larrea, "La Cultura," 18–9.
47. Rowe, "Absolute Chronology," 276.
48. Wedin, "El Concepto," 135.
49. Wedin, *La Cronología*, 26–9.
50. Salomon, "Vertical Politics," 90–2.
51. Meyers, "Die Inka," 180–2.
52. Cieza, *Crónica*, 143–4.
53. Pease, "Las Fuentes," 108.
54. Salomon, *Native Lords*, 145.
55. Bauer, *Development*, 8.
56. Zuidema, "Dynastic Structures," 503.
57. Topic, "Territorial Expansion," 192.
58. Barlow, "Extent," 45–84.
59. *Declaración*, 5.
60. Hemming, *Conquest*, 259.
61. Toledo, *Informaciones*, 122–7.
62. Hemming, *Conquest*, 339.
63. Espinosa Soriano, "Las Colonias," 241–2.
64. Salomon, "Vertical Politics," 102.
65. Pease, *Los Últimos*, 42, 56.
66. Chaumeuil, "La Canela," 58.
67. Saignes, "El Piedemonte," 158.

Chapter 5: The Inca State

1. Cobo, *History*, 185.
2. Pizarro, *Relación*, 501.
3. Cieza, *Señorío*, 102.
4. Ibid., 103.
5. Cobo, *History*, 248.
6. Estete, *Noticia*, 391–9.
7. Zuidema, "El Ushnu," 325–7.
8. Duviols, *Un Inédit*, 24.
9. Sancho de la Hoz, *Relación*, 328–31.
10. McEwan, *Middle Horizon*, 23, 68.
11. Betanzos, *Suma y Narración*, 75, 77.

12. Zuidema, "Guaman Poma," 179.
13. Rostworowski, *Pachacutec*, 170.
14. Kendall, *Everyday Life*, 113.
15. Calvo, *La Traza*, 134–5.
16. Cieza, *Crónica*, 215.
17. Rowe, "What Kind," 60.
18. Demarest, "Viracocha," 45–6.
19. Cobo, *History*, 187.
20. Conrad and Demarest, *Religion*, 172–3.
21. Castro and Ortega, *Relación*, 480.
22. Rostworowski, "Succession," 420.
23. Santillán, *Historia*, 387.
24. Rostworowski, "Succession," 419–20.
25. Cieza, *Señorío*, 136.
26. Rostworowski, "Succession," 422.
27. Sarmiento, *Historia*, 137–9.
28. Cabello, *Miscelánea*, 358–60.
29. Ziólkowski, "El Sapan," 59–60.
30. Ibid., 61, 67.
31. Cobo, *History*, 211.
32. Polo de Ondegardo, *Relación*, 127.
33. Murra, *La Organización*, 66–7, 74.
34. Rostworowski, "Nuevos Datos," 130–4.
35. Rostworowski, "Las Tierras," 32.
36. Moore, *Power and Property*, 47.
37. Santillán, *Historia*, 417; Cieza, *Señorío*, 53.
38. Murra, *La Organización*, 53.
39. *Relaciones Geográficas*, I, 338.
40. Betanzos, *Suma y Narración*, 77.
41. Garcilasco, *Comentarios*, Book VII, chapter I.
42. Cobo, *History*, 208–9.
43. Sarmiento, *Historia*, 88.
44. Ibid., 118, 125, 129.
45. Ibid., 112.
46. Ibid., 142.
47. Sarmiento, *Historia*, 141, 143; Cabello, *Miscelánea*, 361; Cobo, *History*, 203.
48. Kirchhoff, "Social," 54.
49. Katz, *Ancient*, 285.
50. Schaedel, "Early State," 302.
51. Huaman Poma, *Nueva Corónica*, I, 130.
52. Bandera, *Relación*, 495–6.
53. Gibson, *Inca Concept*, 43.
54. Murúa, *Historia*, 206, 209.
55. Moore, *Power and Property*, 111.
56. Murra, *Formaciones*, 225–33.
57. Choy, "Desarollo," 90–1.

58. Rostworowski, *Etnía y Sociedad*, 35.
59. Cabello, *Miscelánea*, 368.
60. Hyslop, *Inca Road System*, 2–3.
61. Ibid., 317.
62. Ibid., 301.
63. Morris, "From Principles," 478–85.
64. Murra, *Formaciones*, 23.
65. Schaedel, "Early State," 301–6.
66. Murra, *Formaciones*, 182–3; Ramírez, "The Inca Conquest," 509–10.
67. Wedin, "El Concepto," 36–7.
68. Cieza, *Señorío*, 46.
69. Murra, *La Organización*, 225.
70. Ascher, *Code*, 14–5, 32–3.
71. Ibid., 53.
72. Murra, *Formaciones*, 23–43.
73. Murra, "Expansion," 52.
74. Santillán, *Historia*, 402–3.
75. Cieza, *Señorío*, 66–71.
76. Moore, *Power and Property*, 66.
77. Rowe, "What Kind," 62.
78. Cieza, *Señorío*, 87.
79. Espinosa Soriano, "Los Chambillas," 421–5.
80. Murra, *Organización*, 253–4.
81. Cieza, *Señorío*, 57–9.
82. Rostworowski, "Pescadores," 325.
83. Morris, "From Principles," 478–83.

Chapter 6: The Empire and Its Infrastructure

1. Morris, "From Principles," 478.
2. Lumbreras, "Acerca de la Aparición," 103.
3. Ibid., 107.
4. Schaedel, "Formation," 113.
5. Julien, *Hatunqolla*, 41.
6. Murra, *Formaciones*, 193, 208.
7. Julien, *Hatunqolla*, 256.
8. Hyslop, "El Area," 61–4.
9. Castelli, "Dioses," 111.
10. Cieza, *Señorío*, 187.
11. Cobo, *History*, 139.
12. Cieza, *Señorío*, 210.
13. Netherly, "El Reino," 112.
14. Cieza, *Crónica*, 183–4.
15. Cieza, *Señorío*, 212–3.

16. Shady Solis, "La Cultura," 58–9.
17. Pizarro, *Relación*, 478.
18. Xerez, *Verdadera*, 248.
19. Cieza, *Crónica*, 207; Cobo, *History*, 161.
20. Rostworowski, *Etnía y Sociedad*, 26–33.
21. Ibid., 214.
22. Day, "Storage," 335.
23. Hyslop, *Inca Road System*, 39.
24. Rowe, "Kingdom," 28–40.
25. Kolata, "Urban Concept," 137.
26. Ibid., 138.
27. Cabello, *Miscelánea*, 327–30.
28. Donnan, "An Assessment," 243–5.
29. Ibid., 268–70.
30. Keatinge and Conrad, "Imperialist Expansion," 261.
31. Conrad, "Burial Platforms."
32. Day, "Storage," 338.
33. Cabello, *Miscelánea*, 331–3; Cieza, *Senorío*, 206.
34. Schaedel, "City," 26.
35. Rowe, "Kingdom," 40–7.
36. Hyslop, *Inca Road System*, 40.
37. Netherly, "El Reino," 118.
38. Cieza, *Señorío*, 206.
39. Carrera, *Arte*, 8–9.
40. Hyslop, *Inca Road System*, 56–9.
41. Morris and Murra, "Dynastic," 273.
42. Morris and Thompson, "Huánuco," 352.
43. Morris, "Establecimientos Estatales," 132.
44. Ortiz de Zúñiga, *Visita*, 39.
45. Morris, "Huánuco Pampa," 150.
46. Morris and Murra, "Dynastic," 274.
47. Morris, "From Principles," 479.
48. Hyslop, *Inca Settlement Planning*, 40, 61, 69.
49. Bonavía, "Ecological Factors," 394–8.
50. Hyslop, *Inca Settlement Planning*, 255.
51. Dillehay, "Tawantinsuyu," 400–3.
52. Trimborn, "Archäologische Studien," 115; Byrne de Caballero, "Incarracay," 309.
53. Nordenskíöld, "Incallacta," 170, 174.
54. Gonzáles, "Inca Settlement," 358–9.
55. Hyslop, *Inca Road System*, 284.
56. Beck, "Ancient Roads."
57. Hyslop, *Inca Road System*, 272–4.
58. Ibid., 264–5.
59. Ibid., 257.
60. Ibid., 228–33.
61. Ibid., 317–34.

62. Ibid., 275–84.
63. Cieza, *Señorío*, 80.
64. Hyslop, *Inca Road System*, 309.
65. Cieza, *Crónica*, 104–5; Garcilasco, *Comentarios*, Book II, chapter 3.
66. Moseley, *The Incas*, 163.
67. Raffino, *Los Inkas*, 258.
68. González, "Inca Settlement," 350.
69. Polo de Ondegardo, *Relación*, 98.
70. Salomon, "Vertical Politics," 100.
71. Cieza, *Señorío*, 232–7; *Crónica*, 102–3.
72. Plaza Schuller, *La Incursión*, 115–7.
73. Ibid., 120.
74. Quiroga Ibarrola, "Ensayo," 38.
75. Ibid., 390–3.
76. Benson, *Mochica*, 22.
77. Xerez, *Verdadera*, 231–3.
78. Cieza, *Señorío*, 78, 91.
79. Gorenstein, "Differential Development," 96.
80. Trimborn, "Archäologische Studien," 10–1.
81. Cieza, *Señorío*, 73.
82. Rowe, "Inca Culture," 277.
83. Murra, "Expansion," 54.
84. Cieza, *Señorío*, 85.

Chapter 7: The Imperial System

1. Wedin, "El Concepto," 56–60.
2. Santillán, *Historia*, 381; Bandera, *Relación*, 495–6.
3. Wedin, *El Concepto*, 61–3.
4. "Relación del Origen," 77.
5. "Relación del Origen," 71; Bandera, *Relación*, 505.
6. Murra, *Organización*, 69–72.
7. Cieza, *Señorío*, 75–7.
8. *Relaciones Geográficas*, I, 177.
9. Murúa, *Historia General*, 206–7.
10. Polo de Ondegardo, *Los Errores*, 56.
11. Sarmiento, *Historia*, 101, 120, 132, 135.
12. Moore, *Power and Property*, 30–2.
13. Murra, *Organización*, 165–6.
14. Castro and Ortega, *Relación*, 83.
15. Bandera, *Relación*, 502–7.
16. Santillán, *Historia*, 385.
17. Sarmiento, *Historia*, 120–1, 132.
18. Cieza, *Señorío*, 70.

19. Murra, "Inca Political Structure," 33.
20. Murra, *Formaciones*, 172–3.
21. Murra, *Organización*, 178–81; *Formaciones*, 155.
22. Murra, *Formaciones*, 29–30.
23. Garcilasco, *Primera Parte de los Comentarios*, Book V, chapter 2.
24. Wachtel, *La Visión*, 112–4.
25. Cobo, *History*, 190.
26. Murra, *Organización*, 141.
27. Bandera, *Relación*, 507.
28. Cobo, *History*, 200.
29. Cieza, *Crónica*, 114.
30. Castro and Ortega, *Relación*, 485–6.
31. Bandera, *Relación*, 507.
32. Ibid., 505.
33. Garcilasco, *Primera Parte de los Comentarios*, Book VI, chapter 23.
34. Moore, *Power and Property*, 69.
35. Polo de Ondegardo, *Relación*, 135.
36. Murra, *Formaciones*, 191, 209.
37. Rostworowski, *Senoríos*, 91.
38. Rostworowski, *Estructuras*, 118, 124.
39. Laurencich-Minelli, "El Trabajo," 55.
40. Demarest, "Viracocha," 44.
41. Castro and Ortega, *Relación*, 488.
42. Cobo, *History*, 181; Cieza, *Señorío*, 65.
43. Cieza, *Crónica*, 122–3.
44. Cieza, *Señorío*, 89.
45. Toledo, *Informaciones*, xviii.
46. Salomon, *Native Lords*, 189.
47. Raffino, *Los Inkas*, 245.
48. Julien, *Hatunqolla*, 45, 50–1.
49. Menzel, "Inca Occupation," 127.
50. Dillehay, "Tawantinsuyu," 398.
51. Netherly, "El Reino," 118.
52. Hyslop, "El Area," 72.
53. Meyers, *Die Inka*, 181.
54. Stehberg, "La Fortaleza," 34.
55. Raffino, *Los Inkas*, 163–8.
56. Ibid., 169.
57. Moseley, *The Incas*, 74.
58. Cieza, *Crónica*, 122.
59. González, "Inca Settlement," 358–9.
60. Cobo, *History*, 211–3.
61. Murra, *Organización*, 63.
62. Ibid., 67.
63. Ibid., 72–3.
64. Moore, *Power and Property*, 30–1.

65. Schaedel, "Formation," 130.
66. Polo de Ondegardo, *Relación*, 58.
67. Bandera, *Relación*, 509.
68. González, "Inca Settlement," 344.
69. Niemayer, "La Ocupación," 182–3.
70. Berthelot, "Extraction," 71–3.
71. Lechtman, "Issues," 30–1.
72. Murra, *Organización*, 123–4.
73. *Relaciones Geográficas*, I, 338.
74. Murra, *Organización*, 126, 130.
75. Ibid., 94, 102.
76. Ibid., 93.
77. Murra, "Historic Tribes," 810.
78. Espinosa Soriano, "Los Mitmas," 353–7.
79. Cieza, *Señorío*, 85–7.
80. Cobo, *History*, 189–90.
81. Díez de San Miguel, *Visita*, 65–114.
82. Espinosa Soriano, "Los Mitmas," 355–7.
83. Wachtel, "Les Mitimas," 298–300.
84. Santillán, *Historia*, 400–2.
85. Cobo, *History*, 209–10.
86. Murra, *Organización*, 143–6.
87. Ibid., 161.
88. Murra, "New Data," 36.
89. Huaman Poma, *Nueva Corónica*, II, 28.
90. Espinosa Soriano, "Los Mitmas," 9–14.
91. Murra, *Organización*, 245–8.
92. Bandera, *Relación*, 496–8; Castro and Ortega, *Relación*, 479–80; Sarmiento, *Historia*, 132; Santillán, *Historia*, 382; Cobo, *History*, 198.
93. Murra, *Organización*, 154.
94. Moore, *Power and Property*, 49.
95. Cieza, *Señorío*, 76–7.
96. Morris, "Storage," 64.
97. Ibid., 61.
98. Huaman Poma, *Nueva Corónica*, I, 251.
99. Salomon, *Native Lords*, 170.
100. Flores Ochoa, *Pastoreo*, 181.
101. Murra, "El Control Vertical," passim.
102. Murra, *Formaciones*, 71–9.
103. Murra, Wachtel, and Revel, "Introduction," 4–5.
104. Salomon, "Vertical Politics," 106–9.
105. Oberem, "El Acceso," 54.
106. Murra, "Los Límites," 77.
107. Ibid., 78.
108. Moseley, *The Incas*, 46.
109. Pease, "Cases and Versions," 144.

110. Cieza, *Señorío*, 87.
111. Morris, "Storage," 67.
112. Rostworowski, *Etnía y Sociedad*, 96–140.
113. Cieza, *Crónica*, 241.
114. Murra, *Organización*, 198.
115. Ramírez, "Inca Conquest," 527.
116. Samano-Xerez, "Relación," 65–6.
117. Murra, *Organización*, 199–200.
118. Rostorowski, *Etnía y Sociedad*, 115.
119. Salomon, "Vertical Politics," 102.
120. Netherly, "El Reino," 112.
121. Ramírez, "Inca Conquest," 527–8.
122. Murra, *Organización*, 198.

Chapter 8: The Decline and Fall

1. Sarmiento, *Historia*, 150.
2. Cieza, *Señorío*, 250.
3. Betanzos, *Suma y Narración*, 31.
4. Sarmiento, *Historia*, 152–3.
5. Santacruz Pachacuti, "Relación," 267–8.
6. Cabello, *Miscelánea*, 396–407.
7. Cobo, *History*, 165.
8. Ibid., 166.
9. Sarmiento, *Historia*, 155–8; Cobo, *History*, 166.
10. Betanzos, *Suma y Narración*, 210.
11. Ibid., 237–45.
12. Ibid., 216.
13. Ibid., 250.
14. Huaman Poma, *Nueva Corónica*, I, 87.
15. Sarmiento, *Historia*, 164–5.
16. Ibid., 152.
17. Betanzos, *Suma y Narración*, 199.
18. Sarmiento, *Historia*, 152.
19. Betanzos, *Suma y Narración*, 210.
20. Cobo, *History*, 165.
21. Rostworowski, *Pachacutec*, 246–8.
22. Pease, *Los Ultimos*, 106–10.
23. Hemming, *Conquest*, 30.
24. Ibid., 31.
25. Estete, *Noticia*, 374–5.
26. *Relación Francesa*, 178.
27. Hemming, *Conquest*, 152–68.
28. Ibid., 179.

29. Ibid., 95–6.
30. Ibid., 127.
31. Estete, *Noticia*, 400.
32. Molina, *Conquista*, 340–3.
33. Hyslop, *Inca Settlement*, 148.
34. Pease, *Los Últimos*, 115.
35. Ibid., 107–9.
36. Betanzos, *Suma y Narración*, 221.
37. Ibid., 223.
38. Ibid., 264–5.
39. Hemming, *Conquest*, 114–5.
40. Davies, *The Aztecs*, 250.
41. Hemming, *Conquest*, 88.
42. Davies, *The Aztecs*, 258–61.
43. Finley, *Ancient*, 48.
44. Ibid., 49.
45. Ibid., 52.
46. Trigger, *Time and Traditions*, 38.
47. Davies, *Aztec Empire*, 4.
48. Himmelfarb, *New History*, 14.
49. Adams, *Evolution*, 34.
50. Hemming, *Conquest*, 488–94.
51. Topic, *Territorial Expansion*, 170, 180, 189.
52. Trigger, *Time and Traditions*, 42–5.
53. Conrad and Demarest, *Religion*, chapter 4.
54. Ibid., chapter 3.
55. Demarest, "Viracocha," 31–3.
56. Davies, *Aztec Empire*, 250.
57. Hyslop, *Inca Settlement*, 298.
58. Hemming, *Conquest*, 135.
59. Conrad, "Cultural Materialism," 3–10.
60. Salomon, personal communication.
61. Berthelot, "Extraction," 78–9.
62. Salomon, "Vertical Politics," 114–5.
63. Vogt, *Decline*, 72.
64. Davies, *Aztec Empire*, 292.

Bibliography

Acosta, Joseph de. 1962. *Historia Natural y Moral de las Indias.* Mexico City: Fondo de Cultura Económica.

Adams, Robert McC. 1966. *The Evolution of Urban Society.* Chicago: Aldine Publishing Company.

Ascher, Marcia, and Robert. 1978. *Code of the Quipu Databook.* Ann Arbor: University of Michigan Press.

Aveni, Anthony. 1981. "Horizon Astronomy in Incaic Cuzco." In *Archaeoastronomy in the Americas*, ed. Ray Williamson, pp. 305–15. Los Altos, CA: Ballena Press.

Bandera, Damián de la. 1968. *Relación.* Biblioteca Peruana, Primera Serie, Vol. 8, pp. 491–512. Lima: Editores Técnicos Asociados.

Barlow, R. H. 1949. *The Extent of the Empire of the Culhua Mexica.* Berkeley and Los Angeles: University of California Press.

Baudin, Louis. 1961. *A Socialist Empire: The Incas of Peru.* Princeton, NJ: Van Nostrand Reinhold.

Bauer, Brian S. 1992. *The Development of the Inca State.* Austin: University of Texas Press.

Beck, Coleen M. 1979. "Ancient Roads on the North Coast of Peru." Unpublished doctoral thesis, Department of Anthropology, University of California, Berkeley.

Bennett, Wendell C. 1936. "Excavations in Bolivia." Anthropological Papers of the American Museum of Natural History, Vol. 35, part 4, New York.

Benson, Elizabeth P. 1972. *The Mochica: A Culture of Peru.* New York: Praeger.

Berthelot, Jean. 1977. "Une Région Minière des Andes Péruviennes: Carabaya Inca et Espagnole (1480–1630)." Thesis, Ecole des Hautes Etudes, Université de Paris X, Nanterre.

———. 1986. "The Extraction of Precious Metals at the Time of the Inca." In *Anthropological History of Andean Polities*, eds. John V. Murra, Nathan Wachtel, and Jacques Revel, pp. 69–88. Cambridge and New York: Cambridge University Press.

Betanzos, Juán de, 1987. Suma y Narración de los Incas. Madrid: Atlas.

Bibar, Gerónimo de. 1966. *Crónica y Relación Copiosa y verdadera de los Paynos de Chile.* Santiago: Fondo Histórico y Bibliográfico José Torribio Medina.

Bingham, Hiram. 1930. *Machu Picchu — A Citadel of the Incas.* New Haven: National Geographic Society and Yale University Press.

Bonavía, Duccio. 1979. "Ecological Factors Affecting the Urban Transformation in the Last Centuries of the Pre-Columbian Era," in *Advances in Andean Archaeology*, ed. David L. Browman, pp. 393–410. Chicago: Aldine Press.

Brundage, Burr Cartwright. 1963. *Empire of the Inca*. Norman: University of Oklahoma Press.

Bushnell, Geoffrey. 1956. *Peru*. Ancient Peoples and Places Series. London: Thames and Hudson.

Byrne de Caballero, Geraldine. 1978. "Incarracay: Un Centro Administrativo Incáico." *Arte y Arqueología*, Vols. 5–6, pp. 309–16.

Cabello de Balboa, Miguel. 1951. *Miscelánea Antártica*. Lima: Universidad de San Marcos.

Calancha, Antonio de. 1639. "Corónica Moralizada del Orden de San Augustín en el Perú." Barcelona: Imprenta Lacavallería.

Calvo, Santiago Algurto. 1979. *La Traza Urbana de la Ciudad Incáica*. Lima: Instituto Nacional de Cultura del Perú.

Carrera, Fernando de la. 1939. *Arte de la Lengua Yunga de los Valles de Obispado de Trujillo del Perú*. Lima: J. Contreras.

Casevitz, France-Marie Renard de. 1981. "Las Fronteras de las Conquistas en el Siglo XVI en la Montaña Meridional del Perú." *Boletín del Instituto Francés de Estudios Andinos*, Vol. 10, Nos. 3–4, pp. 113–40.

Castelli, Amalia. 1991. "Dioses y Arquetipos en una Jerarquía Sacerdotal." In *El Culto Estatal del Imperio Inca*, ed. Mariusz S. Ziólkowski, pp. 109–13. Warsaw: Center of Latin American Studies, University of Warsaw.

Castro, Cristóbal de, and Diego Ortega Morejón. 1974. "Relación y Declaración del Modo que este Valle de Chincha se Governavan antes que hubiese Ingas." In *Biblioteca Peruana*, Primera Serie, Vol. 3, pp. 55–85. Lima: Editores Técnicos.

Céspedez Paz, Ricardo. 1982. "La Cerámica Incáica en Cochabamba." *Cuadernos de Investigación*, Serie Arqueológica, No. I, pp. 1–154. Instituto de Investigaciones Antropológicas, Universidad Mayor de San Simón, La Paz, Bolivia.

Chaumeuil, Jean-Pierre, and Josette Fraysse-Chaumeuil. 1981. "La Canela y El Dorado: Les Indigènes du Napo et du Haut-Amazone au XVI e Siècle." *Boletín del Instituto Francés de Estudios Andinos*, Vol. X, Nos. 3–4, pp. 55–85.

Choy, Emilio. 1959. "Desarollo del Pensamiento Especulativo en la Sociedad Esclavista de los Incas." In *II Congreso Nacional de Historia del Perú*, Vol. 2, pp. 87–102. Lima: Centro de Estudios Histórico-Militares del Perú.

Cieza de León, Pedro de. 1973a. *La Crónica del Péru*. Lima: Promoción Editorial SA.

———. 1973b. *El Señorío de los Incas.* Lima: Editorial Universo.

Cobo, Bernabé. 1979. *History of the Inca Empire*, tr. Roland Hamilton. Austin: University of Texas Press.

Collier, Donald, and John V. Murra. 1943. "Survey and Excavation in Southern Ecuador." Anthropological Series of the Field Museum of Natural History, Vol. 35, Chicago.

Conklin, William J. 1982. "The Information of Middle Horizon Quipus." In *Ethnoastronomy and Archaeoastronomy in the American Tropics*, eds. Anthony Aveni and Gary Urton, pp. 261–82. New York: Annals of the New York Academy of Sciences.

Conrad, Geoffrey W. 1981. "Cultural Materialism, Split Inheritance and the Expansion of Ancient Peruvian Empires." *American Antiquity*, Vol. 46, No. I, pp. 3–27.

———. 1982. "The Burial Platforms of Chan Chan: Some Social and Political Implications." In *Chan Chan: Andean Desert City*, eds. Michael E. Moseley and Kent C. Day. Albuquerque: University of New Mexico Press.

———. 1990. "Farfan, General Pacatnamu and the Dynastic History of Chimor." In *The Northern Dynasties*, eds. Michael E. Moseley and Alana Cordy Collins, pp. 227–42. Washington, DC: Dumbarton Oaks.

Conrad, Geoffrey W., and Arthur Demarest. 1984. *Religion and Empire. The Dynamics of Aztec and Inca Expansionism*. Cambridge and New York: Cambridge University Press.

Cook, Anita G. 1983. "Aspects of State Ideology in Huari and Tiwanaku Iconography: The Central Deity and the Sacrificer." In *Investigations of the Andean Past*, ed. Daniel H. Sandweiss, pp. 161–85. Ithaca, NY: Cornell University.

Cordy Collins, Alana. 1990. "Fonda Sidge, Shell Purveyor to the Chimu Kings." In *The Northern Dynasties*, eds. Michael E. Moseley and Alana Cordy Collins, pp. 393–418. Washington, DC: Dumbarton Oaks.

D'Altroy, T. N., and T. Earle. 1985. "Stable Wealth, Finance and Storage in the Inca Political Economy." *Current Anthropology*, Vol. 25, No. 2, pp. 187–206.

Davies, Nigel. 1973. *The Aztecs: A History*. London: Macmillan.

———. 1987. *The Aztec Empire: The Toltec Resurgence*. Norman: University of Oklahoma Press.

Day, Kent C. 1982. "Storage and Labour Service: A Production and Management Design for the Andean Area." In *Chan Chan: Andean Desert City*, eds. Michel E. Moseley and Kent C. Day, pp. 333–50. Albuquerque: University of New Mexico Press.

"Declaración de los Quipocamayos a Vaca de Castro." 1921. In *Colección de Libros y Documentos Referentes a la Historia del Perú*, eds. Carlos A. Romero and Horacio H. Orteaga, Serie II, Vol. 3, Lima.

Demarest, Arthur. 1981. "Viracocha. The Nature and Antiquity of the Andean High God." Peabody Museum Monographs, No. 6, Harvard University, Cambridge, MA.

Díez de San Miguel, Garci. 1964. *Visita Hecha a la Provincia de Chucuito por Garci Díez de San Miguel en el Año 1567*. Lima: Casa de Cultura.

Dillehay, Tom D. 1977. "Tawantinsuyu Integration of the Chillón Valley, Peru: A Case of Inca Geopolitical Mastery." *Journal of Field Archaeology*, Vol. 4, pp. 397–405.

———. 1988. "La Actividad Prehispánica de los Incas y su Influencia en la Araucania." In *La Frontera del Estado Inca*, eds. Tom D. Dillehay and Patricia Netherly, pp. 215–34. Oxford: BAR International Series, No. 422.

———. 1990. *Araucania, Presente y Pasado*. Santiago: Editorial Andrés Bello.

Dillehay, Tom D., and Patricia Netherly. 1988. *La Frontera del Estado Inca*. Oxford: BAR International Series, No. 442.

Donnan, Christopher B. 1990. "An Assessment of the Validity of the Naymlap Dynasty." In *The Northern Dynasties*, eds. Michael E. Moseley and Alana Cordy Collins, pp. 243–74. Washington, DC: Dumbarton Oaks.

Donnan, Christopher B., and Carol J. MacKey. 1978. *Ancient Burial Patterns of the Moche Valley, Peru*. Austin: University of Texas Press.

Donnan, Christopher B., and Guillermo A. Cock, eds. 1986. *The Pacatnamu Papers*. Vol. I. Los Angeles: Museum of Culture History, University of California.

Dumézil, Georges. 1949. *L'Héritage Indo-Européen à Rome*. Paris: Gallimard.

———. 1970. *The Destiny of the Warrior*. Chicago: University of Chicago Press.

Duviols, Pierre. 1967. *Un Inédit de Cristóbal de Albornoz*. Paris: Journal de la Société des Américanistes, Vol. LVI, No. I, pp. 7–40.

———. 1979. "La Dinastía de los Incas: Monarquía o Diarquía?" *Journal de la Société des Américanistes de Paris*, Vol. 46, pp. 67–83.

Eliade, Mircea. 1943. *Myth and Reality*. New York: Harper and Row.

Ellefsen, Bernardo. 1973a. "La División en Mitades de la Ciudad Incáica." *Bulletin de 1'Institut Français d' Etudes Andines*, Vol. 2, No. 4, pp. 23–8.

———. 1973b. "El Patrón Urbano según el Prof. Zuidema y su Relación con Incallacta." *Bulletin de L'Institut Francais d' Etudes Andines*, Vol. 2, No. 4, pp. 29–35.

Espinosa Soriano, Waldemar. 1970a. "Los Mitmas Yungas de Collique en Cajamarca." *Revista del Museo Nacional*, Vol. 36, pp. 9–59.

———. 1970b. "Los Mitmas Huayacuntas en Cajabamba y Antamarca, Siglos XV y XVI." *Historia y Cultura*, Vol. 4, pp. 77–96.

———. 1973. "Las Colonias de Mitmas Múltiples en Abancay, Siglos XV y XVI." *Revista del Museo Nacional*, Vol. 39, pp. 225–99.

———. 1982. "Los Chambillas y Mitmas Incas y Chinchasuyos en Territorio Lupaqa, Siglos XV–XX." *Revista del Museo Nacional*, Vol. 46, pp. 419–506.

Estete, Miguel de. 1968. *Noticia del Perú*. Biblioteca Perusea, Primera Serie, Vol. I, pp. 345–404. Lima: Editores Técnicos Asociados.

Falcón, Franco. 1918. "Representacion hecha sobre los Daños y Molestias que hacen a los Indios." In *Colección de Libros y Documentos Referentes a la Historia del Perú*, eds. Carlos A. Romero and Horacio H. Orteaga, Serie I, Vol. II, Lima.

Finley, Sir Moses. 1985. *Ancient History: Evidence and Models*. London: Chatto and Windus.

Flores Ochoa, Jorge A. 1983. "Pastoreo de Llamas y Alpacas," *Revista Andina* I, pp. 175–218.

Galdames, Luis. 1941. *A History of Chile*. Chapel Hill: University of North Carolina Press.

Garcilasco de la Vega, El Inca. 1943. *Primera Parte de los Comentarios Reales de los Incas*. Buenos Aires: Angel Rosenblat.

Gibson, Charles. 1948. *The Inca Concept of Sovereignty and the Spanish Administration in Peru*. Austin: University of Texas Press.

Gómara, Francisco López de. 1952. *Historia General de las Indias*. Biblioteca de Autores Españoles, Vol. 22. Madrid: Imprenta de Rivadeneyra.

González, Alberto Rex. 1963. "Cultural Development in Northwestern Argentina." In *Aboriginal Cultural Development in Latin America*, eds. Betty Meggers and Clifford Evans, Smithsonian Miscellaneous Collections, Vol. 146, No. I, pp. 102–17. Washington, DC: Smithsonian Institute.

———. 1983. "Inca Settlement Patterns in a Marginal Province of the Empire." In *Prehistoric Settlement Patterns*, eds. Evon Z. Vogt and Richard M. Leventhal. Albuquerque:

University of New Mexico Press.

González Corrales, Jose. 1984. "La Arquitectura y Cerámica Killke del Cusco." In *Current Archaeological Projects in the Central Andes*, ed. Ann Kendall, pp. 189–204. Oxford: BAR International Series, No. 210.

Gorenstein, Shirley. 1966. "The Differential Development of Military and Political Organization in Prehispanic Mexico and Peru." Doctoral dissertation, University of Chicago.

Gutiérrez de Santa Clara, Pedro. 1963–1965. *Quinquenarios o Historias de Las Guerras Civiles del Perú (1544–1550) y de otros Sucesos de las Indias.* Biblioteca de Autores Españoles, Vol. 164. Madrid: Ediciones Atlas.

Haas, Jonathan, Sheila Pozorski, and Thomas Pozorski. 1987. *The Origins and Developments of the Andean State.* Cambridge and New York: Cambridge University Press.

Hagen, Victor W. von. 1957. *Realm of the Incas.* New York: New American Library.

———. 1976. *The Royal Realm of the Inca.* London: Gordon Cremonosi.

Hemming, John. 1970. *The Conquest of the Incas.* London: Macmillan.

Himmelfarb, Gertrude. 1987. *The New History and the Old.* Cambridge, MA: Harvard University Press.

Huaman Poma de Ayala, Felipe. 1956. *Nueva Corónica y Buen Gobierno.* 2 vols. Lima: Editorial Cultura.

Hyslop, John. 1976. "An Arqueological Investigation of the Lupaca Kingdom and Its Origins." Unpublished doctoral dissertation, Department of Anthropology, Columbia University, New York.

———. 1977. "Hilltop Cities of Peru." *Archaeology,* Vol. 30, No. 4, pp. 218–25.

———. 1979. "El Area Lupaca Bajo el Dominio Incáico — un Reconocimiento Arqueológico." *Histórica,* Vol. 3, No. 1, pp. 53–79. Lima: Departamento de Humanidades, Pontífica Universidad Católica del Perú.

———. 1984. *The Inca Road System.* New York: Academic Press.

———. 1985. *Inkawasi, The New Cuzco.* Oxford: BAR International Series, No. 234.

———. 1988. "Las Fronteras Extremas del Tawantinsuyu." In *La Frontera del Estado Inca,* eds. Tom D. Dillehay and Patricia Netherly, pp. 35–57. Oxford: BAR International Series, No. 442.

———. 1990. *Inka Settlement Planning, Cañete, Lunahuana, Perú.* Austin: University of Texas Press.

Idrovo, Jaime. 1988. "Tomebamba: Primera Fase de Conquista Incásica en los Andes Septentrionales." In *La Frontera del Estado Inca,* eds. Tom D. Dillehay and Patricia Netherly, pp. 87–124. Oxford: BAR International Series, No. 442.

Isbell, William H. 1984. "Huari Urban Prehistory." In *Current Archaeological Projects in the Central Andes,* ed. Ann Kendall, pp. 95–132. Oxford: BAR International Series, No. 210.

———. 1985. "El Origen del Estado en el Valle de Ayacucho." *Revista Andina,* Ano 3, No. 1.

———. 1988. "City and State in Middle Horizon Huari." In *Peruvian Prehistory,* ed. Richard W. Keatinge, pp. 164–89. New York and Cambridge: Cambridge University Press.

Ixtlilxóchitl, Fernando de Alva. 1952. *Obras Históricas*. 2 vols. Mexico City: Editora Nacional.

Julien, Catherine. 1983. *Hatunqolla, A View of Inca Rule from the Lake Titicaca Region*. Berkeley: University of California Press.

Katz, Friedrich. 1969. *The Ancient American Civilizations*. London: Weidenfeld and Nicolson.

Keatinge, Richard W. 1988. "A Summary View of Peruvian Prehistory." In *Peruvian Prehistory*, ed. Richard W. Keatinge, pp. 303–16. Cambridge and New York: Cambridge University Press.

Keatinge, Richard W., and Geoffrey W. Conrad. 1983. "Imperialist Expansion in Peruvian Prehistory: Chimu Administration of a Conquered Territory." *Journal of Field Archaeology*, Vol. 10, pp. 255–83.

Kendall, Ann. 1973. *Everyday Life of the Incas*. London: Batsford.

———. 1976. "Descripción e Inventario de las Formas Arquitectónicas Inca." *Revista del Museo Nacional*, Vol. 42, pp. 19–36.

Kirchhoff, Paul. 1949. "The Social and Political Organization of the Andean Peoples." *Handbook of South American Indians*, Vol. 5, pp. 293–311. Washington, DC: Smithsonian Institute.

Kolata, Alan Louis. 1982. "Tiwanaku: Portrait of an Andean Civilization." *Field Museum of Natural History Bulletin*, Vol. 53, No. 8, pp. 13–28.

———. 1990. "The Urban Concept of Chan Chan." In *The Northern*

Dynasties, eds. Michael E. Moseley and Alana Cordy Collins, pp. 107–44. Washington, DC: Dumbarton Oaks.

Kroeber, Alfred L. 1930. "Archaeological Explorations in Peru — Part II — The Northern Coast." *Memoirs of the Field Museum of Natural History, Anthropology*, Vol. 2, No. 2.

Kubler, George. 1983. "Written Sources on Andean Cosmogony." In *Recent Studies in Andean Prehistory and Protohistory. Papers from the Second Annual Conference on Andean Archaeology and Ethnohistory*, eds. Peter Kvietok and Daniel Sandweiss. Ithaca, NY: Cornell University Press.

Larco-Hoyle, Rafael. 1938–1939. *Los Mochicas*. 2 vols. Lima: Casa Editora La Crónica.

Larrea, Carlos Manuel. 1971. "La Cultura Incásica del Ecuador." Publicaciones No. 253, pp. 1–41, Instituto Panamericano de Geografía e Historia, Mexico City.

Las Casas, Barolomé de. 1958. *Historia de las Indias*. Madrid: Biblioteca de Autores Españoles.

Laurencich-Minelli, Laura. 1991. "El Trabajo como Forma de Culto Estatal en el Imperio Inca." In *El Culto Estatal del Imperio Inca*, ed. Mariusz S. Ziólkowski, pp. 55–8. Warsaw: Centro de Estudios Latinoamericanos, Warsaw University.

Lechtman, Heather. 1979. "Issues in Andean Metallurgy." In *Precolombian Metallurgy of South America*, eds. Elizabeth Benson and Michael Coe, pp. 1–40. Washington, DC: Dumbarton Oaks.

León, Leonardo. 1983. "Expansión Inca y Resistencia Indígena en Chile." *Chungara*, No. 10, pp. 95–115.

Levillier, Roberto. 1940. "Origen e Historia Crítica de las Informaciones Hechas por Orden Del Virrey Toledo." In *Informaciones que Mandó Levantar el Virrey Toledo Sobre los Incas*, pp. i–xxxi. Buenos Aires: Editores Emece.

Lévi-Strauss, Claude. 1962. *La Pensée Sauvage*. Paris: Plon.

Leyenda de los Soles. 1945. *Códice Chimalpopoca*, ed. Primo Feliciano Velázquez, pp. 119–28. Mexico City: Imprenta Universitaria.

Loredo, Rafael. 1958. *Los Repartos. Bocetos para la Nueva Historia del Perú*. Lima: Instituto de Estudios Peruanos.

Lumbreras, Luis Guillermo. 1958. "Sobre los Chancas." *Actas y Trabajos del II Congreso Nacional de Historia del Perú*, Vol. 2, pp. 211–42.

———. 1959. "Acerca de la Aparición del Estado Inca." *II Congreso Peruano El Hombre y la Cultura Andina*, ed. Ramiro Matos, Vol. I, pp. 101–9.

———. 1974. *The Peoples and Cultures of Ancient Peru*, tr. Betty Meggers. Washington, DC: Smithsonian Institute.

Markham, Sir Clements Robert. 1910. *The Incas of Peru*. London and New York.

McEwan, Gordon F. 1987. *The Middle Horizon in the Valley of Cuzco*. Oxford: BAR International Series, No. 372.

———. 1990. "Investigations at the Pikillacta Site." In *The Northern Dynasties*, eds. Michael E. Moseley and Alana Cordy Collins, pp. 93–120. Washington, DC: Dumbarton Oaks.

Means, Philip Ainsworth. 1928. "Biblioteca Andina." *Transactions*, Vol. 29, pp. 271–525, Connecticut Academy of Arts and Sciences, New Haven.

———. 1931. *Ancient Civilizations of the Andes*. New York: Gordian Press.

Menzel, Dorothy. 1959. "The Inca Occupation of the South Coast of Peru." *Southwestern Journal of Anthropology*, Vol. 15, No. 2, pp. 124–42.

———. 1971. "Estudios Arqueológicos en los Valles de Ica, Pisco, Chincha y Cañete." *Arqueología y Sociedad*, No. 6, Museo de Arqueología y Etnología de la Universidad Nacional Mayor de San Marcos, Lima.

———. 1976. *Pottery Style and Society in Ancient Peru: Art as a Mirror of History in the Inca Valley, 1350–1570*. Berkeley: University of California.

Métraux, Alfred. 1970. *The History of the Incas*. New York: Schocken Books.

Meyers, Albert. 1976. "Die Inka in Ecuador." *Bonner Amerikanistische Studien*, No. 6, Bonn.

Molina, Cristóbal de. 1968. *Conquista y Población del Perú*, Biblioteca Peruana, Primera Serie, Vol. 3, pp. 297–374. Lima: Editores Técnicos.

Montesinos, Fernando. 1957. *Memorias Antiguas, Historiales y Políticas del Perú*, ed. Horacio Orteaga. Lima: Imprenta Gil.

Moore, Sally Falk. 1973. *Power and Property in Inca Peru*. Westport, CT: Greenwood Press.

Morris, Craig. 1973. "Estabelecimientos Estatales en el Tawantinsuyu: Una Estrategía de Urbanismo Obligado." *Revista del Museo Nacional*, Vol. 39, pp. 127–42.

———. 1978–1980. "Huánuco Pampa: Nuevas Evidencias Sobre el Urbanismo Inca." *Revista del Museo Nacional*, Vol. 44, pp. 139–52.

———. 1984. "Architecture and the Structure of Space at Huánuco Pampa." In *Tecnología, Urbanismo y Arquitectura de los Incas*, eds. Graziano Gasparini and Luise Margelies. Caracas: Ediciones Venezolanas de Antropología.

———. 1985. "From Principles of Ecological Complementarity to the Organization and Administration of Tawantinsuyu." In *Andean Ecology and Civilization*, ed. Shozo Mazuda, pp. 477–89. Tokyo: University of Tokyo Press.

———. 1986. "Storage Supply and Redistribution in the Economy of the Inca State." In *Anthropological History of Andean Polities*, eds. John V. Murra, Nathan Wachtel, and Jacques Revel. Cambridge and New York: Cambridge University Press.

———. 1988. "Progress and Prospect in the Archaeology of the Inca." In *Peruvian Prehistory*, ed. Richard W. Keatinge, pp. 233–56. Cambridge and New York: Cambridge University Press.

Morris, Craig, and Donald E. Thompson. 1970. "Huánuco Viejo, an Inca Administrative Center." *American Antiquity*, Vol. 35, No. I, pp. 345–60.

Morris, Craig, and John Murra. 1976. "Dynastic Oral Tradition, Administrative Records and Archaeology in the Andes." *World Archaeology*, Vol. 7, pp. 270–77.

Moseley, Michael E. 1990. "Structure and History in the Dynastic Lore of Chimor." In *The Northern Dynasties*, eds. Michael E. Moseley and Alana Cordy Collins, pp. 1–42. Washington, DC: Dumbarton Oaks.

———. 1992. *The Incas and Their Ancestors*. London: Thames and Hudson.

Moseley, Michael E., and Kent C. Day. 1982. *Chan Chan: Andean Desert City*. A School of American Research Book. Albuquerque: University of New Mexico Press.

Murra, John V. 1946. "The Historic Tribes of Ecuador." In *Handbook of South American Indians*, ed. Julian H. Steward, Vol. 2, pp. 785–821. Washington, DC: Smithsonian Institute.

———. 1958. "On Inca Political Structure." Proceedings of the 1958 Annual Spring Meeting of the American Ethnological Society, pp. 30–422, University of Washington, Seattle.

———. 1964. "Una Apreciación Etnológica de la Visita Hecha a la Provincia de Chucuito." In Visita Hecha a la Provincia de Chucuito por Garci Díez de San Miguel, pp. 419–44. Casa de Cultura, Lima.

———. 1966. "New Data on Retainers and Servile Populations in Tawantinsuyu." Proceedings of the XXXVI International Congress of Americanists, Vol. 2, pp. 35–45, Seville.

———. 1972. "El Control Vertical de un Máximo de Pisos Ecológicos en la Economía de las Sociedades Andinas." In *Ortiz de Zúñiga, Visita de la Provincia de Huánuco*, Vol. II, pp. 429–76. Huánuco: Universidad de Hermilio Valdizán.

———. 1975. *Formaciones Económicas y Políticas del Mundo Andino*. Lima: Instituto de Estudios Peruanos.

———. 1978a. *La Organización Económica del Estado Inca*. Lima: Instituto de Estudios Peruanos.

———. 1978b. "Los Límites y Limitaciones del Archipiélago Vertical en los Andes." *Avances*, No. 1, pp. 75–80.

———. 1982. "The Mit'a Obligations of Ethnic Groups to the Inca State." In *The Inca and Aztec States 1400–1800*, ed. George A. Collier. New York: Academic Press.

———. 1984. "Andean Societies Before 1532." In *The Cambridge History of Latin America*, Vol. I, pp. 59–90. New York and Cambridge: Cambridge University Press.

———. 1985. "El Archipiélago Vertical Revisited." In *Andean Ecology and Civilization*, ed. Shozo Mazuda, pp. 3–149. Tokyo: University of Tokyo Press.

———. 1986. "The Expansion of the Inca State: Armies, War, and Rebellions." In *Anthropological History of Andean Politics*, eds. John Murra and Nathan Wachtel, pp. 49–58. Cambridge and New York: Cambridge University Press.

Murra, John, Nathan Wachtel, and Jacques Revel. 1986. "Introduction." In *Anthropological History of Andean Politics*, pp. 1–8. Cambridge and New York: Cambridge University Press.

Murúa, Martín de. 1962. "Historia General del Perú." Madrid: Joyas Bibliográficas.

Netherly, Patricia J. 1988. "El Reino de Chimor y el Tawantinsuyu." In *La Frontera del Estado Inca*, eds. Tom Dillehay and Patricia Netherly, pp. 105–29. Oxford: BAR International Series, No. 442.

Niemayer, Hans F. 1986. "La Ocupación Inca de la Cuenca Alta del Río Copiapo." In *El Imperio Inca*, ed. Rodolfo Paffino, pp. 165–318. Córdoba: Comechingonia.

Nordenskӧld, Erland von. 1915. "Incallacta, eine Befestigte und von Inca Tupac Yupanqui Angelegte Stadt." *Ymer*, Heft 2, pp. 169–85, Stockholm.

Oakeshott, Michael. 1978. *Experience and Its Modes*. Cambridge and New York: Cambridge University Press.

Oberem, Udo. 1978. "El Acceso a Recursos Naturales de Diferentes Ecologías en la Sierra Ecuatoriana." In *Organización Social y Complementaridad Económica en los Andes Centrales*, ed. Jorge A. Flores Ochoa. Proceedings of XLII International Congress of Americanists, Vol. 4, pp. 51–64, Paris.

Ortiz de Zúñiga, Ínigo. 1967 and 1972. *Visita de la Provincia de León de Huánuco*. 2 vols. Huánuco: Universidad Hermilio Valdizán.

Patterson, Thomas C. 1991. *The Inca Empire: The Formation and Disintegration of a Pre-Capitalist State*. Oxford and Providence, RI: Berge Ltd.

Pease, G. Y. Franklyn. 1976. *Los Ùltimos Incas del Cuzco*. Lima: Villanueva.

———. 1978a. "Las Fuentes del Siglo XVI y la Formación del Tawantinsuyu." In *Del Tawantinsuyu a la Historia del Perú*, pp. 31–114. Lima: Instituto de Estudios Peruanos.

———. 1978b. *Del Tawantinsuyu a la Historia del Peru*. Lima: Instituto de Estudios Peruanos.

———. 1983. "Notas Sobre Historia Incáica." *Historia y Cultura*, Vol. 16, pp. 95–112.

———. 1985. "Cases and Versions of Verticality in the Southern Andes." In *Andean Ecology and Civilization*, ed. Shozo Mazuda. Tokyo: Tokyo University Press.

———, ed. 1986. *Los Cronistas del Péru 1528–1650 y Otros Ensayos*. Lima: Ediciones del Centenario, Banco de Crédito.

Pizarro, Pedro. 1968. *Relación del Descubrimiento y Conquista del Peru*. Biblioteca Peruana,

Primera Serie, Vol. I, pp. 439–586. Lima: Editores Técnicos.

Plaza Schuller, Fernando. 1976. "La Incursión Inca en el Septentrión Andino Ecuatoriano." Instituto Otavaleno de Antropología, Serie Arqueológica No. 2, Otavalo.

Polo de Ondegardo, Juan. 1916a. "Los Errores y Supersticiones de los Indios, Sacadas del Tratado y Averiguación que Hizo el Licenciado Polo." Colección de Libros y Documentos Referentes a la Historia del Perú, Serie I, Vol. 3, pp. 3–43.

———. 1916b. "Relación de los Fundamentos Acerca del Notable Daño que Resulta de no Guardar a los Indios sus Fueros." Colección de Libros y Documentos Referentes a la Historia del Perú, Serie I, Vol. 3, pp. 45–186.

Prescott, William H. 1847. *History of the Conquest of Peru.* 2 vols. London: Richard Bentley.

Puento, Hierónimo. 1974. "Probanza de Don Hierónimo Puento Cacique Principal del Pueblo de Cayambe." Documentos para la Historia Militar, Casa de la Cultura, Quito.

Puhvel, Jean. 1987. *Comparative Mythology.* Baltimore and London: Johns Hopkins University Press.

Quiroga Ibarrola, César A. 1962. "Ensayo Monográfico de la Organización del Ejército y Armas Empleadas por los Soldados del Tahuantinsuyu y por los Conquistadores Españoles." In *Actas y Trabajos del II Congreso Nacional de Historia del Perú*, Vol. 2, pp. 358–416. Lima: Centro de Estudios Histórico-Militares del Perú.

Raffino, Rodolfo. 1982. *Los Inkas del Kollasuyu!* La Plata, Argentina: Editora Ramos Americana.

———. 1986. *El Imperio Inka. Actualización y Perspectivas por Registros Arqueológicos y Ethnohistóricos.* Córdoba, Argentina: Comechingonia.

Ramírez, Susan E. 1990. "The Inca Conquest of the North Coast: A Historian's View." In *The Northern Dynasties*, eds. Michael E. Moseley and Alana Cordy Collins, pp. 489–506. Washington, DC: Dumbarton Oaks.

Ravines, Rogger. 1978. *Tecnología Andina.* Lima: Instituto de Estudios Peruanos.

Reinhard, Johann. 1991. *Machu Picchu: The Sacred Center.* Lima: Editorial Cultura.

Relación del Origen e Gobierno que los Ingas Tuvieron y del que había antes que ellos Señoreasen a los Indios de este Reino. 1921. Colección de Libros y Documentos Referentes a la Historia del Perú, Serie II, Vol. 3, Lima.

Relación Francesa (anómina) de la Conquista del Perú. 1968. Biblioteca Peruana, Primera Serie, Vol. I, pp. 171–90, Lima.

Relaciones Geográficas de Indias (1557–1586). 1965. Biblioteca de Autores Españoles, ed. Marcos Jiménez de la Espada, 4 vols, Madrid.

Romoli de Averi, Kathleen. 1977–1978. "Las Tribus de la Antigua Jurisdicción de Pasto en el Siglo XVI." *Revista Colombiana de Antropología*, Vol. 21, pp. 11–51.

Rostworowski, María de Diéz Canseco. 1953. *Pachacutec Inca Yupanqui.* Lima: Imprenta Torres Aguirre.

———. 1959. "Una Hipótesis sobre el Surgimiento del Estado Inca." II Congreso Peruano, El Hombre y la Cultura Andina, Vol. 1, pp. 39–100, Lima.

———. 1960. "Succession, Cooption to Kingship and Royal Incest Among the Inca."

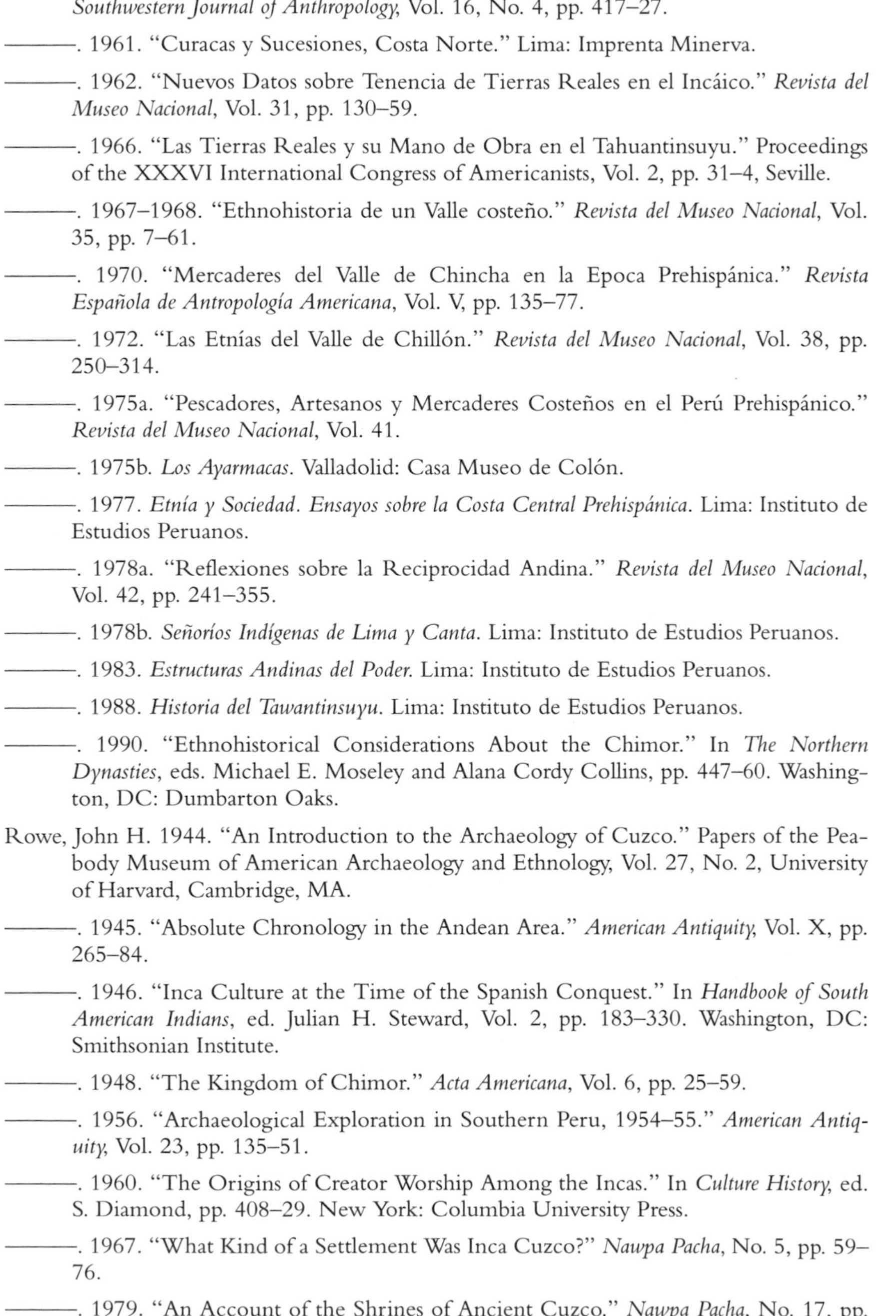

Southwestern Journal of Anthropology, Vol. 16, No. 4, pp. 417–27.

———. 1961. "Curacas y Sucesiones, Costa Norte." Lima: Imprenta Minerva.

———. 1962. "Nuevos Datos sobre Tenencia de Tierras Reales en el Incáico." *Revista del Museo Nacional,* Vol. 31, pp. 130–59.

———. 1966. "Las Tierras Reales y su Mano de Obra en el Tahuantinsuyu." Proceedings of the XXXVI International Congress of Americanists, Vol. 2, pp. 31–4, Seville.

———. 1967–1968. "Ethnohistoria de un Valle costeño." *Revista del Museo Nacional,* Vol. 35, pp. 7–61.

———. 1970. "Mercaderes del Valle de Chincha en la Epoca Prehispánica." *Revista Española de Antropología Americana,* Vol. V, pp. 135–77.

———. 1972. "Las Etnías del Valle de Chillón." *Revista del Museo Nacional,* Vol. 38, pp. 250–314.

———. 1975a. "Pescadores, Artesanos y Mercaderes Costeños en el Perú Prehispánico." *Revista del Museo Nacional,* Vol. 41.

———. 1975b. *Los Ayarmacas.* Valladolid: Casa Museo de Colón.

———. 1977. *Etnía y Sociedad. Ensayos sobre la Costa Central Prehispánica.* Lima: Instituto de Estudios Peruanos.

———. 1978a. "Reflexiones sobre la Reciprocidad Andina." *Revista del Museo Nacional,* Vol. 42, pp. 241–355.

———. 1978b. *Señoríos Indígenas de Lima y Canta.* Lima: Instituto de Estudios Peruanos.

———. 1983. *Estructuras Andinas del Poder.* Lima: Instituto de Estudios Peruanos.

———. 1988. *Historia del Tawantinsuyu.* Lima: Instituto de Estudios Peruanos.

———. 1990. "Ethnohistorical Considerations About the Chimor." In *The Northern Dynasties,* eds. Michael E. Moseley and Alana Cordy Collins, pp. 447–60. Washington, DC: Dumbarton Oaks.

Rowe, John H. 1944. "An Introduction to the Archaeology of Cuzco." Papers of the Peabody Museum of American Archaeology and Ethnology, Vol. 27, No. 2, University of Harvard, Cambridge, MA.

———. 1945. "Absolute Chronology in the Andean Area." *American Antiquity,* Vol. X, pp. 265–84.

———. 1946. "Inca Culture at the Time of the Spanish Conquest." In *Handbook of South American Indians,* ed. Julian H. Steward, Vol. 2, pp. 183–330. Washington, DC: Smithsonian Institute.

———. 1948. "The Kingdom of Chimor." *Acta Americana,* Vol. 6, pp. 25–59.

———. 1956. "Archaeological Exploration in Southern Peru, 1954–55." *American Antiquity,* Vol. 23, pp. 135–51.

———. 1960. "The Origins of Creator Worship Among the Incas." In *Culture History,* ed. S. Diamond, pp. 408–29. New York: Columbia University Press.

———. 1967. "What Kind of a Settlement Was Inca Cuzco?" *Nawpa Pacha,* No. 5, pp. 59–76.

———. 1979. "An Account of the Shrines of Ancient Cuzco." *Nawpa Pacha,* No. 17, pp.

2–80.

Rowe, John H., Donald Collier, and Gordon R. Willey. 1950. "Reconnaissance Notes on the Site of Huari, near Ayacucho, Peru." *American Antiquity*, Vol. 16, pp. 120–37.

Ruiz de Arce, Juán. 1933. "Advertencias que Hizo al Fundador del Vínculo y Mayorazgo a los Sucesores en el 1545." *Boletín de la Real Academia de Historia*, Vol. 102, pp. 327–85.

Sahlins, Marshall. 1985. *Islands of History*. Chicago: University of Chicago Press.

Saignes, Thiery. 1981. "El Piedemonte Amazónico de los Andes Meridionales: Estado de la Cuestión y Problemas Relativos a su Ocupación en los Siglos XVI y XVII." *Bulletin de L'Institut Français d'Etudes Andines*, Vol. 10, Nos. 3–4, pp. 146–76.

Salomon, Frank. 1985. "The Dynamic Potential of the Complementarity Concept." In *Andean Ecology and Civilization*, eds. Shozo Mazuda and Craig Morris, pp. 511–27. Tokyo: University of Tokyo Press.

———. 1986a. *Native Lords of Quito in the Age of the Incas*. Cambridge and New York: Cambridge University Press.

———. 1986b. "Vertical Politics on the Inka Frontier." In *Anthropological History of Andean Polities*, eds. John V. Murra, Nathan Wachtel, and Jacques Revel, pp. 89–118. Cambridge and New York: Cambridge University Press.

———. 1988. "Frontera Aborigen y Dualismo en el Ecuador Prehispánico: Pistas Onomasticas." In *La Frontera del Estado Inca*, eds. Tom Dillehay and Patricia Netherly, pp. 59–86. Oxford BAR International Series 442.

———. 1991. *The Huarochiri Manuscript: A Testament of Ancient and Colonial Andean Religion*. Austin: University of Texas Press.

Sámano-Xerez (1527–1528). 1937. "Relación de los Primeros Descubrimientos de Francisco Pizarro y Diego de Almagro!" *Cuadernos de Historia del Perú,* Vol. 2, No. 1, Paris.

Sancho de la Hoz, Pedro. 1968. *Relación para su Majestad*. Biblioteca Peruana, Primera Serie, Vol. I, pp. 275–344. Lima: Editores Técnicos.

Santacruz Pachacuti Yamqui, Juán de. 1927. *Relación de las Antiguedades deste Reyno del Piru*, eds. Carlos Romero and Horacio Urteaga. Colección de Libros y Documentos Referentes a la Historia del Perú, Second Series, No. 9, Lima.

Santillán, Hernando de. 1968. *Historia de los Incas y Relación de su Gobierno.* Biblioteca Peruana, Primera Serie, Vol. 3, pp. 375–464. Lima: Editores Técnicos.

Sarmiento de Gamboa, Pedro. 1943. *Historia de los Incas.* Buenos Aires: Editores Emece.

Schaedel, Richard P. 1951. "Major Ceremonial Population Centers in Northern Peru." Proceedings of the XXIX International Congress of Americanists, Vol. 2, pp. 232–43, Chicago.

———. 1959. "Formation of the Inca State." In *II Congreso Peruano, El Hombre y La Cultura*, ed. Pamiro Matos, Vol. I, pp. 112–56. Lima: Editorial Cultura.

———. 1966. "Urban Growth and Ekistics on the Peruvian Coast." Proceedings of the XXXVI International Congress of Americanists, Vol. I, pp. 532–39, Seville.

———. 1972. "The City and the Origin of the State in America." Proceedings of the XXXIX International Congress of Americanists, Vol. 2, pp. 15–33, Lima.

———. 1981. "Early State of the Incas." In *The Early State*, eds. Henry Claessens and Peter Skalnek, pp. 289–320. The Hague: Mouton.

———. 1985. "Coast-Highland Interrelationships and Ethnic Groups in Northern Peru." In *Andean Ecology and Civilization*, eds. Shozo Mazuda and Craig Morris, pp. 443–74. Tokyo: University of Tokyo Press.

———. 1988a. "Andean World View: Hierarchy or Reciprocity, Regulation or Control?" *Current Anthropology*, Vol. 29, No. 5, pp. 768–74.

———. 1988b. "Comentario: Las Fronteras del Estado Inca." In *La Frontera del Estado Inca*, eds. Tom Dillehay and Patricia Netherly, pp. 261–72. Oxford: BAR International Series, No. 442.

Schjellerup, Inge. 1984. "Cochabamba — An Incaic Administrative Center in the Rebellious Province of Chachapoyas." In *Current Archaeological Projects in the Central Andes*, ed. Ann Kendall, pp. 161–89. Oxford: BAR International Series, No. 210.

Schobinger, Juan. 1964. "Investigaciones Arqueológicas en la Provincia de San Juán, República Argentina." Proceedings of the XXXV International Congress of Americanists, Vol. I, pp. 615–19, Mexico City.

Shady Solis, Ruth. 1982. "La Cultura Nieveria y la Interracción Social en el Mundo Andino en la Epoca Huari." *Arqueológica,* No. 19, pp. 5–108, Museo Nacional de Antropología e Arqueología, Lima.

Silva Galdames, Osvaldo. 1982. "Apuntes sobre el Desarrollo de la Teoría Arqueológica en America." *Cuadernos de Historia,* No. 2, pp. 27–62. Santiago: Universidad de Chile.

———. 1983. "Detuvo la Batalla del Maule la Expansión Inca hacia el Sur de Chile?" *Cuadernos de Historia*, No. 3, pp. 7–27.

———. 1986. "Donde Estuvo la Frontera Meridional del Imperio Inca en Chile?" In *El Imperio Inka: Actualización y Perspectivas por Registros Arqueológicos y Etnohistóricos*, pp. 45–61. Córdoba: Comechingonia.

Stehberg, L. Ruben. 1976. "La Fortaleza de Chena y Su Relación con la Ocupación Incáica de Chile Central." *Publicación Ocasional del Museo Nacional De Historia Nacional,* No. 23, Santiago.

Strube Erdmann, León. 1963. "Vialidad Imperial de los Incas." *Serie Histórica,* No. 33, Instituto de Estudios Americanistas, Universidad Nacional de Córdoba, Argentina.

Thompson, Donald E. 1968. "Incaic Installations at Huánuco and Pumpu." Proceedings of the XXXVII International Congress of Americanists, Vol. I, pp. 64–74, Mar de Plata, Argentina.

Toledo, Francisco de. 1940. *Informaciones que mandó levantar el Virrey Toledo Sobre los Incas*, ed. Roberto Levillier. Buenos Aires: Editores Emece.

Topic, John R. 1990. "Craft Production in the Kingdom of Chimor." In *The Northern Dynasties*, eds. Michael E. Moseley and Alana Cordy Collins, pp. 145–76. Washington, DC: Dumbarton Oaks.

Topic, Theresa Lange. 1990. "Territorial Expansion and the Kingdom of Chimor." In *The Northern Dynasties*, eds. Michael E. Moseley and Alana Cordy Collins, pp. 177–94. Washington, DC: Dumbarton Oaks.

Trigger, Bruce. 1978. *Time and Traditions: Essays in Archaeological Interpretation*. Edinburgh: Edinburgh University Press.

Trimborn, Hermann. 1959. "Archäologische Studien in den Kordilleren Boliviens." *Baessler Archiv, Beitrage zur Völkerkunde*, Heft 2.

———. 1967. "Archäologische Studien in den Kordilleren Boliviens." *Baessler Archiv, Beitrage zur Völkerkunde*, Heft 5.

Troll, Karl. 1931. "Die Geographischen Grundlagen der Andinen Kulturen und des Inkareiches." *Ibero-Amerikanisches Archiv*, No. 5, pp. 258–94.

Uhle, Max. 1903. *Pachacamac: A Report of the William Pepper Peruvian Expedition of 1896.* Philadelphia: University of Pennsylvania.

Uribe, Maria Victoria. 1977–1978. "Asentamientos Prehispánicos en el Altiplano de Ipiales, Colombia." *Revista Colombiana de Antropología*, Vol. 21, pp. 57–196.

Urton, Gary. 1990. *Pacariqtambo and the Origin of the Incas.* Austin: University of Texas Press.

Valcárcel, Luis E. 1943–1948. *Historia de la Cultura Antigua del Perú.* Lima: Imprenta del Museo Nacional.

Valera, Blas. 1879. "Relación de las Costumbres Antiguas de los Naturales del Perú." In *Tres Relaciones de Antiguedades Peruanas*, ed. Jiménez de la Espada, pp. 135–227.

Van Zantwijk, Rudolph. 1985. *The Aztec Arrangement.* Norman: University of Oklahoma Press.

Vogt, Joseph. 1965. *The Decline of Rome.* London: Weidenfeld and Nicolson.

Wachtel, Nathan. 1971. *La Vision des Vaincus.* Paris: Gallimard.

———. 1980. "Les Mitimas de la Vallée de Cochabamba, la Politique de Colonisation de Huayna Capac." *Journal de la Société des Américanistes de Paris*, Vol. 47, pp. 297–324.

Wedin, Ake. 1963. *La Cronología de la Historia Incáica.* Gotemburg, Sweden: Instituto Ibero-Americano.

———. 1965. *El Sistema Decimal en el Imperio Incáico.* Gotemburg, Sweden: Instituto Ibero-Americano.

———. 1966. "El Concepto de lo Incáico y las Fuentes, Estudio Crítico." *Studia Histórica Gothoburgensia*, No. 7, Uppsala, Sweden.

Xerez, Francisco de. 1968. *Verdadera Relación de la Conquista de la Nueva Castilla.* Biblioteca Peruana, Primera Serie, Vol. I, pp. 191–274. Lima: Editores Técnicos.

Zárate, Augustín de. 1947. *Historia del Descubrimiento y Conquista de la Provincia del Perú, y de las Guerras y Cosas Señaladas en ella.* Madrid: Biblioteca de Autores Españoles, Vol. 26.

Ziólkowski, Mariusz. 1991. "El Sapan Inca y el Sumo Sacerdote: Acerca de la Legitimización del Poder en el Tawantinsuyu." In *El Culto Estatal del Imperio Inca*, ed. Marius Ziólkowski, pp. 59–74. Warsaw: Centro de Estudios Latino-americanos, University of Warsaw.

Zuidema, R. T. 1964. *The Ceque System of Cuzco: The Social Organization of the Capital of the Inca.* Leiden: E. J. Brill.

———. 1966a. "El Ayllu Peruano." Proceedings of the XXXVI International Congress of Americanists, Vol. 3, pp. 407–11, Seville.

———. 1966b. "El Calendario Inca." Proceedings of the XXXVI International Congress of Americanists, Vol. 2, pp. 25–30, Seville.

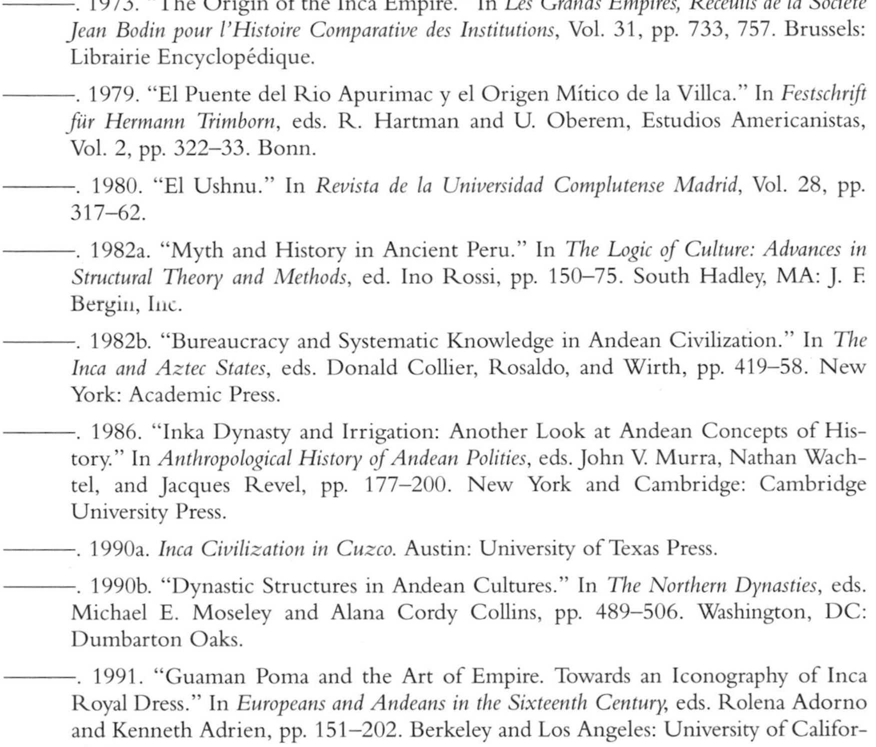

———. 1973. "The Origin of the Inca Empire." In *Les Grands Empires, Receuils de la Société Jean Bodin pour l'Histoire Comparative des Institutions*, Vol. 31, pp. 733, 757. Brussels: Librairie Encyclopédique.

———. 1979. "El Puente del Rio Apurimac y el Origen Mítico de la Villca." In *Festschrift für Hermann Trimborn*, eds. R. Hartman and U. Oberem, Estudios Americanistas, Vol. 2, pp. 322–33. Bonn.

———. 1980. "El Ushnu." In *Revista de la Universidad Complutense Madrid*, Vol. 28, pp. 317–62.

———. 1982a. "Myth and History in Ancient Peru." In *The Logic of Culture: Advances in Structural Theory and Methods*, ed. Ino Rossi, pp. 150–75. South Hadley, MA: J. F. Bergin, Inc.

———. 1982b. "Bureaucracy and Systematic Knowledge in Andean Civilization." In *The Inca and Aztec States*, eds. Donald Collier, Rosaldo, and Wirth, pp. 419–58. New York: Academic Press.

———. 1986. "Inka Dynasty and Irrigation: Another Look at Andean Concepts of History." In *Anthropological History of Andean Polities*, eds. John V. Murra, Nathan Wachtel, and Jacques Revel, pp. 177–200. New York and Cambridge: Cambridge University Press.

———. 1990a. *Inca Civilization in Cuzco*. Austin: University of Texas Press.

———. 1990b. "Dynastic Structures in Andean Cultures." In *The Northern Dynasties*, eds. Michael E. Moseley and Alana Cordy Collins, pp. 489–506. Washington, DC: Dumbarton Oaks.

———. 1991. "Guaman Poma and the Art of Empire. Towards an Iconography of Inca Royal Dress." In *Europeans and Andeans in the Sixteenth Century*, eds. Rolena Adorno and Kenneth Adrien, pp. 151–202. Berkeley and Los Angeles: University of California Press.

Index

Aconquija, 143
Acos, 152
Acosta, Joseph de, "Historia Natural y Moral de las Indias," 31
Administration, 151; of Collao, 128–30; of Inca state, 117–21, 125–26, 179–80; provincial, 138–40, 154–58; and road system, 140–42
Agriculture. *See* Food production
Aguapante, 192
Alcavizas, 23, 24, 28, 33, 36
Almagro, Diego de, 189
Alpacas, 165
Alva Ixtlixóchitl, Fernando de, 19
Alvarado, Pedro de, 188
Alzire (Voltaire), 1
Amaru, 49
Amaru Tupac, 58, 61
Amaru Yupanqui, 109–10
Ambato, 182
Anca Ayllo, 57
Ancient Civilizations of the Andes (Means), 7, 21
Ancient Roads on the North Coast of Peru (Beck), 140
Andahuaylas, 46, 47
Angaraes, 65
Angasamayo, Río, 81
Anonymous History of Trujillo, 133
Antalongo, 85
Antisuyu, 35, 37, 70, 71, 73, 78, 84, 101
Apoc Achache, 110
Apo Capac, 72
Apoc Hualpaya, 110
Apo Guacal, 166
Apo Mayta, 32, 41, 115
Arapa, 72
Araucanos, 88, 206
Archaeology, 46, 57, 105, 127, 172; at Chanchan, 134, 135; contributions of, 8–12, 196–99; of fortifed sites, 143–44; and Inca imperial expansion, 61, 82, 86–87, 88, 160–61; at Lambayeque, 132–33; pre-Inca, 136–40; of road systems, 140–42; on trade, 178–79
Archipelagos: vertical, 174–77
Architecture, 11, 161, 198–99; of provincial centers, 137–39
Archivo de Indias, 5
Arequipa, 21, 56
Argentina, 72, 80, 143, 159, 164; Inca sites in, 87–88, 161, 196
Arica, 174
Armies. *See* Military
Arnoldsson, Sverker, 62
Artisans, 123, 124–25, 136, 152, 168
Ascher, Marcia, 121
Asillo, 72
Astu Huaraca, 48
Atacama Desert, 141
Atahualpa, 1, 104, 146, 188; and Huascar, 110, 181–86; and Pizarro, 4, 90, 91, 131, 186–87; as ritual leader, 191–92
Atoco, 182
Aucaypata, 106
Auqui Francisco Tupac, 100
Auqui Topa, 32, 82
Avery, Romoli de, 81
Ayacucho, 46
Ayahuaca, 71, 78
Ayar Auca, 22, 30, 34, 37
Ayar Cachi, 22, 37
Ayamarca, Ayarmacas, 22, 28, 36–37, 52
Ayar Manco, 30–31, 34, 37
Ayar Uchu, 22, 37
Ayavaca, 72
Ayllus, 24, 52, 107, 113, 120, 124; role of, 34–35, 111
Aymara, 5, 12, 19, 24, 129, 166
Aymara language, 46, 159–60
Aztecs: chronicles of, 96–97; comparisons to, 202, 203–5

Bandera, Damián de la, 4, 32, 116, 164, 171; on government, 150, 151, 152, 153, 156
Barlow, R. H., 96–97
Baudin, Louis, 4, 60, 173; *A Socialist Empire: The Inca of Peru,* 7
Bauer, Brian, 25–26, 93
Beck, Coleen, *Ancient Roads on the North Coast of Peru,* 140
Benalcázar, Sebastián de, 188
Beni, Río, 87
Bennett, Wendell C., 9, 11
Benson, Elizabeth, 146
Berkhofer, Robert, 197
Berthelot, Jean, 164, 207
Betanzos, Juán de, 4, 16, 22, 30, 34, 47, 94, 95, 98; on Atahualpa, 191–92; on Cuzco, 105–6; on rulers, 41, 42, 72, 79, 93, 183, 184–86
Bibar, Gerónimo de, 88
Bingham, Hiram, 9, 199
Bío Bío, Río, 88
Bolivia, 72, 80, 86, 87, 161, 165, 166, 188, 196; mines in, 206–7
Bonavía, Duccio, 138–39
Bonbón, 57, 58, 71, 78, 136, 151, 182
Borregán, Alonso de, 80
Bracamoros, 71, 78, 79, 89, 167
Bridges, 118, 141–42
Brundage, Burr Cartwright, *Empire of the Inca,* 26
Bushnell, Geoffrey, 11

Caballero, Byrne de, 139
Cabello de Balboa, 5, 13, 25, 48, 59, 94–95, 96, 99, 100, 120, 121, 151, 167; on conquests, 56, 57, 58, 64, 65, 67(table), 70, 71, 73, 75(table), 80, 81, 82, 83, 84, 85, 89, 144, 147; on Lambayeque, 133–34; on rulers, 22, 23, 24, 29, 30, 32, 36, 41–42, 44, 49, 56, 58, 90, 91, 110, 182, 211–16
Cacha, 43, 49
Cajamarca, 4, 57, 58, 70, 78, 83, 124, 130, 134, 136, 139, 172; Pizarro in, 186–87, 192
Cajamarquilla, 131
Cajas, 186
Calancha, 18, 129
Calendrical system, 35, 198
Callo, 140
Calvo, Santiago, 107
Cameloids, 165. *See also* Llamas
Cañaris, 29, 85, 91, 166, 192; and Huascar, 182, 183, 184, 185, 188
Candide (Voltaire), 1
Cañete Valley, 130, 137
Cantares, 97
Capac Huari, 110
Capac Yupanqui, 21, 23, 41
Capac Yupanqui (Pachacutec's brother), 57
Carabaya mines, 164, 207
Carabayllo, 133
Carangas, 168
Caranquis, 81–82, 166, 167
Caras, 166
Carchi, Río, 81
Cari, 43, 84, 129
Cari, Martín, 30
Carlos Inca, 95, 96
Carrera, Fernando de la, 136
Casana, 51, 73, 106
Casevitz, France-Marie Renard de, 84
Casma Valley, 143
Castelli, Amalia, 129–30
Castro, Cristóbal de, 108, 150, 151, 153, 156, 158, 171
Caxas, 78
Cayambi, 80, 82, 168
Cayocache, 95
Cayo Tupac, 21–22, 95
Ceque system, 35, 37
Ceque System of Cuzco, The (Zuidema), 31, 35
Ceramics, 11, 25, 135; Inca-style, 86, 160–61
Chachapoyas, 70, 72, 73, 78, 167
Chalco Chima, 182, 183
Chanapata culture, 25
Chancas, 28, 29, 37, 41, 43, 44, 57, 115, 167, 201; origins of, 45–46; wars with, 46–49, 58, 59–60, 61, 62, 128
Chanchan, 29, 132, 134, 135, 147
Chanquillo, 143
Charcas, 70, 71, 79, 84, 148, 168, 189, 201
Chasquis, 142
Chena, 88, 160
Chile, 9, 58, 64, 141, 143, 152, 164, 206; conquest of, 84–85, 88, 101; Huayna Capac in, 78, 79; Inca settlement in,

160, 161, 196, 207; Spanish in, 188, 189; Tupac Inca's conquests in, 70, 71, 72, 80
Chillón, Río, 131, 133, 139, 160
Chimo-Capac, 133
Chimor, 8, 12, 29, 49, 57, 58, 59, 93, 94, 120, 147, 160, 176, 199; conquest of, 70, 71, 72, 80, 83, 132–36; rulers of, 154, 158
Chimu, 94, 132
Chincha, Chinchas, 70, 71, 83, 117, 130, 160, 177, 180
Chinchasuyu, 35, 42, 58, 71, 115, 167, 168
Chincha Valley, 130, 132, 155
Chipihuayco, 87
Chiponahuas, 70
Chiriguanos, 73, 78, 101, 149
Choy, 117
Chronicles, chroniclers, 2–3, 4, 18; evaluating, 7–8, 13–14, 79–85, 93–94; information available to, 94–100; language used in, 5–6. *See also by name*
Chronology, 198; of conquests and reigns, 89–92
Chuchi Capac, 56
Chucuito, 5, 21, 43, 56, 71, 84, 129, 144, 157, 176
Chunchos, 70, 71, 84, 87, 101, 149, 167
Chuquiago, 87, 207
Chuquisguaman, 65
Cieza de León, 3, 36, 57, 59, 94, 95, 97, 113, 121, 122, 136, 142, 158, 161, 172, 177; on Chancas, 47, 48; on conquests, 64, 65, 68(table), 70–71, 76(table), 78–79, 80, 82–83, 84, 85, 89, 129, 130, 131, 134, 144; on creation myths, 16–17; *La Crónica del Peru,* 4, 92; on Cuzco, 103, 107, 123; on fortresses, 143, 144; on mitimaes, 166–67, 176; on Pachactutec, 51, 56; on provincial centers, 151–52; on rulers, 21–22, 23, 31, 41, 42, 43, 44, 45, 55, 185; *El Señorío de los Incas,* 4, 92
Ciquinchara, 192
Cium, 134
Civil war: after Huayna Capac's death, 181–86, 191
Clergy. *See* Priests
Coast, 130–32, 176
Coati, 161
Cobo, Bernabé, 116; on conquests, 64, 65, 69(table), 71–72, 73, 77(table), 78, 83, 89, 130, 167, 171; on Cuzco, 103–4; on government, 151, 152, 154, 169; *Historia del Nuevo Mundo,* 5; on land tenure, 112, 162; on Pachacutec, 51, 56, 59, 106; on religion, 55, 108, 158; on rulers, 22, 23, 24, 41, 42, 43, 46, 49
Cochabamba, 73, 79, 119, 139–40, 148, 168, 176, 205
Codex Ramírez, 96
Colla, 12, 57
Colla Capac, 56
Collao, Collas, 17, 21, 29, 30, 38–39, 42, 45, 70, 72, 114, 118, 158, 160, 164, 177, 189, 201; conquest of, 56, 57, 64, 71, 78, 79, 83–84; Inca administration of, 128–30, 154, 166; Viracocha Inca in, 44, 59
Collasuyu, 35, 52, 57, 71, 78, 128, 161, 165, 167. *See also* Collao
Collier, Donald, 9
Collins, Alana, *The Northern Dynasties,* 94
Collique, 125, 131
Colombia, 81, 86, 91
Communication system, roads and, 140–42
Con, 17–18
Conchopata, 12
Condesuyu, 23, 35, 70, 71
Conquest of Peru (Prescott), 1
Conquests: of Chancas, 46–49; of Chimor, 132–36; chroniclers of, 4, 6; chronology of, 89–92; coastal, 82–83, 130–32; Collao, 83–84, 129; Ecuadorian, 80–82; historical context of, 92–94, 100–102; under Huayna Capac, 72–79; and imperial cult, 158–59; by Incas, 21–22, 23–24, 25–29, 40–41, 42, 43, 44, 62, 196; under Pachacutec, 51, 55–58; politics of, 147–48; reasons for, 205–6; resettlement after, 166–68; Spanish, 186–87, 191–94; under Tupac Inca, 64–72
Conrad, Geoffrey, 93, 200, 201, 204, 206
Copacabana, 56, 73, 129–30
Copalimayta, 36
Copiapo, 164, 189

Copper mines, 165
Coquimbo, 70, 85
Corichanca, 23, 24, 30, 36; elite and, 114, 185; rule of, 32–33; Temple of the Sun at, 18, 22, 50, 53, 103, 104, 135
Cotapampa, 182, 186
Coya, 109
Creation, myths of, 16–20, 24–25, 38, 39, 201–2
Crime, 153, 156–57
Croce, Benedetto, 195
Crónica del Peru, La (Cieza de León), 4, 92
Crónica "X," 96–97
Cuellar, Juán de, 100
Cuenca, 92
Cuenca Valley, 85
Cugma, 55
Cults: ancestral, 107–8; imperial, 158–59; sun, 33, 52, 153, 159; Viracocha, 19, 20, 53
Culunchimas, 23
Cumpi, 165
Cuntisuyu. *See* Condesuyu
Curacas, 51, 107, 169; governmental role of, 154–58, 173, 179; labor and, 170–71; land distribution by, 162, 163; mining by, 122–23; property rights of, 112, 113
Cusi, 129
Cusi, Martín, 30
Cuzco, 2, 4, 6, 9, 35, 141, 177, 179, 184, 190; central, 105–7, 114; creation myths and, 16, 19; descriptions of, 103–5; divisions of, 23, 24, 29, 30; origins of, 26, 27, 38; Pachacutec and, 50–52, 59–60; religion in, 158, 159; rulers of, 32–33,43; social engineering in, 123–24; symbolic importance of, 103, 191; warehousing, 172, 202–3
Cuzco Huanca, 22
Cuzco Valley, 9, 11; conquest of, 55–56; cultures in, 25, 36, 105; mitimae system in, 123–24; Incas in, 21–22, 26, 28
Cuzqueno, el. *See* Molina, Cristóbal de

Day, Kent, 132
Decimal system, 170–71
Declaración de los Quipocamayos, 49, 97–98, 120
Deities, 12, 194; creation, 17–18; manipulation of, 158–59; roles of, 52–55
Demarest, Arthur, 19, 200, 201, 206; on religion, 53–54, 55, 158
Dillehay, Tom D., 88, 139
Donnan, Christopher, 134
Dumézil, Georges, 20
Durán, Diego, 96, 97
Duviols, Pierre, 93; "The Dynasty of the Incas: Monarchy or Duarchy?," 31, 32
"Dynasty of the Incas: Monarchy or Duarchy?, The" (Duviols), 31, 32

Early Intermediate Period, 11
Ecological zones, 127; and economy, 174–77, 180
Economy, 132, 180, 198; goods and, 172–74; regional self-sufficiency of, 174–77; trade and, 177–79
Ecuador, 9, 29, 79, 91, 118, 130, 152, 159, 166, 170, 173, 175, 193; conquests in, 58, 64, 65, 72, 78, 80–82, 186, 207; forts in, 143–44; Inca frontier in, 86, 101, 196; Spanish in, 188–89; trade with, 177, 178; wars in, 13, 100, 147
Eliade, Mircea, 16, 19, 62
Elite, 2, 159; administration by, 117–18; in Cuzco, 106–7; goods redistribution by, 173–74; as provincial governors, 151–54; social order and, 114–17
Empire of the Inca (Brundage), 26
Envoys, 153
Esmeraldas, 101
Espinosa, Waldemar, 91, 101, 124, 166, 167–68, 170
Espinosa Soriano, Waldemar, 148
Estete, Miguel de, 104, 105, 186–87, 190
Ethnohistory, 7–8

Fábulas y Ritos de los Incas (de Molina), 31–32
Fempellec, 134
Field of Cuzco, 22
Finney, M. I., 195
Floods, 17, 18
Flores Ochoa, Jorge, 174
Food production, 171–72, 176–77
Fortresses: conquest of, 72, 81; construction of, 73, 78; locations of, 86–87; and military system, 142–44

Garci Díez de San Miguel, 5, 124, 167, 168, 174; *Visita Hecha a la Provincia de Chucuito,* 62, 129
Garcilasco de la Vega (El Inca), 6–7, 51, 52, 55, 113, 114, 157; on conquests, 72, 79, 82; on creation myths, 17, 19; on government, 154, 155; on Pachacutec, 48–49, 50, 56, 59, 60; on rulers, 21, 29, 37, 40–41, 43, 46
Gibson, Charles, 116
Gift exchange, 156, 169
Gold, 113, 131, 135; in Cuzco, 104, 105, 106; Inca use of, 50–51; mining of, 122–23, 164
Gómara, López de, 17–18, 31, 124
González, Alberto Rex, 143
González Corrales, 25
Goods: ritual, 203–4; storage and distribution of, 172–74
Gorenstein, Shirley, 146
Government: curacas and, 154–158; of early rulers, 29–32; mitimae system and, 166–68; organization of, 116–17, 125–26, 150–51; provincial, 152–54. *See also* Adminstration
Governors, provincial, 151–54
Guaitaira, Río, 81
Guaman Chinchay Suyu, 32
Guata, 55
Guayaquil, 82
Gutiérrez de Santa Clara, Pedro, 18

Hanan Chillo, 173
Hanan Cuzco, 23, 24, 29, 30, 37, 52, 106, 123; and civil war, 185–86; rule of, 31, 33
Hanansaya, 29–30
Hanansora, 30
Handbook of South American Indians, 8
Hatunqolla, 56, 128, 129
Hatun Xauxa, 158
Hemming, John, 188, 193, 194
Himelfarb, Gertrude, 197
Historia del Nuevo Mundo (Cobo), 5
"Historia Natural y Moral de las Indias" (Acosta), 31
History: ambiguities in, 92–94; and mythology, 20–25, 26–28; nature of, 14–15; Pachacutec's role in, 58–63; validity of, 195–98
History of the Incas (Métraux), 26–27
Hochaycacamayoc, 153
Hoz, Sancho de la, 105
Huacas, 22, 35
Huallas, 36
Huamachuco, 136, 183
Huamanantupa, 24
Huamanga, 4, 30, 56, 150, 151, 152
Huaman Poma de Ayala, 4–5, 18, 25, 72, 162, 170, 173; on rulers, 21, 32, 116, 183
Huanacauri, 22, 23
Huanca Auqui, 182
Huancabamba, 72, 78
Huancavilcas, 70
Huancayo Alto, 139
Huánuco Pampa, 9, 57, 125, 138(fig.), 157, 174, 176; archaeology of, 136–37, 161
Huarcos, 71, 130–31
Huari, 9–11, 12, 26, 51, 105
Huari Urban History Project, 11
Huascar, 110, 187, 188; and Atahualpa, 181–86
Huatanay River, 31, 36, 106
Huayacuntus, 166
Huaylas, 71
Huayllacan, 37
Huayna Capac, 9, 13, 14–15, 22, 23, 27, 34, 42, 51, 53, 62, 64, 92, 97, 144, 159, 168, 170, 190, 191; accession to rule of, 18, 108, 110; advisors to, 32, 95; and Atahualpa, 184–85; campaigns of, 72–79, 80, 81–82, 83, 84, 85, 98, 100–101, 115, 166, 214–16; death of, 90–91, 131, 181, 194; reign of, 90–91, 101, 125, 130, 155, 176, 195, 205
Hurin Chillo, 173
Hurin Cuzco, 23, 24, 29, 30, 37, 50, 52, 123; and civil war, 185, 191; rule of, 31, 32, 33
Hurinsaya, 30
Hurinsora, 30
Hyslop, John, 51, 82, 118, 129, 191; on Inca borders, 85–86; on Lambayeque, 132–33; on Lupaqas, 56–57; on roads, 140, 141–42

Ica, 70, 130, 177
Ica-Chincha culture, 12

Iconography, 12, 132
Idrovo, Jaime, 85
Illapa, 12, 20, 53, 55, 165
Imbabura, 207
Inca, El. *See* Garcilasco de la Vega
Inca, the, 116–17; post-conquest, 95–96. *See also* Rulers
Inca Empire, ii(map), 35, 127, 198, 207–9; borders of, 85–88; and Collao, 128–30; expansion of, 46–49, 80–85, 101, 130–32, 204–5; extent of, 8, 9, 12–13, 206–7; founding of, 40–41, 42; inhabitants of, 36–37; mythology of, 61–62; Pachacutec and, 49–52, 59, 60; Spanish control of, 95–96, 188–94
Incahuasi, 137–38
Incallacta, 139, 161
Inca Manco II, 106
Incaracay, 148, 161
Inca Road Project, 140
Inca Roca, 21, 22, 23, 24, 27, 28–29, 31, 32, 37, 46
Inca Roca (Pachacutec's brother), 41, 47, 56, 115
Incas o la Destruction de Pérou, Les (Marmontel), 1
Incas of Peru, The (Markham), 21
Inca Yupanqui, 42, 44. *See also* Yahuar Huaca
Informaciones (Toledo), 36
Inti, 20, 53, 54, 107–8, 158
Inti Pata, 199
Inti Raymi, 190
Introduction to the Archaeology of Cuzco, An (Rowe), 9
Isbell, William, 11, 12

Judicial system, 120, 153
Julien, Catherine, 129

Katz, Friedrich, 59
Kendall, Ann, 106–7
Killke period, 25–26
Kingship. *See* Monarchies
Kin groups, 34–35, 52, 119–20. *See also* Ayllus
Kolata, Alan, 133
Kroeber, Alfred L., 9
Kubler, George, 17, 18

Labor, 51, 52, 155; control of, 202, 205; decimal system and, 170–71; possession of, 161–62; skilled, 124–25; state, 121–23, 171–72; as tribute, 169–70
Lacatunga, 71, 78
Lambayeque, 70, 94, 132–34
Land, 35, 176; control of, 163–64, 202; curacas and, 155–56; distribution of, 151, 162–63; labor taxation on, 171–72; provincial governors and, 152–53; rights to, 112–14
Larco-Hoyle, Rafael, 132
Larecaja mines, 164
Larecaxa, 174–75
Larrea, Carlos Manuel, 80, 90
Late Horizon, 160, 197
Late Intermediate Period, 11, 12, 136, 160
Laurencich-Minelli, Laura, 158
León, Leonardo, 85
Lévi-Strauss, Claude, 14
Lima Valley, 131, 133
Lives of the Emperors (Molina), 100
Llamas, 113–14, 165
Lloqui Yupanqui, 21, 22, 23–24, 28, 35
Lumbreras, 11, 46, 128
Lupaqa kingdom, 12, 29–30, 56–57, 117, 124, 128, 129, 157, 160, 168, 173, 200–201; economy of, 174–75

McEwan, Gordon, 105
Machu Picchu, 9, 199
Madre de Dios, Río, 87
Maipo Valley, Río, 88, 160
Mamaconas, 153
Mama Ocllo, 22, 110
Mama Tacucary, 24
Manco, 189–90
Manco Capac, 21, 22, 28, 29, 36, 48; as mythic, 61, 62
Manosuyos, 70
Mapocho, Río, 88
Maranga, 158
Markham, Clement, *The Incas of Peru,* 21
Marmontel, Jean François, *Les Incas o la Destruction de Pérou,* 1
Matahua, 22
Maule, Río, 70, 71, 88
Mayo, Río, 81
Mayta Capac, 21, 23–24, 28, 31, 36

Means, Philip Ainsworth, 41, 89, 171; *Ancient Civilizations of the Andes,* 7, 21
Menzel, Dorothy, 160
Merchants, 177–78, 180
Mesoamerica, 18–19
Métraux, Alfred, *History of the Incas,* 26–27
Mexicas, 202
Mexico, 18, 96
Meyers, Albert, 91–92, 160
Michimalongo, 70, 85
Middle Horizon, 11, 12, 197
Militarism, 11, 94
Military, 57, 118, 120; fortresses and, 142–44; mitimaes and, 166–67; organization of, 145–49, 171
Minchançaman, 133
Mining, 113, 122–23, 164–65, 206–7
Mit'a, 121–22, 169–70
Mitimaes, 52, 91, 125, 148, 176; control of, 155–56, 205; in Cuzco, 107, 123–24; imperial use of, 113, 119, 136; mass resettlement of, 166–68, 170
Moche, 132, 146, 176
Moche Valley, 160
Moieties, 29–30, 37. *See also* Hanan Cuzco; Hurin Cuzco
Mojos, 71, 73, 78, 84, 87, 149, 167
Molina, Cristóbal de (el Cuzqueno), 105, 190; *Fábulas y Ritos de los Incas,* 31–32; *Lives of the Emperors,* 100
Monarchies: dual, 29–32; organization of, 33–34
Montesinos, 21, 31, 151
Moore, Sally, 152–53, 157, 163, 171
Moquegua, 174
Morris, Craig, 8, 119, 125, 127, 137, 172, 176–77
Mortuary practices, 33, 34
Moseley, Michael, 26, 29, 143; *The Northern Dynasties,* 94
Muina, 24
Murra, John, 5, 8, 13, 30, 59, 63, 81, 82, 117, 129, 137, 148, 153, 169, 170, 197; on administration, 119, 124, 154–55, 166, 173; on labor, 121–22, 171; on land, 162–63; on llama ownership, 113–14; on Pachacutec, 60–61; on trade, 177, 178; on verticality, 127, 175–76
Murúa, Martín de, 18, 124, 152; on quipus, 120–21; on rulers, 21, 22, 37, 44, 116
Myths, 39; creation, 16–20, 201–2; and history, 20–25, 26–27; and Pachacutec, 58–63; of rulers, 27–29, 38

Ñançenpinco, 133
Naylamp dynasty, 133–34
Nazca, Nazcas, 9, 70, 71, 83, 130
Niemayer, Hans, 164
Ninan Cuyochi, 181
Nobility, 106–7, 119–20. *See also* Elite
Nordensköld, Erland von, 139
Northern Dynasties, The (Moseley and Collins), 94
Nos, 88
Numerical system, 120–21, 170–71

Oakeshott, Michael, 14
Oberem, Udo, 175, 176
Ochacamayo, 153
Officials, 153–54
Ollantaytambo, 55
Oma, 22
Opataris, 70
Oral tradition, 2–3
Orejones, 81, 107, 111, 119, 148, 152, 169, 179; as informants, 95–96; in social order, 114–17
Oroya, 142
Ortega Morejón, Diego, 108, 150, 151, 153, 156, 158, 171
Ortiz de Zúñiga, Iñigo, 5, 86, 137, 174
Otavalo, 91, 143, 144, 159, 178
Oviedo y Valdés, Gonzalo Hernández de, 166

Pachacama, 17–18, 19
Pachacamac, 4, 8, 83, 131, 132, 139
Pachacutec, 6, 19, 20, 21, 25, 27, 28, 32, 33, 37, 43, 84, 98–99, 109, 120, 128, 194; ascent to throne of, 43–45, 111; campaigns of, 55–58, 65, 130, 147; and Chancas, 47–49; and Cuzco, 105, 106; ashistorical figure, 58–63; panacas and, 34, 35; relatives of, 114–15; as ruler, 31, 40, 41, 42, 49–52, 90, 116; and state religion, 52–55, 158

Pachacuti, Santacruz, 47, 182
Pacsamayo River Valley, 70
Palaces, 29, 51, 106, 134
Palloca, 181
Palta, 166
Panacas, 21, 33–34, 35, 108, 111, 113, 119–20, 164, 183
Pastos, 78, 81, 86, 144, 184
Paucarcolla, 160
Paucartambo, 22, 23, 24, 25, 38, 39
Paullu Inca, 95, 98, 189
Pease, Franklyn, 5, 8, 20, 38, 55, 92, 176; on rulers, 61–62, 101, 186, 191
Peru, 8, 57, 86, 188; pre-Inca cultures in, 136–40
Philip II, 99
Pikillacta, 11, 26, 105
Pinahua Capac, 37
Pizarro, Francisco, 106, 189, 207; and Atahualpa, 4, 90, 131, 186–87, 192
Pizarro, Hernando, 50
Pizarro, Pedro, 51, 80, 103, 131; *Relación*, 4
Planning, 125; central, 118–19, 127
Plaza Schuller, Fernando, 13, 80, 144
Pocona, 73, 78, 84, 168
Pocras, 46
Polo de Ondegardo, 5, 99, 143, 152, 156; on government, 151, 157; on land, 164, 171; on property, 112, 162; on rulers, 30–31, 62
Pomorcaes, 88
Popayan, 81
Porto Viejo, 82, 86
Potosí, 177, 206–7
Pre-Inca Period, 11
Prescott, William: *Conquest of Peru,* 1
Priests, 24, 32, 107, 111, 185
Principalities, 136
Property rights, of rulers, 112–14
Provincial centers, 137–39; government of, 151–54; mitimae in, 166–68; tribute in, 172–73
Public works, 51, 122, 170. *See also* Road system; Temples
Pucara, 84
Pucara de Andalgala, 143
Pucarane, 72
Puento, Hieronimo, 80
Puhvel, Jean, 20
Pumap Chupan, 106
Pumpu, 137
Puná, 73, 83, 178, 186
Puno, 29
Puruaes, 78
Puruha, 91, 166, 175

Quechuan, 18, 98; as imperial language, 159–61
Quechuas, 47, 65, 87–88, 201
Quetzalcoatl, 19
Quijos, 178
Quillacas, 168
Quipocamayos, 3, 97–98, 121, 173
Quipus, 3, 59, 89, 118, 120–21, 153
Quishuarcancha, 53
Quito, 32, 44, 70, 71, 72, 73, 78, 79, 92, 143, 159, 160, 166, 168, 173, 178, 188; conquest of, 80, 90, 91, 101, 187
Quizqiz, 182, 183, 187, 188–89

Raffino, Rodolfo, 87, 143, 161
Ramírez, Susan, 177–78
Ranke, Leopold von, 195
Rebellions, 109, 130, 190
Reciprocity, 156, 169
Record-keeping, 3, 120–21. *See also* Quipus
Relación (Pizarro), 4
Relación del Origen e Gobierno Que Los Incas Tuvieron, Por Señores Que Sirvieron al Inca Yupangui y a Topa Yupanqui, La, 150
Relaciones Geográficas de Indias, 30, 62, 114, 152, 178
Religion, 38, 125; land control and, 162, 163–64; Pachacutec and, 50, 52–55, 60–61; in provinces, 158–59; sun cult and, 107–8
Resettlement, after conquest, 166–68
Revenues, state, 116
Ríobamba, 78
Rituals, 190; Atahualpa's, 191–92; goods for, 203–4; panaca, 33, 34
River crossings, 36. *See also* Bridges
Road systems, 11, 35, 51, 105, 118, 140–42
Rostworowski, Maria, 8, 38, 41, 60, 131, 132; on labor, 52, 124; on property, 112–13; on rulers, 36–37, 40, 42, 44,

46, 50, 61, 185; on social organization, 29–30, 34, 157–58; on trade, 177, 178
Rowe, John, 7–8, 47, 53, 93, 148; on ayllus, 34–35, 52; on Chimor, 133, 135; on conquests, 89–90; on Cuzco, 38, 107, 123; on iconography, 12, 19, 20; *An Introduction to the Archaeology of Cuzco,* 9; on rulers, 21, 25, 26, 49, 61, 194
Rubinos y Andrade, Justo, 134
Rucanas, 46
Ruiz de Arce, Juán, 106, 107
Rulers, 198; ancestral cult and, 33–34, 107–8; conquests of, 25–29; dual, 29–32, 37, 157–58; early history of, 20–24, 38; government of, 32–33; historical veracity of, 58–63; imperial development and, 49–52; property rights of, 112–14; provincial, 154–58; social hierarchy and, 114–15; under Spanish, 189–94; succession of, 42–45, 108–12, 181–86, 194–95, 208. *See also by name*
Rumichaca, 81, 144
Rumiñavi, 188, 189
Runaquipo, 153

Sacrifices, 50, 103, 165
Sacsahuaman, 4, 9, 25, 51, 72, 105, 106
Sahagún, Bernardino de, 97, 195, 204
Sahlins, Marshall, 15, 63
Saignes, Thiery, 84, 87
Salomon, 80, 91, 92, 143, 175, 178, 207
Samaipata, 87, 148
Sámano-Xerez, 178
Sancho, Pedro, 202–3
San José de Maipo, 88
Santiago, 9
Santiago del Estero, 87–88
Santillán, Hernando de, 4, 32, 109, 122; on government, 150, 151, 153, 168
Sarmiento de Gamboa, Pedro, 5, 6, 17, 47, 94, 95, 96, 152, 171; on conquests, 55, 57, 64, 65, 66(table),70, 72, 73, 74(table), 80, 84–85, 89, 144; on government, 151, 153; on Pachacutec, 61, 98–99; on rulers, 22, 23, 24, 32, 34, 37, 41–42, 43, 58, 181, 184, 185, 211–16; on social organization, 29, 30
Sausirays, 36
Sayri Tupac, 21
Schaedel, Richard, 8, 52, 119–20, 128, 134; on Chancas, 45–46; on landholding, 163–64
"Señores, Los." *See Relación del Origen e Gobierno Que Los Incas Tuvieron, Por Señores Que Sirvieron al Inca Yupangui y a Topa Yupanqui, La,* 150
Señorío de los Incas, El (Cieza de León), 4, 92
Services, state, 121–23
Settlement patterns, and ecological zones, 174–77
Shady, Ruth, 131
Shrines. *See* Coriancha; Pachamac; Sacsahuaman
Sillustani, 161
Silva Galdames, Osvaldo, 88
Silver mines, 113, 164
Sinchi Roca, 21, 22, 23, 28, 31, 35, 73
Social class, 13. *See also* Elite
Social engineering, 123–24
Socialist Empire: The Inca of Peru, A (Baudin), 7
Social organization, 4–5, 15, 37–39: duality in, 29–33; hierarchical, 114–17; mitimaes and, 166–67; Pachacutec and, 60–61; regional, 157–58
Songs, 3
Soras, 30, 46, 56
Soto, Hernando de, 186
Spanish, 208, 209; as chroniclers, 1, 5–6; conquest by, 4, 90, 131, 186–87; imperial control by, 188–94; on mines, 206–7
Stehberg, L. Ruben, 160
Stones, sacred, 22
Storage systems, 11, 172–74, 199, 202–3
Sun, 18, 165; cults of, 33, 52; land control and, 162, 163–64; in religion, 53, 54, 55, 107–8, 158. *See also* Inti

Tahuantinsuyu, 35, 38, 62. *See also* Inca Empire
Tampus, 142
Taxation, 168, 171–72. *See also* Labor; Tribute
Taycanamo, 133
Tello, Julio C., 7, 9, 46
Temple of the Sun, 18, 22, 34, 50, 53, 103, 135

Temples, 4, 18, 22, 105, 151, 159, 161
Temucu, 88
Tezozómoc, Alvarado, 96, 97
Thompson, Donald, 137
Thunapa, 12, 19, 55
Tici Viracocha, 16, 17. *See also* Viracocha
Tihuanaco, 8, 9, 12, 16, 21, 56, 71
Tiquizambi, 78
Titicaca, Lake, 21, 29, 89, 124, 128, 140, 161, 170, 175; creation myths and, 16, 17, 19, 24, 38; Inca expeditions to, 56, 73. *See also* Collao, Collas; Collasuyu
Tito Cusi Hualpa, 110. *See also* Huayna Capac
Titu Atauchi, Alonso, 96
Titu Cusi Yupanqui. *See* Pachacutec
Tocay Capac, 37
Tocoyrioc, 120, 153. *See also* Officials
Tocricoc, 120, 153. *See also* Governors
Toledo, Francisco de, 6, 42, 95, 96, 99, 109, 159, 190; *Informaciones,* 36
Tombebamba, 9
Topic, Theresa Lange, 94, 199
Tovar, Juán de, 97
Toynbee, Arnold, 208
Trade, 177–79, 202
Transportation, 120, 170. *See also* Road system
Treasures, 4, 105, 131; at Coriancha, 103–4
Tribute, 122, 153, 168, 202–3; labor service as, 169–70; in provincial centers, 172–73
Trigger, Bruce, 196
Trimborn, Hermann, 139, 148
Tucumán, 48, 71, 85
Tullumayo River, 36, 106
Tumay Huaraca, 48
Tumbez, 70, 71, 72, 79, 83, 86, 92, 133, 186
Tumebamba, 70, 78, 80, 90, 92, 101, 159, 160, 161, 186, 188, 191; Atahualpa in, 181, 182
Tupac Amaru, 96, 190
Tupac Huallpa, 189
Tupac Inca (Yupanqui), 27, 23, 34, 35, 41, 48, 49, 62, 98, 113, 158, 167, 183; accession to rule of, 58, 109–10; campaigns of, 64–72, 78–79, 80, 83, 84, 85, 89, 92, 94, 130, 131, 134, 147, 166, 168, 194, 211–13; and Copacabana, 129–30; as ruler, 90, 115, 116, 125, 195

Uhle, Max, 8–9, 91–92
Umasuyu, 167
Uramarca, 152
Urco, 41, 44–45, 47, 60, 112
Urton, Gary, 24
Urus, 73, 117
Uscovilca, 47–48
Ushnu, 105

Vaca de Castro, 3, 97, 99
Valcárcel, Louis, 7
Valdivia, Pedro de, 88
Valera, Blas, 48
Verticality, 127, 174–76
Vicaquirao, 41, 115
Vicuñas, 165
Vilcabamba, 190
Vilcanota River, 37
Vilcas, 152
Vilcashuaman, 46
Villacastín, Francisco de, 98
Viracocha, 12, 16, 19, 20, 38–39, 62, 194; role of, 52–53, 54, 202
Viracocha Inca, 25, 28, 37, 48, 55, 109, 195; and Chancas, 46–47, 49, 60; as ruler, 40–41, 42–43, 59
Visita Hecha a la Provincia de Chucuito por Carci Díez de San Miguel, 62, 129
Visitors, official roles of, 153–54
Vogt, Joseph, 208
Voltaire: *Alzire,* 1; *Candide,* 1
Von Hagen, Victor, 140

Wachtel, Nathan, 155–56, 168, 175
Warehouses, 172–73
Wars, 13, 81–82, 100, 108, 110, 201; with Chancas, 46–49, 59, 61, 62, 128; with Huarcos, 130–31; military organization and, 145–49; under Pachacutec, 55–58; with Spanish, 192–93, 194. *Seealso* Conquests
Weapons, 145–46, 193
Wedin, Åke, 18, 31, 120; on dynastic history, 62, 63, 90–91; on imperial government, 150–51
Willca Chanca, 46

Willey, Gordon, 9
Winay Wayna, 199

Xaquixahuana, 47
Xauxa, 57, 70, 78, 121, 136, 151, 182, 189
Xerez, Francisco de, 4, 90, 103, 131, 146

Yahuarcocha, 78, 79, 82, 91, 92, 100, 207
Yahuar Huaca, 21, 22, 37, 41, 42, 43, 109
Yanacayo, 70, 72
Yanas, 52, 107, 117, 119, 121, 123, 170
Ychma, 131
Yucay Valley, 72
Yungas, 29, 158

Zantwijk, Rudolf van, 26
Zárate, Augustíne de, 178
Ziólkowski, Mariusz, 111
Zuidema, Tom, 6, 8, 13, 27, 30, 61, 93, 105, 106; *The Ceque System of Cuzco,* 31, 35